DATE DUE

DEMCO 38-296

WITHIN THE CIRCLE

The History and Society of the Modern Middle East Series

Leila Fawaz, General Editor

WITHIN THE CIRCLE

Parents and Children
in an Arab Village

Andrea B. Rugh

Columbia University Press

New York

Columbia University Press
Publishers Since 1893
New York   Chichester, West Sussex
Copyright © 1997 Columbia University Press
All rights reserved

Library of Congress Cataloging-in-Publication Data
Rugh, Andrea B.
    Within the Circle: parents and children in an Arab village / Andrea B. Rugh.
        p.   cm. — (The History and society of the modern Middle East series)
    Includes bibliographical references and index.
    ISBN 0-231-10678-5 (alk. paper). — ISBN 0-231-10679-3 (pbk.: alk. paper)
    1. Child rearing—Syria—Case studies. 2. Parent and child—Syria—Case
    studies. 3. Rural families—Syria—Case studies. I. Title. II. Series.
HQ769.R7675   1997
649'.1'095691—dc20   96-31447

∞
Casebound editions of Columbia University Press books are printed on permanent
and durable acid-free paper.

Printed in the United States of America
c 10 9 8 7 6 5 4 3 2 1
p 10 9 8 7 6 5 4 3 2 1

Contents

PREFACE

———

Turn the pot on its head; the daughter becomes the mother.

— Syrian proverb

The idea for this book came to me in 1981 when I was living in Damascus, Syria, during my husband's diplomatic assignment to the American embassy there. At the time, I was finishing a book about Egyptian family life, so it was tempting to look for a quiet place to complete the final chapters. In retrospect, the Egyptian book was probably an excuse to satisfy my curiosity about a side of Syrian life different from that of cosmopolitan Damascus and the "international" set of Syrians that tended to congregate around diplomats.

In September, with the help of a Syrian acquaintance, I arranged to rent a room from October to May with a family in a village about an hour away from Damascus. As the Egyptian manuscript progressed, I became increasingly dissatisfied with the parts describing relations between parents and children. There had been little opportunity for me to observe Egyptian families in intimate enough detail to understand the complexities of child rearing in Arab society. But in the Syrian family with whom I was living, I realized, I was immersed in a wealth of these details. Not only did my prolonged visits to the Syrian village give me a unique opportunity to supplement my work on the Egyptian family, but the descriptions of Syrian family life also might illuminate the then current debates in the United States about the deteriorating situation of American families. The U.S. debate was fueled by statistics of high divorce rates, fewer and later marriages, and more single-parent and two-career households, all suggesting less commitment to traditional patterns of family life. Some media reports even claimed that families as they were once known now barely existed in the United States, with more than half of families having no children and a third consisting of single-parent households.

If we hope to resolve the problems of family in America, we need to know more about how families in other cultures establish strong ties. We need to know what practices and mechanisms hold families together and what contexts are conducive to family cohesion. Through contrast, we can determine which practices in American life detract from family commitment. Is it possible for people to commit themselves to others in family groupings and still realize their potential as separate individuals? How might children be brought up to suppress their own interests in favor of the broader interests of the group? What examples can we take from societies in which strong family ties are a priority? How do these societies cope with the fragmenting effects of modern life? A "thick" (to use Clifford Geertz's term) description of such a society seemed useful to me to shed light on critical aspects of our own American society.

Perhaps the most important lesson to be gained from a detailed account of child rearing in another culture is to see the broad consistency that emerges in the practices of parents as they raise their children. This consistency comes from strong "feelings of what is right," that is, from the "deep-structure" conditioning of culture. Without this largely unconscious, commonly held set of expectations, it would be difficult, if not impossible, for the people of a particular culture to interact smoothly with one another. Indeed, it is probably very difficult for people holding strong views about, for example, the positive qualities of individualism to internalize values regarding the superiority of affiliation with groups. But by becoming aware of this fact, we might better understand the implications of our actions and design strategies for living that are more compatible with the values that we do hold. At the very least, we become aware of the extent to which some of our routine behaviors contradict the cooperative practices we need to build more cohesive family ties.

This is not to suggest that after reading this book, Americans will immediately want to imitate Syrian patterns of family life—they would find some of these patterns exceedingly uncongenial—rather, they might become aware, as I did while living in the village, of how other people organize their daily lives to produce strong family connections. Americans could decide for themselves if any of the practices from the Syrian village might be effective in an American setting.

With a general audience in mind, therefore, I have tried to avoid an academic study "explaining" child rearing in a foreign culture. Instead, the aim of this book is a simple one: to report the day-to-day life of parents and children in a Syrian village and to note my reactions as an American woman and mother to what I saw there. Because children grow up in a world governed by cultural rules and peopled by adult role models, my descriptions go beyond the immediate relations between parents and children to the world that surrounds them. Children's understandings are molded over time by the consistent worldviews of those around them, mainly parents but others as well. For that reason, this book seeks to identify the wider premises on which family relations are based.

With the exception of the last chapter, this book is a narrative of events during my stay in Wusta. The last chapter reviews and analyzes these observations. There I show how the daily household activities organized by adults with a consistent view of life shape their children's perception of the world and prepare them to take their place in the community of adults.

This book is not a study in the formal sense. Perhaps "observations while spending the winter in a Syrian village" is a more apt way of expressing what is found here. It is not the limited number of people described in these pages that makes me refrain from calling it a study, for anthropologists often use limited case histories to illuminate general principles. In fact, if culture can be defined broadly as a shared set of deep-structure meanings that help organize daily living, then all but the exceptional individuals of a culture will employ these general meanings to rationalize their behavior. I am not overly concerned, therefore, that the comparisons in this book are between the practices of a rural Syrian family and those of my own upper-middle-class urban American family. With caution, both examples can be used as expressions of two fundamentally different approaches to life. Like many anthropologists, I work from the base of my own cultural experiences. In this book I simply make the comparison more explicit.

I also do not refrain from labeling this book a study because I think my observations are less objective than a formal study requires. It is true that as the circle of people narrows, the relationship between observer and observed becomes more intense, making a distanced "objectivity" more difficult. This is a common hazard for anthropologists who deal intimately with people and their lives. Although I tried to intrude as little as possible into the routines of the Wusta families, I never doubted that as an outsider, I affected how they behaved and, in some cases, what activities they undertook. On the other hand, the most interesting insights came to me when, as an outsider, I made "mistakes" and was corrected by my hosts. Because I was so much a part of the action, it was clear to me from the beginning that for accuracy I would have to become a conscious part of the story told in this book.

Finally, I have refrained from calling the book a formal study because of the way I approached the subject—in what I would say was a less systematic, more relaxed, and less exhaustive style than I have approached work in the past. But even though I have absorbed rather than pursued insights, I do not consider them less valid. Indeed, by treating the conclusions more tentatively, I may have been able to report in more detail the essential differences between Syrian culture and our own. These differences are well known to those who go back and forth between the two worlds but are often considered too trivial to dignify in scholarly writing.

During my stay in Syria, relations between the Syrian and the American governments were not good, and the strain intensified during the buildup to the Israeli invasion of Lebanon. From one day to the next, I expected to find authorities wanting to know what I was doing in the village, and I worried that my presence might compromise my hosts or, on a different level, my husband in his position as a diplomat. However, with the exception of one visit by a high Baathi Party government official who spent the summer in a house nearby, I was never bothered or, as far as I know, restricted in any of my activities. It is reasonable to assume that permissions for my stay in the village were given at some official level without my knowledge.

The level of tension surrounding foreigners is perhaps best exemplified by an incident that occurred one day on the edge of Damascus. An anthropologist friend and I were taking pictures of artists painting trucks with the elaborate and beautiful designs that are characteristic of trucks all over the Middle East, when a Baathi official appeared at the workshop and arrested us—the charge was "taking pictures in an industrial area." After an hour of being checked out by a series of officials, including some unidentifiable men with Kalashnikov rifles lounging on a street corner, we were released. No incident of this kind occurred in the village of Wusta while I stayed there, but perhaps this fact alone was unusual and showed that I was given some level of official protection of which I was not aware.

A number of people should be acknowledged for their help in making it possible for me to write this book. There are the obvious ones mentioned in these pages and the not so obvious ones that I am reluctant to draw attention to for reasons that are clear to those who understand the sensitivities of the area.

My own family—my husband and three grown sons—are the first to be thanked for their patience in the face of what has become a time-consuming obsession. The boys are the "American" foil—the basis for comparison that has been held up against these Syrian families—and although I am proud of how well they have turned out, I feel it is to their credit and not to my skill in mothering. I wish I had known then what I know now about raising children. Further thanks should go to the Honorable Robert Paganelli, then the U.S. ambassador in Syria, who, when I explained my desire to live in the village, encouraged me to do so, even though as a member of the diplomatic community, any problems I encountered there might have caused him official difficulties.

Andrea Rugh
February 1996

ONE

Beginnings

What connects us [Americans] back through history to our founders and across space to each other is, ironically, a shared sense of the importance of our own separateness. Together we defend our right to be independent of others, including each other. Together, we value self-reliance. And together we often forget our togetherness.

—Ellen Goodman, "Our Finding Fathers"

Two small boys, barely more than toddlers, walked hand in hand along a busy street leading into one of the famous vegetable *suqs* (markets) of old Damascus. The younger, not more than a hand's breadth smaller than his companion, tilted his head up to the other to ask earnestly and respectfully, "Tell me, Samir, is it true . . ." and the rest of the question was lost in the noise of cars and hawkers. I watched them absently as they progressed along the busy street and was in time to see the bigger one disengage his hand from that of the younger one, place it firmly in the small of his back, and propel him carefully across a narrow space between two momentarily stalled cars. I waited to see the younger one twist away with the "I-can-do-it-myself" defiance I expected from a child of that age, but instead he showed nothing but happy compliance with the directions of the older child.

His unexpected reaction brought me back to an awareness of how absently I was observing the scene. If I had been conscious of my presence on a public street in an Arab country, I would automatically have altered my expectations of the children's behavior to ones that had become familiar during my twenty years of residence in the Middle East. Instead, I reacted as an American mother who had raised three boys with the individualistic, competitive behaviors that seem an inevitable part of growing up in the Western world. I felt a twinge of guilt that perhaps if I had raised my own children in a more "Arab way," they might have exhibited a greater sense of the shared connection that seemed so appealing in these Damascene children. Another voice inside me wondered what it would take to produce that "Arab behavior."

A week later at a social gathering in Damascus, someone asked me the question that had become routine since I arrived in the country: What did I think of Syria and the Syrian people in comparison with other Arab countries where I had lived? I answered impatiently that until I knew more about people and places outside Damascus, it would be unfair to answer. The small international set of Damascenes I was meeting, with their strong overlay of European culture, did not seem representative of the "authentic" Syrian culture about which I had been asked to comment. I mentioned my wish to find a quiet place where I could finish writing a book and learn more about Syrian rural life. One woman standing near me said that if I was serious, she would speak to a relative who owned a vacation house in a Christian village not far away from Damascus, to see whether I could rent a room there. I quickly cautioned that I was not interested in a resort village like Bludan or Zebdani in the mountains east of Damascus, and she reassured me that the place she had in mind was not that kind of village.

She was right, Wusta[1] was definitely not a fashionable resort town, even though its mountain air made it attractive enough so that a few Damascenes had built vacation homes there. Even without many summer visitors, however, it was a village that in recent years had become substantially more prosperous than many others—an economic success story in the same Syria about which economists reported gloomy statistics showing depleted foreign exchange, growing inflation, and low productivity in most sectors. Official statistics, it became apparent, hid a vibrant informal economy that flourished in many parts of Syria, making the economically successful Wusta, if not representative of all Syrian villages, at least not atypical of many where individual households managed to conceal their true wealth.

On the following Friday, my husband and I visited the relative of the helpful Damascene woman. The relative, a holiday visitor to Wusta, was a woman doctor with a thriving practice in Damascus. She and her husband, rather atypically, held Rousseauian beliefs about the charm and wholesomeness of country living. They prepared lunch for us, and then after a cup of thick

Turkish coffee, the Doctora took me for a walk to see the village where I would be living if all went well with the rental negotiations.

A ten-minute walk on the town's one asphalted road was enough for me to see most of the points of interest in town: the primary school, a bakery, the only grocery store that was more than a kitchen business, a mosque, and the village's two major churches. The village buildings seemed little more than a sediment caught in a long loop of road that exited and then returned to a Damascus–Aleppo highway that bisected the valley. Seven additional loops of irregularly positioned houses strung between the entrance and exit roads formed the remainder of the village. Older houses from the original village were located in widely spaced intervals on the outermost loop, with the newer constructions and most of the family-owned shops filling in the spaces between. It was a simple plan, born haphazardly but with a natural logic.

As we walked, we noticed trucks everywhere—tanker trucks in empty lots or parked next to grape arbors, trucks up on lifts being repaired in makeshift workshops, trucks unhitched from their trailers, trucks being refueled, cabs circling the village as young men honed their driving skills, stake trucks, goods trucks, refrigerator trucks—big, medium, and small trucks. The village was filled with their presence, and our conversation was drowned by their noise. We retraced our steps back down the road until we stood before the small house belonging to the man who had a room to rent. The house was located on the edge of the village, not far from a row of summer homes at the periphery of Wusta's settled area. Two of these summer homes, across the street from "our" house, were surrounded by walls with gates that could be locked during the winter months.

The house we were standing next to was modest by comparison and even modest by village standards. It had one story and was of modern stone and cinder block construction. Rough concrete pillars as high as the house supported a primitive grape arbor along one side. A cement apron on all four sides kept mud away from the entrance doors. Facing us was a flight of stairs leading to the flat roof where fruits, vegetables, and grains could be dried for winter use, away from the incursions of household animals. As was true for most houses in Wusta, reinforcing steel from the first floor protruded spaghetti-like from each corner of the roof, awaiting plans for future additions. I felt a momentary regret that the available room was in this unremarkable dwelling and not in one of the more graceful older houses of the village.

We turned in at the front path and knocked on the door of Um and Abu Abdalla.[2] The door opened, and I saw Um Abdalla for the first time. She surprised me with her vivid red hair and her sweater and skirt, which were a more typically urban fashion. Five children stood behind her, two teenage girls and three boys. Four of the five had their mother's fair skin and red hair. The oldest boy had his arm in a sling; the second was a carbon copy of the first; and the third boy—younger, thinner, and darker—hung his head shyly when he saw me. The Doctora introduced them one by one, saying something nice about each, while Um Abdalla beamed at the compliments. In comparison with the sophisticated Doctora, the villagers seemed slightly awkward and rough hewn, yet she had obviously taken pains to know each one, and it was clear that they had a genuinely warm relationship.

Um Abdalla was prepared for our visit but appeared incredulous that an American would want to live in her modest home. Emigrants to America, it seemed, came back to the village with exaggerated tales of the standards Americans expected. For a moment, her anxiety made me unsure. Could I cope with difficulties that arose once I made the commitment? Was there something intolerable about this living arrangement that I had somehow missed? I looked around to see what she might think objectionable but saw only a hallway of rough unplastered walls and freshly scrubbed floor tiles.

In my room-to-be off the hallway, they had not had time to clear away the sacks of grain and excess household furniture that had been stored there. Figs were drying on a cloth laid out on the floor, and an acrid smell rose from a cheesecloth full of grapes suspended from a tripod and draining into a bucket on the floor. "We will move all these things if you are interested in the room," Um Abdalla said quickly, noticing the direction of my gaze. Overhead, a picture of Jesus and a lamb gazed benignly down on us.

She led me to a small kitchen off the main room, which had a shallow stone sink and counters and a few wooden cupboards, and then took me to the bathroom where a modern toilet stood next to an older hole-in-the-floor version. There was a rudimentary bathtub and a kerosene heater that I could light to heat water whenever I wanted a bath. Everything I needed was there, plus the privacy I thought I would want to finish my book.

The room itself was nothing special, but it was light and spacious with a western exposure. I had two doors to the outside, a small porch of my own, and a view that stretched across the valley to the mountains beyond. From this window I could see, at the other end of the valley, the spectacular church of neighboring Mafraq rising like a fairy-tale palace from its mound in the center of town. The quiet of this place and the view enchanted me, and I quickly made up my mind to take the room.

As if reading my thoughts, the Doctora began the negotiations on my behalf: "She will need a curtain rod so she can cover the windows and feel more at ease." I shrank at the possibility that her demands might make me too much of an inconvenience but remained silent, trusting the Doctora, though not sure she represented my best interests. The Doctora took it for granted that she knew what I needed and didn't bother to consult me about the furnishings I might want.

We were still standing in "my" room as the negotiation continued. To hide my embarrassment, I wandered over to look out the windows again. My outside door, in the direction of Mafraq, opened on a small veranda shaded by some dusty green grapevines of late summer. In fall and spring, I could imagine this would be a pleasant place to sit and look out over the valley. In winter, I soon learned, this face of the house collected snow to the depth of several feet, and after the pleasant months of fall, I kept this door tightly closed. At the back of the house, off my tiny kitchen, was another door to a veranda that I shared with Um Abdalla's household. It was sunny and hot and not given to long, sweeping views because of the sheltering enclosure of a sloping hill. This recessed spot with its inviting warmth from the midday sun turned out to be our favorite sitting place, even in the dead of winter. I watched three chickens snatch a few grains from the wheat drying on the concrete floor of the veranda before two small children chased them away with sticks. A bearded goat strained at his tether as though also relishing the grains spread temptingly before him.

I turned back to the negotiations. The Doctora was reviewing the points they had agreed on. Together they would assemble most of the necessities— the Doctora would bring me a bed, a table, a sitting bench, and a wardrobe from her extra furnishings, and Um Abdalla would provide curtain rods, a canister of *butagaz*, and a stove for winter. I would bring a hot plate and all the sheets, blankets, and kitchen things I needed. Everything was settled except the price, which Um Abdalla had to ask her husband about when he returned. I heard her ask the Doctora what she thought an American might be charged, but the Doctora was noncommittal. My decision to take the room "no matter what" made me vulnerable to any price they wanted to set, and indeed, when I returned a few days later, Abu Abdalla asked for more than I wanted to pay. But with the help of the Doctora, he reduced the price and we came to an agreement.

Before leaving, the Doctora reassured me in the presence of Um Abdalla that I would be perfectly safe under the protection of Um and Abu Abdalla—"It will be as though this were your own home." These words, though spoken to me, were meant for Um Abdalla, to charge her with responsibility for my welfare. "People in this village," she continued, "like foreigners, especially Americans, because so many have relatives who emigrated to the United States." "Also, in this village, they are all Christians. . . ." She didn't need to finish the sentence—she was indicating that I was trustworthy on the religious front. "Christians know their place. They may be reserved about greeting you, but it's only because they don't want to bother you. If you speak to them, they will be friendly with you." I thought back to our walk through the village and the way she greeted two girls sitting in the open window of a bus with a wave and a "Hello, Ya Helwiin (you beauties)!" and how they shouted back cheerfully, "Hello, Doctora!" I remembered also the reluctant greetings of an older woman sitting on her balcony. I was not afraid of the dangers of Wusta or of a possible lack of friendliness, but I did feel comforted that someone was charged with my welfare, even though at that moment I had no idea what such a responsibility might entail. I could see they were anxious that I form a good impression of Wusta.

The Doctora continued pointedly: "It is because the village is Christian and so safe that even government officials who are Muslim come here to build vacation homes where they can feel secure. They are afraid of the Muslim Brotherhood in Damascus, but you won't find that here in this village." I was feeling uncomfortable with the Doctora's emphasis on the Christian connection, even though I knew it was her way of drawing a common bond between us.

We said our good-byes, with the Doctora again directing a few words to each child who reappeared to see our departure, and returned to her house to tell our husbands the good news and arrange for the next visit to settle the matter of the rent.

We returned to Damascus that evening, as if to another world. The last rays of the sun were lighting the tops of the mountains behind the city, and in their shadows, the street lights gave an artificial brilliance to the broad avenues of the "smart" quarters of Abu Rumani. I thought once again how much these neighborhoods reminded me of affluent residential areas in

European cities, with their carefully tended parks and formal flower beds in the median strips of palm-lined avenues. There was no doubt that Damascus was a beautiful city—but a city of noise, tension, and pretension. Solid, placid Wusta seemed a good antidote, and I felt highly satisfied with the visit to the Doctora and Um Abdalla.

Two weeks later, it was time to settle into my new home in Wusta, and although I had looked forward with impatience to this day, when it finally came, I suddenly felt reluctant to get started on an adventure that contained so many unknowns. Our car was packed full of the necessities I was likely to need in my new home, and we drove slowly, trying to enjoy the countryside as we went. My husband was in a good mood, enjoying being away from the confines of his Damascus office, and I tried to concentrate on the scenery to alleviate my anxieties.

After half an hour, we rounded a spectacular cliff with clinging houses and came to the high plateau that announced the entrance to Wusta's valley. Here the plateau broadens out into spacious fields of ground-trained grapes whose stems in winter hug the earth in grotesque shapes and in early summer restore a vivid green to the pastel grays and browns of the rolling hills. It is as though one has reached the top of the world, though farther east, just out of sight, are even more spectacular and rugged peaks in the Lebanon range. The impression of height is fostered by low hills that prevent one from seeing beyond their limited circumference. On any day, the landscape is bleak, but on a cold day with glowering clouds hanging low over the hills, the landscape is forbidding and the urge irresistible to seek a warm and friendly place. At this spot, I would anticipate the warm stove in the cozy family room at Um Abdalla's, just a few minutes down the valley.

From monochrome to pastel shades takes only a few surprisingly short weeks in springtime, when the brilliant blue skies with their wind-chased clouds bring new life to the valley. The colors brighten and then slowly deepen into the dull shades of late summer, signaling that the time for harvest is near. Along this roadside in the fall, a farmer sits next to his rag-festooned shack, and when you stop, he sells you an excellent *dips*, a thick molasses made from these same grapes, or you might stock up for the winter on raisins and figs from his donkey's saddlebags. I never learned much about land use in this specific area, but since it was clear that the farmer came from some distance to tend his fields, I suspected that the land use pattern was similar to that of Wusta, where fields are often rented far from a farmer's village.

Finally and spectacularly, because one waits for its appearance, the monastery and the church of Mafraq, for which the region is famous, rise like a Brigadoon out of the mists. Set high on a hill in the center of a small town, the outline of its buildings comes and goes on stormy days in winter, first spotlighted by a shaft of sunlight and then disappearing again when an ungenerous gloom descends over the valley. So often does this miracle of weather occur that it is scarcely remarked by local inhabitants, who have long since stopped noticing the persistently spectacular beauty of their valley. Their attentions are drawn instead to a different kind of miracle, a small discoloration shaped like the figure of the Madonna, which appeared a few years before on the stone steps leading to the monastery. This miracle attracts the pious on Sundays who hope to obtain some benefit from its special powers.

Mafraq is a fascinating and lively place to visit—all the more so when you have lived in a smaller village for a while. But for this first visit to Wusta, we passed it by and continued up the valley until we came to the narrower and more deeply rutted lane that led to Wusta. Tall dark cypress trees lined the roadway, a reminder of some long-ago resident's foresightedness. At the end of the road, we turned into a dirt lane and stopped in front of the home of Abu and Um Abdalla.

No life was immediately visible in the house, so since I already had a key to my room, we unloaded the car and, without stopping to arrange things, walked up into the low hills directly behind the village. The view over the houses to the valley completed the transition from city to village, to lodge me securely in the place I would stay for the next eight months.

When my husband had left, it took me only a few minutes to arrange the furniture waiting there and even less time to put away the few things I had brought with me. I pulled the Doctora's bed to a space along the wall with the room's only light socket so I could read at night, arranged the iron child's bed converted to a daybed along a second wall, placed the table and chair against a window to catch the light, hung my clothes on hooks scattered around the walls, and distributed a few utensils and cans of food among the shelves of the small room that served as a kitchen. Jesus and the lamb stared down from their spot near the ceiling, unperturbed by all this activity. In the two windows, I hung print curtains already sewn to size and found to my delight that their designs replicated the bird and flower patterns of the wrought iron protective grills. I set the satchel with my papers on the floor under the table, and the room was ready.

As promised, the Doctora had provided the items of furniture I needed, and Um Abdalla's boys had carried them to my room before I arrived. Um Abdalla stopped by for a few minutes to inquire whether the curtain rod was acceptable, and Abu Abdalla helped me attach the propane canister to the two-burner hot plate I had bought in Damascus. Both then quickly retreated, and quiet returned, except for the distant noise of children playing at the neighbor's house.

I pulled the papers out of their satchel and slowly arranged them in piles. But not ready for work and hoping to attract some attention, I went out to pick wildflowers for my table. Lying by the roadside was a tin can—not too badly rusted—to serve as a flower vase. No one was visible along the lane, and after walking slowly for a hundred meters or so, I returned to my room, disappointed at finding no one, and pondered again how I might make some contact with my neighbors.

Suddenly, the sound of an amplified voice broke the silence. I looked out the window to see a man with a loudspeaker and a small three-wheel truck circling the neighborhood. Um Abdalla and the neighbor next door emerged from their homes and waved the driver to a stop. Soon they were hanging over the back of the vehicle, where large baskets of produce, as yet invisible to me, were stacked. I joined them, feigning interest in buying from the peddler. My neighbors were casually straining handfuls of green olives through their fingers and letting them fall back into the baskets. The peddler all the while pointed out the quality of the olives in each basket and dwelt particularly long on the special excellence of his most expensive variety. They asked the price, and he responded with the graduated prices of each before revealing the price of the ones in which they had shown the most interest. They looked disinterested but finally offered a price for his best variety that was a great deal lower than the price he had mentioned earlier. He looked annoyed that his time was being wasted and started to climb back in his truck. "All right, then, give us a good price so we can buy several kilos," the women urged. Then the bargaining started in earnest, though both parties were still far apart.

They began to talk about other things. Where did he come from? He came from the next village; they forgot about the bargaining and began to discuss mutual acquaintances who lived in his village. He described the house of someone in Wusta who had bought a large quantity of olives from him, and they supplied the name of the family who lived there. The two women suddenly suggested a slightly higher price than their previous one, and he responded with a slightly lower one than he had asked earlier.

Abu Abdalla joined the group and continued the bargaining in a more authoritative tone. Finally, after half an hour, they took away fifteen kilos of green olives for S£90,[3] enough of the green variety to supply the two households for the winter. The peddler weighed out the quantities, using a stone they all took for granted was a correct weight, and added a handful to each of their purchases to make them feel he was generous.

I asked the women how they made these hard green olives edible. They seemed surprised that I didn't know and suggested that I come with them to see how it was done. It was the opportunity I had wanted, and I quickly agreed. We spent the rest of the day until the sun went down working on the olives, first in the house of the neighbor next door and then later on the back porch of our house.

They explained to me the process of preserving olives: "You make three slits in each olive and then let them sit for twenty days in water that you change frequently." I worked along with them in the slitting operation. The men and children congregated around our work area, and occasionally one of the women made a cup of tea for everyone. There was an easy informality among them that made it difficult to distinguish who belonged to which spouse and children. The men did not slit olives but helped care for the smaller children, who alternated between crawling over them and playing by themselves independent of their parents.

The women wanted to know whether I had children and what their names were. They exclaimed at my good fortune of having three boys and wanted to know where they were living and why I wasn't taking care of them, since they were unmarried. They also wanted to know how my husband managed to get along without me to cook and clean for him in Damascus, and they thought it strange that it would be enough for him to have a cook and a maid to take care of him without my being there to give them orders. Finally, they wanted to know my name, which until then they had not known except for a brief introduction by the Doctora when we first came to ask about renting the room. They didn't feel comfortable with the Mrs. Rugh she had used and were searching for a better way of referring to me. We discussed this for a while, and I offered my first name, Andrea, as a possibility, to which Um Abdalla returned that her name was Laila. Abu

Abdalla liked the idea of calling me Um Dawud, after my oldest son, David, and so adopted that name for the rest of my stay in Wusta.

These questions were the sum of the interest they expressed in me, except a few weeks later in what came to be our customary morning coffee hour, when Um Abdalla and the neighbor wanted to know about my parents and my parents-in-law—what their names were and whether they were still alive. Perhaps they considered other questions too personal or my life in America so far outside their experience that they were unable to think of questions to ask. These few personal details appeared to be enough for them to form an impression of me. They never expressed an interest in that paramount question of first concern to Americans: what my occupation was or the occupation of any other member of my household. When I volunteered this information by telling them about my sons' interests in economics and art, they fell silent, their faces expressing the sympathy they felt that the boys were not interested in more distinguished fields such as medicine and engineering. They knew that from time to time I traveled to Egypt to work on education projects, but what interested them in these travels was where I stayed and who my friends were rather than what my professional activities were.

On that first day, I learned that Um and Abu Abdalla had five children. Lisa, the fifteen-year-old, was the oldest, followed by Abdalla (fourteen), Muna (twelve), Hanna (eleven), and Boulos (nine). Um Abdalla was just thirty-two, and Abu Abdalla about forty-five. When I asked him, Abu Abdalla told me he worked in the local village government office (*baladiyya*) next to the primary school. It was characteristic of him to release information slowly and let me find out later that he was engaged in a number of other commercial activities, including a large chicken-farming operation that provided a substantial part of his income. It was only later that I learned he was also the *mukhtar* of the village, the main government official in the community.

In the course of the day, I discovered that the neighbor who had been buying olives with us was Um Abdalla's younger sister, Um George. Um George also had five children. George (twelve), the oldest, was the son of her first husband, who had been killed in a trucking accident. I learned this fact not because it was offered but because I mistakenly called Um George's husband Abu George, as would have been correct if he had been the father of her oldest child. The four younger children, Miriam (five), Lisa (four), Adil (three), and Ilyas (one), all preschoolers, were fathered by this second husband, Abu Adil, who was the brother of both her first husband and Abu Abdalla.

Um George's two forms of marriage, I knew, were not uncommon in the Arab world: the first, the marriage of herself and her sister to siblings of an unrelated family, Abu Abdalla and Abu George, and the second, to her deceased husband's brother, Abu Adil, who was supposed to be the best substitute husband and father for his brother's family. Both types of marriage were thought to keep families emotionally close to each other and ensure a warm nest of related kin in which to raise children. This was the theory, even though in practice, some families found that involving closely related people in marriage only complicated and intensified irritations between spouses. For example, if one couple were not getting along, the difficulty might spread to the other couple, who were likely to be more loyal to their own siblings than to their spouses. This never appeared to be the case in these Wusta families, however, who gave every evidence of having a warm and congenial relationship as both couples and relatives.

Meanwhile, the olive slitting continued in Um George's kitchen. Um George and Um Abdalla did the work with a deftness that the rest of us—myself and Um Abdalla's two teenage daughters—could not imitate successfully. Um George did not encourage the young children to help in the operation, and in truth her preschoolers were too small to be very helpful. But on their own initiative, they "worked" along with us, even when their work only consisted of putting a slit olive in the pail of finished ones. Um George ignored the children most of the time until their insistent cries for attention became too loud for our talk to continue, and then she distracted them with something to eat or a comment that made them forget the immediate problem.

Watching this tranquil scene, I found it impossible to conjure up the images of oppression sometimes associated with Arab women. The women orchestrated the olive splitting with instructions to the children to fetch a pot or remove debris and called on the men, without hesitation, to take care of whatever ailed the younger children. True, the women worked long hours on this simple, repetitive task, but everyone in the two families was drawn to the kitchen to watch them work, and the easy conversations made the time fly. Much more stressful, according to the stories they told, were the troubles the men encountered in their uncertain efforts to earn money.

Of the two men, Abu Adil was the more animated, telling stories and teasing the children. He would gather them up in his arms and let them go again, all the while engaging in the general conversation as he addressed his remarks to one or another of those present. I soon learned that he owned the large refrigerator truck parked behind the house. He complained vaguely about the difficulties he faced from governmental restrictions, but it was a long time before he trusted me enough to tell me in detail about these restrictions and how truckers circumvented them. He had just returned from a trucking journey to Saudi Arabia and was savoring the moments—apparently never long enough—when he could be with his family. His beaming face told the story. The children crawled all over him and even drew him away from the kitchen to let them sit in the cab of his truck. When he returned, he looked appreciatively at Um George, who returned his glance with a flirtatious remark and then blushed at his answer. They appeared more like newlyweds than a married couple with five children.

In his corner, the quieter Abu Abdalla also was assaulted by his young nephews and nieces to such an extent that it was difficult to determine who was the father and who was the uncle to these little children.

The men continued with their stories about trucking, a subject that I soon learned was a favorite among men in the village. Um George said that her husband had started working on trucks eight years earlier and, when I showed an interest, went on to explain how, since it took about twelve days for a round trip to Saudi Arabia, Doha, Dubai, or Bahrain, he usually had time to make about two trips a month. First he went to Lebanon to load up with vegetables and fruits, and then he headed back into Syria and down through Jordan and into the Gulf States. The actual driving time from Chtura in Lebanon to Dubai was about three days one way, but considerable time was lost in formalities at the borders, so the trip actually took much longer. When he became tired, Abu Adil would stop by the side of the road to sleep. The roads then were in good condition, but not long before, when they had not yet been paved, the trip was more dangerous and took longer. Usually when Abu Adil returned, he would bring something for Um George—a Molinex blender, cans of vegetable oil, blankets, perfume, whatever he thought she would like, and occasionally gifts for his brother's family. At one point, Abu Adil unexpectedly turned to me and said that he didn't really like truck driving very much, but "you have to work at something and it pays well."

They were amused by my questions about trucking, which they didn't think was a topic that should interest women. And when the conversation moved to the gifts that Abu Adil brought back, it gave them an excuse to turn to another favorite topic enjoyed equally by men and women—the price of things. For a while they compared the prices of the goods he brought back from the Gulf with the prices for the same items in Syria. Eventually I managed to ask about the cost of the trucks. Abu Adil's truck, it seemed, cost S£800,000 (about $200,000). Because it was a refrigerator truck, it was particularly expensive, but as Abu Adil noted when referring to other villagers' trucks, it sometimes was possible to find a stripped-down truck for S£500,000 or less. I was astonished by the price, which seemed an enormous amount of money for anyone to pay, especially for villagers who didn't appear so affluent. They reverted again to the more interesting topic of price comparisons, with each person arguing over which seller and which store gave the best prices. I turned back to the olive splitting and my own thoughts.

Finally, Um George put down the olives and began preparations for the midday meal. Um Abdalla took this cue to remove her own family tactfully from Um George's house. I returned home with them and continued to slit olives on the back porch while the oldest daughter, Lisa, kept me company preparing the salad for their own meal. I watched as she meticulously lined up sprigs of parsley, piece by piece, so the leafy portions could be gathered together and cut in tiny pieces without including any of the stems. She worked slowly and carefully, totally absorbed in what she was doing. When she finished, she took in the parsley to add to the rest of the ingredients that Um Abdalla was preparing in the kitchen.

At their urging I remained for the meal, and afterward, while the girls washed the few dishes, Um Abdalla and I slit more olives on the back porch until the sun was about to go down. Then, feeling that I had outstayed my welcome on a first visit, I excused myself, to protests that it was too early for me to leave and that I should join them in watching television inside. I remained adamant but took a pot of olives with me to finish slitting in my room—an umbilical cord to continued contact with them the next day.

A while later, one of the older girls knocked at my door with a plate of food for my evening meal and very skillfully pressed this hospitality on me despite my refusals.

Alone again, I was elated that the first day had gone so well.

TWO

———

Days

Within all of Syria's communities, life centers around the family. The individual's loyalty to his family is nearly absolute and generally overrides all other obligations. . . . To ask a Syrian where he is from usually draws a response not of geographical region, but of family origin.

— Dawn Chatty, "The Anthropology of Syrian Society"

In our household, most days began around five-thirty. Um Abdalla would slip out of bed quietly so as not to disturb Abu Abdalla and quickly dress before heading to the kitchen to start the kettle heating before she roused the sleeping children. Muna and Lisa were the first to stumble through the house collecting their belongings, each compelled by the urgency to get a favorite pair of socks or other piece of clothing in the girls' closet before her sister reached it. After a momentary disagreement, the loser—usually the younger Muna—would search for a missing sock to complete another favorite pair. Next they would reach for their school uniforms—unisex military-style trousers and jacket with epaulets, a yellow neck scarf, and a cap—all hanging over the cupboard door, ironed and ready from the night before. The girls stuffed the caps in their pockets, putting them on only at the last minute before entering school. They thought the caps unattractively masculine and would gladly have skipped wearing them were it not for the school's strict dress code.

By this time, Um Abdalla had set white cheese, flat bread, olives, and tea on a tray on the floor of the girls' room, and one by one, as soon as they were ready, the children would start to eat. Boulos ate silently and, with his characteristic economy of motion, was ready first, his books and clothes all neatly organized from the night before. Muna would throw herself down on the floor before the tray and sit gloomily contemplating the food until her mother brusquely commanded her to eat. With excruciating slowness she would wrap pieces of bread around the cheese and thrust them one after another into her mouth, washing each down with a splash of tea. Lisa always came late to the meal, carrying her open school book and continuing to mumble the lessons she had memorized the night before, her sentences hanging in midair when she took a mouthful and then resuming when her mouth once again became free. Abdalla also entered late, coming in from checking on the tractor and water truck outside the backdoor. Abu Abdalla slept on, unconscious of the preparations taking place in the rooms on the other side of the corridor.

Each day, the children from our house and cousin George from next door left for school about seven or seven-thirty, the older children a little earlier to catch the bus to Mafraq, where the intermediate school was located. When the door closed behind them, Um Abdalla cleaned away the dirty dishes, set the kettle back on the stove, and reorganized the food neatly on the tray before calling Abu Abdalla. He ate quickly, all the while telling Um Abdalla his plans for the day—he might try to catch a ride into town after work to buy the weekly meat supply, pick up some bags of chicken feed, or stop to see how a worker on a construction site was doing. Then he would disappear on his motorbike up the hilly track behind the house to check on the chickens in their sheds half a mile away. Fifteen minutes later, he would reappear again down the road on his way to his office in the village—the noisy motorbike echoing down the valley. His official work was supposed to start about eight, but no one took particular notice if he was a few minutes late. I would listen for the returning bike—if it came back soon, then all was well with the chickens, if not, we would hear about the problems at the sheds during the noonday meal.

Next door at Um George's, by eight at the latest, after their brother George was off to school and their mother had had time to dress them, three of the preschoolers, except for baby Ilyas, would be shooed outside to play while their mother cleaned up the messes of the night before. Usually the first I heard of them was the scraping of a stool being dragged across the porch and then little faces peering in the window by my bed to find out whether I was awake yet. They followed their mother's injunction not to disturb me, and according to their own narrow interpretation of what "not disturb" meant, they were careful not to wake me. Since I was the main novelty in sight, it was hard for them to suppress the temptation to visit, especially when they saw me writing at my desk.

By the time they arrived, I had usually been working on my manuscript for an hour or two, rushing to get as much done as possible before the social part of the day began. When the preschoolers arrived, my work effectively ended. On the first day they came to visit, wanting to be friendly, I invited them in and tried to engage them in conversation, but either my Arabic accent was strange or shyness overcame them, and they only stood silently observing me. Finally, five-year-old Miriam, the oldest, started circling the room and examining each object she found, picking up one item at a time to show her sister, little Lisa, four years old, and giggling as she set it down again. Trailing behind her sister and intent on what she was being shown, Lisa drew a line with her finger absently along the outlines of the furniture—up over the day bed, down across the seat of the chair, up over the table, and across the bed—I raced to catch the neatly piled chapters as they slid in a jumble in the wake of little Lisa's finger. I felt annoyed that these children, who were old enough to know better, had not been taught to "respect" someone else's private property. And then in a rush of anthropological self-correction, I realized that everything in the narrowly circumscribed world of their experience up until then had been common property and that it was too much to expect that they would suddenly recognize the privateness of my things. I was torn between a desire to teach them "the right way" and reluctance to admonish them, for fear they might run away and not come back.

Little Adil, three, crowded in next to the girls, also wanting to see the objects. But he soon tired of being the recipient of her instruction and began to imitate Miriam with all her characteristic gestures, striding around the room making her inspection. I began to feel like a Gulliver in a room full of jolly Lilliputians who had effectively assumed control of the action. Eventually, their circlings brought them to the kitchen, where Miriam again was the first to notice a pile of dirty dishes from the night before sitting in the sink. Watching me for a reaction and seeing none, she dragged a chair to the sink and began organizing the two other children to do a thorough and most professional job of washing up.

From that day on, the pattern was set, thanks to my equivocating on how to handle my relations with the children. Each morning they took over my housework, at first hesitating to see whether I would discourage them, as their mother would have done, but eventually relaxing and assuming prioritorial rights over the work. They knew their mother would not have approved of their "messes," her reasoning being that when they were old enough to do the job right was time enough to teach them how to do it properly and that in the meantime it was frivolous indulgence to allow them anywhere near tasks that might increase her workload.

My allowing them to do "forbidden" work prepared the way for a reversal of roles to develop between the children and myself. When we were alone, they assumed the role of adults helping me and in some cases even teaching me the right way to do things. One day, for example, Lisa, assuming her mother's look of annoyance, took the broom away from me after becoming impatient over how long it was taking me to sweep the side porch and finished the job herself.

The guilty secret of the housework I never revealed to their mother, since I sensed it might irritate her enough to prevent their early morning visits. To my "American way of thinking," what they did was praiseworthy and something their mother should have been pleased to have them do so well. Children have so much to learn, I found myself thinking, that any initiative of this sort showing them ready to develop a skill could not be encouraged at too young an age. As an adult, it was surely my duty to encourage such initiatives with patience even when there were major imperfections in the way the children performed the tasks. After all, how many heavy cakes and tasteless cookies had I eaten with relish when my own children were trying their inexperienced hands at baking? It was still many weeks away before I understood more sympathetically that Um George's approach was consistent with her other efforts to train the children and not just a matter of benign neglect.

Each day was the same. Lisa would begin sweeping my small porch while Miriam would climb on a stool and begin the dishes—she knew how to fill the dishpan with water and soap, how to scrub each dish individually, and how to rinse it before placing it in the draining rack. Adil would spin in circles or wait patiently for the work to finish. Eventually the cleaning up would come to an end when the two girls washed down the stone tiles of the kitchen floor and Adil skated happily through the soapsuds. For the most part, the two girls were competent workers, and except for an occasional broken dish or the one time when they washed the floor with so much sudsy dish-washing detergent that it required a lake of water to wash all the suds down the drain, their efforts would improve the appearance of my small quarters. A few minutes cleaning up after them was all that was needed to finish the job.

When their work was done, I tried to interest them in papers and crayons to prolong my work time, but these rarely occupied them for long, and after inspecting the objects in the room for a while longer, they would disappear outside to play. Then it was my turn to look out the window and keep track of their activities for as long as they were within eyesight.

Meanwhile, in their respective homes, Um Abdalla and Um George, like whirlwinds, were scrubbing the tiled floors of their homes until they shone, washing clothes in their wringer washing machines, airing the cushions of their sitting rooms, straightening the displaced articles from the night before, and so on through the innumerable tasks of housekeeping. The thoroughness with which they approached everyday cleaning—what I might have considered necessary only for spring cleaning—never ceased to amaze me. I noticed that whereas I tended to concentrate on drains, sinks, toilets, and furniture surfaces, they concentrated on floors, bringing a new significance to the act of removing our shoes at the outside door.

By ten o'clock, Um Abdalla's house was clean; the clothes were hung out on the line; and wiping the perspiration from her brow even in the coldest weather, Um Abdalla was ready for a cup of tea or coffee. We would meet in good weather on the sunny back porch and, on cold gray winter days, in her family sitting room next to the potbellied stove. In the sitting room, the tea kettle would sizzle comfortably as a background to our talk, and the continually hungry small children would slap pieces of unleavened bread against the hot sides of the stove until they were ready to peel off and eat in crisp warm curls. From Um Abdalla's demeanor, I could tell it was a high point in her day to sit for a time, knowing that the hard work had been accomplished and that yet an hour remained before she had to prepare the noonday meal.

Um George would join us a little later—her chores took longer with four young children—and the conversation would become more lively with her practical, no-nonsense comments on what had taken place since we last saw each other the night before. We discussed what clothes the women planned to buy for the upcoming holidays or Um Abdalla's worries about her son Abdalla, who had accidentally shot himself in the hand with a birdshot pellet, or Um George's concern that it was taking longer than usual for her husband to return with his truck from Saudi Arabia or, on a happier note, speculation on what he might bring as gifts this time. Maybe there would be news about people they knew in the village, brought from the office by Abu

Abdalla the day before or by Um George's neighbor stopping by on her way to the store that morning.

Morning get-togethers differed from family evenings in that we discussed the "women's subjects" that Um George and Um Abdalla felt were inappropriate when men and children were around. We indulged ourselves in emotional stories of people's lives, made better if they were exceedingly tragic or had surprise happy endings—I would tell them stories of the people's lives in the slums of Cairo where I had once worked, and they would tell the stories of acquaintances in the village or secondhand stories from farther away. Sometimes we engaged in spontaneous silliness about how the men reacted to something the women did, or they would laugh at the remembered comments of guests from the night before. We would tell stories of child bearing, travails with parents-in-laws, or concerns about husbands and children. They expressed opinions about controversial decisions made by their husbands that they would not have expressed in front of them, or they talked about projects they would like to see accomplished in the future—additions or improvements to their houses or the building of a store that would bring Um George's family more money. Though infrequent, their grumblings and complaints also were aired more freely in the morning women's times, even though they considered it inappropriate to complain or show strong emotion when the rest of the household was present. In family gatherings, the women presented themselves as paragons of maturity and responsibility.

It surprised me that there was so much to say in these morning sessions when we had just seen one another only the night before. One reason perhaps was that it had been twenty-four hours since we had last had the luxury of unrestrained, relaxed woman talk. Interest hung in the morning sessions on the most minute of daily details—how many loads of wash they had done that day, which beds had been stripped, which floors washed, which child's clothes were wearing out—details that would have seemed inconsequential if repeated in front of the rest of the family but that were of great concern to the women in demonstrating the standards of household cleanliness they kept. Despite the relaxed nature of our meetings, they maintained a formality with each other that rarely revealed either deeply felt emotions or any image of themselves as less than fully in control, competent housewives.

Sometimes during the morning tea, Um Abdalla would make minor sewing repairs, or we would watch Um George's children while she went off on errands to the store. Rarely did neighbors drop in for more than a few minutes during this time, for the break was too brief in the morning to allow for the long visits people preferred. But occasionally, Um Abdalla's and Um George's mother came over for a short visit—in her case, probably choosing the morning time for exactly that reason, that she would not have to stay very long.

After a while, the morning discussions turned to what we would prepare for the noonday meal. With the exception of bread, most villagers did not buy groceries every day, and therefore choosing a menu simply required thinking through the larder for combinations of ingredients they had not eaten too recently. Every week or so, Abu Abdalla would bring meat enough for ten days at a time, and they would put it in the freezing compartment of the refrigerator. Rationed items—sugar, rice, and oil—were bought in bulk in town and stored along with the foods preserved for winter in an open loft over the kitchen. One of the boys or girls would climb up there for things when they were needed in the kitchen. Syrian village women preserve an amazing variety of foods: dried okra on strings, olives pickled in brine, eggplant pickled or dried, numerous types of grains, cheese balls flavored with thyme and stored in olive oil, molasses jams, raisins, and nuts. Up in the loft, one could find the favorite *kishk*—a mixture of goat milk and grain dried into powder or balls to be reconstituted into a sour-tasting soup or added to other dishes. *Kishk* was not one of my favorites, since it tended to attract weevils, which would appear later, floating in the soup.

Occasionally, a child was sent to the store for some greens or other fresh vegetables. When the sun was warm enough, we would chop the vegetables outside on the back porch, and sometimes we listened there to a favorite radio program, *The Family Hour*, which had dramatic vignettes about the proper way to bring up children and care for the household.

Um Abdalla and Um George usually made separate dishes for their two households, but occasionally, for something difficult like *kibbee*, they shared in the preparation, each doing the part she was most skilled at. In the case of *kibbee*, one sister formed the round husk of grains and meat, and the other made the stuffing of spices, pinenuts, and meat. They insisted that each did her task best and that the dish tasted better when they worked together. They usually did not make *kibbee* unless it fit the schedule of both sisters. At such times when they made a joint dish for both families, they divided the expenses for the ingredients proportionately so each household paid its share.

One day they tried to teach me how to form the balls, but the imperfect forms I produced did not satisfy their critical eyes, and they reformed them again into perfect balls. They were not very patient teachers, nor were they willing—even to save my feelings—to compromise their standards of perfection. They were ready to let me sit as a perpetual guest unless I begged to be allowed to help with the preparations—so I could learn, I claimed, how to cook Syrian style but really because it embarrassed me to be continually on the receiving end of their hospitality. Once I read in a book about Pakistan that because generosity and hospitality are admired traits in Muslim-dominated societies, the highest form of these values is the hospitality given to a stranger—a guest with no expectation or even possibility of return.[1] Perhaps something like this value operated here, for Um Abdalla's and Um George's continuous hospitality to me without evidence of irritation seemed far above the call of duty and even made me wonder at times if the cost of entertaining me did not outstrip the value of the rent I paid each month. In any case, helping with the food preparation turned out—surprisingly to one who avoids the kitchen whenever possible—to be a relaxed and enjoyable time working together.

The younger children from both households started coming home from school around twelve-thirty and the older ones at one-thirty, with the times varying slightly, depending on the day of the week and whether they were coming from the primary school in the village or the intermediate school in Mafraq. In Um Abdalla's house, the two older girls threw down their schoolbooks, changed out of their uniforms, and immediately set to work without being told to help prepare the food, and the boys went off to turn on the hoses to fill the water carts they would later take to the chickens. Abu Abdalla came home from the baladiyya office about two, bringing hot bread from the bakery next to his office, and the whole family would take his arrival as a signal to assemble at their places on the carpet around the large tray containing the meal. Each person dipped pieces of freshly baked bread into the main dish or scooped up olives and cheeses using the bread as an encompassing pocket. At first, I thought this a cumbersome way of eating, but the advantages soon became apparent—we ate proportionally larger amounts of bread than more costly foods and avoided using many utensils and dishes that would increase the amount of washing up after meals. It also was hygienic, since a new piece of bread was broken off and dipped in a dish with each bite.

Each day, they repeated the same ritual of asking me to join them for the meal, and if, out of embarrassment at being such a constant guest, I declined the invitation, a plate with more than I could eat appeared later at my door, brought by a small, shy child whom I never could refuse.

After lunch, the adults relaxed over tea while the girls cleaned up the dishes and the boys took the water carts up the road to the chicken houses. During teatime, the talk concentrated on Abu Abdalla's news of the day— what had gone wrong at the chicken house, an observation about someone seeking a permit to build, or an item of news from his work or the village. It was during this time, uninterrupted by children or guests, that I came to know Abu Abdalla best. Like Um Abdalla, he worked hard to carry out the Doctora's charge to make me feel at home in Wusta, but his approach differed from hers. Um Abdalla responded to me in a sympathetic woman-to-woman way that she would have used with any "stranded" female far from home. To her, it was a calamity to be separated from children and family, and the fact that I had voluntarily chosen this path was so incomprehensible to her that she simply avoided thinking about why I had made such a decision. On his part, Abu Abdalla used the only way he knew to make me feel part of the conversations—sly jokes that both included and excluded me, with word plays in an Arabic too complicated for me to understand fully. I knew his approach preserved a distance between us that was appropriate under the conditions in which I, as a stranger female, lived under his roof, and usually I did not feel offended by his jokes at my expense.

Despite his delight in taking me off the deep end with Arabic, Abu Abdalla also spent a great deal of time, when he realized it interested me, patiently explaining his work and teaching me such mundane tasks as how to lay a tile floor correctly. He had learned this skill and a host of others by trial and error while building his own house. After explaining at length how to lay the floor with a slope so that the water could drain off, he would conclude his lesson with a comment about how such work was not for women—always with a twinkle in his eye that let me know he was aware of how his words would irritate me. How he came to know my feminist tendencies I'll never know, but he probably suspected them from the fact of my coming alone to Wusta and leaving my wifely responsibilities in Damascus.

Abu Abdalla was a quiet man, slowly but methodically going about his business with hardly a word. Little roused him to haste or to anger, but when something finally did, he smoldered and occasionally took fire. He knew the value of words and how to make the eloquent speeches of reproach or commitment for which Arab men and women seem to have such a special talent. However, much of the time, his silence and lack of expression could be mistaken for dull passivity, until a sly gleam in his eye gave away the shrewdly calculating mind underneath. I liked and respected Abu Abdalla, and he always treated me with a respect that was not deferential, despite what to him must have seemed a clear class difference between us.

Abu Abdalla was not in any way aggressively chauvinistic—he was always respectful of his wife, though in a familiar way that took for granted his right to make demands on her. I had no reason to think that he behaved any differently when I was not there. At the same time, his quiet ways did not change the fact that the whole family considered him the undisputed authority in the house when it came to conflicts. Um Abdalla and the children made sure, however, that it rarely came to this point. They all waited cautiously to see which way the wind was blowing with Abu Abdalla before taking a position on any family matter.

In appearance, Abu Abdalla typified a certain kind of Syrian physique: he was of medium height, square and solid though not really heavy in build, and with jet black hair slicked back over the crown of his head. As was the case with most male Syrians, his upper lip sported a bristling mustache. He was barely of the first generation in the village that consistently dressed in Western dress, as opposed to an older peasant-style dress of baggy pants and full shirt. His choice of Western dress almost certainly came from a desire to demonstrate his status as a literate man, having completed primary school, and because his employment as a government office worker demanded recognition of his formal education. As did most villagers, even those who wore Western dress, he wrapped a traditional black-and-white checked scarf around his head, not as any sort of statement but, rather, for the practical reason that it protected his head and neck from the sun and cold air as he rode his motorbike around town.

At the end of our relaxed afternoon teatimes, Um Abdalla and Abu Abdalla would settle any matters between them, Um Abdalla perhaps asking Abu Abdalla for permission to go to Damascus in the afternoon to buy some clothes for the children, or he telling her that he would not be back from the chicken houses until after dark, or together deciding if Abdalla should be taken to the doctor to change the dressing on his hand. After a while, and sometimes after a short nap, Abu Abdalla would join the two older boys at the chicken houses to check the grinding of the feed and the day's production of eggs. Father and older sons usually did not return home until five or so in the evening.

Meanwhile, the women were relatively free from housework for the rest of the afternoon. Lisa slipped away to start memorizing her homework for the next day. Muna played with her young cousins until her mother reminded her that she needed to start her schoolwork or finish refilling the stoves' fuel bottles or carry out the scraps to the chickens or sweep the porch. Each chore took much longer than necessary for Muna to do, as she used them to delay returning to her schoolwork. Occasionally, Um Abdalla and Um George would decide to visit someone in the village, and during this time, the older children in each household would be responsible for watching the younger ones to see that they kept out of mischief. Although they were never given explicit directions about babysitting, the older children knew that if anything happened while their mothers were gone, they would be held responsible. The mothers, on the other hand, knew that the older children could not get much homework done while they were watching the little ones and therefore tried not to stay away too long. In addition, the smaller children understood well the boundaries of their territory—the households and yards of the two families—and it was unusual for them to stray from this area or for the older children to have to watch them continuously.

The danger to the children in being casually attended was greatest in winter when the cold weather kept them indoors and near the searing hot stoves. But I was the one who, more anxious than their mothers, worried that in their rough-and-tumble play, they might fall against the stoves. When I mentioned this possibility, the mothers were aghast at the idea, not that it might happen, but that in bringing up the subject I might precipitate that dreadful calamity. I therefore learned to quiet the instincts that made me warn about impending dangers.

More commonly, in the late afternoons we sat together in Um Abdalla's or Um George's house. Um George's house was usually more convenient because her young children were constantly in need of the kind of attention only her house could provide. Often we were joined there by neighbors or relatives coming for informal visits. An older woman, Um Yusef, our neighbor from next door, came frequently, even though to all intents and purposes, because she was deaf, she could enjoy only the visual aspects of our company. Um Abdalla felt sorry for her and sometimes took her gifts of food. But it was Um Yusef who more often sought out our company, since she was in the unusual position for the village of being home alone most of the time and our house—or at least Um George's house—was not more than a few yards from hers. Um Abdalla also maintained good relations with the rest of Um Yusef's family, from whom Um Yusef was at that time estranged. Um Abdalla listened to both sides of their story when she saw them separately but was careful not to take sides.

Another day, the visitor might be Um Abdalla's and Um George's mother, who lived a few lanes away with their brother, Nabil, and his wife. Her obvious preference for her son over her daughters and for his small son at the expense of her other grandchildren caused a strain in her relationships with Um Abdalla and Um George, and therefore visits between them were not as frequent or as cordial as they should have been. Nevertheless, we occasionally made obligatory visits to brother Nabil when he returned safely from his trucking trips or to congratulate him on the birth of his latest baby. The formal nature of the visits reflected the tensions in these relationships; our visits were the very least that had to be done to keep relations from deteriorating further. In this respect, my presence was an advantage, as a conversation that revolved almost totally around me allowed them to avoid personal differences.

On other days, we might visit distant relatives who lived even closer and with whom we had more cordial relations. One time we went to see the trousseau of a bride-to-be and the gifts her bridegroom had given her. Another day, we visited the home of a poor elderly couple, specifically because the old man had broken his wrist. On another occasion, we visited the family of the priest, a little awkwardly because he had asked especially to see me. He was not someone the family would normally visit on their own. Another time, we visited the wife of the alcoholic Abu Munir, for whom everyone felt sorry because her husband spent so much money on his addictions that the family barely had enough to get by. She was lonely, and Um Abdalla brought me to see her so she would have the "exciting" experience of meeting a foreigner.

Um Abdalla and Um George usually visited others out of a sense of obligation: because someone was sick, because someone among the circle of those who had a special connection was lonely and needed company, because someone should be congratulated on a particular event, or simply because it was time to return a call so that people would not be offended. The sisters carried out the calls with a certain amount of resignation, as they required preparation: stockings, high heels, makeup, nicer clothes, and a dressy overcoat. Even if we caught our hostess unaware in her everyday clothes, she would look at us; size up the situation, including the fact of my presence;

and, unless we said something quickly, would throw open the parlor door where we would sit in our overcoats until the heat from the stove penetrated the icy dampness of the infrequently used room. If Um Abdalla and Um George were alone, they would automatically have been ushered into the family room, with a few apologies about the state of disorder. But a stranger needed to be shown the best the family could offer. Um Abdalla would reassure them, saying I was just like one of the family, implying that they need not try to impress me, and usually by the second visit, if we were lucky, this tactic would work.

Much nicer, of course, was to be ushered into the family room in winter where everyone would be sitting on the floor and the children scampering in and out with parental admonitions to close the door quickly so the cold air would not come in. In these rooms, the whole family was present and engaged in whatever was their normal household activity: the children completing their homework for the next day, the father and maybe the grandfather leading the discussion with amusing stories that made everyone laugh, the older girls and women coming in and out with nuts and candies and tea or coffee. These calls lasted from about four-thirty to six-thirty, unannounced in most cases, and provoking warm greetings of welcome when we entered, as if we lived some thousand miles away from one another. In truth, we saw little of these people in winter other than during these formal visits.

At six-thirty, we would take our leave amidst protestations and reminders to come more often. We would walk partway home together and then go our separate ways, to Um Abdalla's or Um George's, for on winter evenings during the week, the two households often carried on their evening activities separately. Back home, there was usually minor chaos in the living room, where, taking advantage of their mother's absence, the children had been tumbling among the scattered seat cushions. The mothers would set about straightening up things and settling everyone back to their homework again. Within minutes, the atmosphere would change to one of orderly concentration.

The main business of evenings during the school year was the children's homework. The family sitting room where everyone gathered to carry out this mission was instrumental in developing a sense among the family members that they "worked together." No one considered studying alone in another part of the house, no matter how noisy the room became. No one left the room except to visit the bathroom or to prepare food, which was brought to the sitting room for everyone to eat later in the evening. When they had finished their homework, the children remained in this room to play quietly until sleep drove them to bed.

We would arrange ourselves in the family room, with each child concentrating on figuring math problems or reciting lessons that had to be memorized by the following morning. The adults sat around the periphery, Um Abdalla folding or ironing laundry or catching up on darning, and Abu Abdalla responding to questions about the homework or listening to a recitation of memorized lessons. I would sit with some needlework and admire the drawing books or sewing patterns that Muna constructed, but I lacked the skill to help with the intricacies of Arabic or social studies.

The children differed considerably in scholastic ability. Lisa, the oldest, was not an intellect, but she had mastered the education system by honing her memorization skills until they were nearly perfect. By dint of hard work and long hours of memorization, she was able to obtain relatively good marks.

The silent Abdalla, next in line of the children, also worked hard and usually did well without asking for help. But during the winter I spent with the family, he was not doing as well as usual because of a series of minor operations for the gunshot wound in his hand, which kept him out of school for significant periods of time. The second daughter, Muna, was a cheerful, good-natured girl, not very interested in any of her schoolwork except the sewing lessons. She had become clever at making her parents think that she had finished her schoolwork, so that she could do other things that interested her more. Her parents continually reminded her that she needed to start her mathematics, Arabic, or religious studies, but no sooner would Muna become immersed in one of these subjects than something was bound to distract her—a conversation between her parents, a question from a sibling, an observation on a piece of clothing Um Abdalla was folding, a request from a brother to go get him a glass of water. The parents contributed to these distractions by asking Muna to serve guests who unexpectedly dropped in to see Abu Abdalla. Even in her slightly clumsy adolescent way, Muna took greater pains to do the serving correctly than her older sister Lisa did, and although the parents did not say so, it seemed they saved Lisa the trouble purposely because she appeared more capable of achieving academic success.

The second son, Hanna, like Abdalla, was a quiet boy who produced satisfactory though not spectacular school results. Hanna was good with his hands, however, and his father seemed to be grooming him for a technical vocation by giving him jobs around the house that used his mechanical abilities. The third son and youngest child, Boulos, was the academic star of the group. He fully absorbed himself in his schoolwork and, mindless of the distractions in the study room, finished his homework in record time. His parents, reviewing his notebooks, found them meticulously written with very few mistakes. Any expectations the family might have for producing a highly educated professional were invested in this boy. He was not given any time-consuming tasks related to chicken production, as were the older two boys, who were more inclined to follow their father's footsteps in entrepreneurial tasks depending on experience rather than academic training.

The parents appeared to have made conscious judgments about each child's special capabilities and gave each one room to develop those capabilities without interference. Often, the differential treatment the children received seemed unfair to me, confirming in them existing tendencies rather than trying to broaden their skills. For instance, I would have liked to see them push Muna to develop her academic skills somewhat more seriously or assign to Boulos more family responsibilities, but the children seemed to have acknowledged these differences and did not themselves expect to develop all aspects of school and household skills to the same degree.

During these evenings at Abu Abdalla's, Abu Munir was likely to drop by. On my first day in town walking with the Doctora, I had met him butchering meat in front of the main store. At that time, he had appeared somewhat too familiar with us for a person of Middle Eastern background, and the Doctora hastily explained that he was known for enjoying his alcohol too much. Abu Munir stayed away from home as much as possible to avoid his wife's scoldings when he returned in his inevitable state of drunkenness. Because there was nowhere else to go on a wintry night in Wusta, he visited any house that would receive him. Um Abdalla explained to me that "her heart was a sensitive one" and overflowed easily, by which she meant she was unable to stand the sight of anyone suffering. She said this was the main reason she fed Abu Munir. "He drinks," she explained, "because he has an unhappy home and his wife doesn't feed him properly or make it pleasant for him, so he goes out and forgets his problems with drink." She had a very clear picture of what both Abu Munir and his wife should be doing to prevent such problems, but she accepted the facts as they were and gave Abu Munir a cup of tea and something to eat whenever he came for a visit. As far as I knew, neither she nor Abu Abdalla drank alcoholic beverages, except during the

New Year's festivities when, according to Um Abdalla, Abu Abdalla invited his brother and Abu Munir for a night of gambling and drinking. I suspected that the grapes hanging in my room on my first visit to Um Abdalla were either for this event or belonged to Abu Munir. In any case, I never saw them give Abu Munir alcoholic beverages on his evening visits, and they pretended not to notice when he brought his own bottle. They didn't think it their business to reform his behavior.

By the time Abu Munir reached our house on a normal evening, he was hardly in need of an additional drink. He fancied himself a linguist and—perhaps to reciprocate the hospitality he received at Um Abdalla's—had decided to tutor Lisa in French. My presence also gave him the opportunity to show off his English skills. Whether in French or English, neither Lisa nor I could distinguish the meanings of the foreign phrases he shouted at us in an explosion of saliva. He would pour out a torrent of words and wait expectantly for our response. I would answer in Arabic (he told me he didn't understand my "dialect" of English) to a question I imagined he had asked, which encouraged him to further discussion, and so we would go back and forth until the children and Abu Abdalla were convulsed with the hilarious performance that we carried out so seriously. Um Abdalla would look sympathetically at me, wishing she could help but understanding even less of the dialogue than I pretended to.

In Um Abdalla's house, the children eventually slipped away to bed when they finished their homework and became sleepy. There was usually no need for the parents to remind them that it was time to go unless they had slipped into the television room to watch the late night serial with the adults. They knew this was forbidden on school nights, but if they were well behaved and quiet, their presence might be overlooked.

In Um George's house, the evening routine was much the same, with the exception that Abu Adil was usually off traveling, and the four younger children had not yet started school so had no homework to complete. Nevertheless, when we visited Um George, we all sat together in the same room so that the only school-aged child, George, would have company while he studied. Um George tried to keep the playful, tumbling children from bothering him, not so much out of concern for the noise as for the toddlers' efforts to seize his papers and engage him in their games. The students of both households were used to a great deal of pandemonium while they studied; they would take part in it for a while and then return to work. The almost continuous interruptions, however, usually prolonged the study period into an all-evening affair.

Sometime during the evening, Um Abdalla or Um George, depending on the household, would prepare a simple meal that everyone sat down to share. Whereas breakfast and the afternoon meal were readied punctually to coincide with work and school schedules, supper was offered when the mother of the house sensed that everyone was ready to eat. The food was informal and likely to include leftovers or prepared foods that were always available in the larder. In the warmer months, the supper might consist of fruit and bread, and in the cold months it might be sliced mortedella (sausage), hot dogs out of a can, olives, cheese, sugared eggplant, and walnuts or other nuts. Flat bread was, of course, served with every meal, and tea usually accompanied the evening meal. The main rule in the evening was to serve simple food that didn't take a great deal of preparation, but of course, Um Abdalla's rationale was not so much preparation time as it was her belief that a lighter meal was better before sleeping. Some nights, grapes would be enough if we had had a heavy meal at noon. At other times, when our spirits over the homework were flagging, Um Abdalla would prepare a special dish like scrambled eggs or the multigrained cereal that we all liked. The kind of food, its amount, and the time for eating it all were decisions she made without consulting the other members of the household. She either gauged these decisions well, or the other family members were used to having these decisions made for them, since it was rare to hear anyone complain. Between meals, the children ate bread if they were hungry, but for anything else they waited until it was presented to them by adults.

After dinner, by nine or nine-thirty at Um George's house, the younger children were dropping off to sleep wherever they found themselves, like little warriors on a battlefield. When enough had fallen, Um George would rouse them one by one, to undress them and then tuck them, two at the top and two at the bottom, in one big bed. Every night they fell asleep in approximately the same order: three-year-old Adil first, then four-year-old Lisa and five-year-old Miriam, and finally baby Ilyas, whose afternoon nap kept him awake longer. George stayed up as long as the adults. Because he was so much older than his half-siblings, he was often treated like an adult.

Around ten o'clock, the adults in both houses finished the day with the Egyptian serial on television. Even though the television had usually been turned on much earlier, rarely could the boring programs hold the viewers' attention if there was any other distraction. Near the end of the homework sessions, Abu Abdalla invariably retired to the television room to stretch out on the cushions and watch the evening program. And anytime guests appeared in the evening—even guests who were as much a part of the family as Um George or Abu Adil, they were ushered immediately into the television room, where, as a gesture of hospitality, the television was turned on for their enjoyment. In those cases, the noise of the television served as a backdrop to conversations, filling the occasional lulls before a new topic was introduced. However, when the nightly serial came on, the conversation ceased and everyone gave full attention to the details of the story.

Egyptian serials—with their intricate plots about romance, family problems, morality, and the rightness and wrongness of financial dealings—have wide appeal to audiences all over the Arab world. The Egyptian actors and actresses are dramatic and lively, especially in contrast to the wooden performances of the actors in many Syrian serials, and they speak in what the Syrians consider to be a quaint though appealing accent. I was grateful for the family's acquaintance with the Egyptian dialect through these programs, since it was the accent I knew best, and it made it easier for them to understand me. I even became somewhat of an expert in helping them understand difficult Egyptian words in the programs, and when I was unable to understand some of their words, they would graciously pass it off as "because she knows only Egyptian."

The serial episodes provoked much comment from viewers. Um Abdalla and Um George often discussed the morality of the characters' behaviors as if they were next-door neighbors, and at first when I heard them talking about Nadia or Fuad, I assumed that they were talking about real people with whom they were intimately acquainted. The same actors and actresses appeared again and again in characteristic roles in the serials, so to their audiences, they were consistent personalities. The characters they played also were so clearly drawn that even without following all the words, it was possible to recognize the coyly innocent eye-fluttering heroine, the evil feminine protagonist who undermined the heroine's relationship with others—most often a significant male, the honorable upstanding hero who was, of course, in love with the heroine but due to misunderstandings had come to question her virtue—and his equally evil male protagonist who was trying to involve the hero in shady business deals. Some event beyond the control of the hero and heroine always interfered with their innocent love, and it took endless turns of the plot and subplots before another fortuitous twist of fate resolved their problems. The twenty or so evening programs of a single drama were ample time to draw out the story in excruciating detail. It mattered to no one that "right and goodness" always triumphed in the end and therefore that the conclusion was completely predictable. Rather, the interest lay in how the stories drew to their inevitable close.

Widely broadcast throughout the Middle East, these programs undoubtedly exert a strong influence on the values of Arab society, especially in rural and conservative communities where there is great receptivity to appealing options packaged in a moral frame. The messages not only are moral—the advantages of virtue, truth, honest dealings, and the like—but also support values such as the acquisition of education for men and women and the importance of young people's seeking compatibility in marriage rather than simply accepting their parents' choices. What in the West was accomplished in a somewhat different way by Horatio Alger stories, showing poor boys working their way to the top through hard work, is shown in these Egyptian episodes as the importance of maintaining virtue in the face of modern society's evil temptations. One difference is that whereas in the Western stories, the results usually are produced by the hero's superior efforts, in the Egyptian serials, they usually hinge on a fate beyond the characters' ability to control. Although Syrians may find little to disagree with in the content of the serials, the fact that they are Egyptian allows Syrians to discard values that do not suit them. For the most part, however, the villagers in Wusta found their own values very much paralleling the middle-class conservatism reflected in the serials.

When the program ended, Abu Munir or any other guest who was present would go home, and the rest of us would disperse to different parts of the house to go quickly off to sleep.

Our days more or less followed this pattern, varying only on holidays when the children were home from school and spending more time on household chores than on homework. Years later as I write this, I wonder if the years have brought any changes to this daily pattern at Um Abdalla's house. At the time, it seemed so invariable, so routine, so ordinary that it was difficult to visualize any other pattern for the day.

———

THREE

Insights

In attempting to answer grand questions . . . , the anthropologist is always
inclined to turn toward the concrete, the particular, the microscopic. . . . We
hope to find in the little what eludes us in the large, to stumble upon general
truths while sorting through special cases.

— Clifford Geertz, *Islam Observed*

I learned very soon to appreciate Abu Abdalla and Um Abdalla and the good
luck that brought me to their door. They were decent, hardworking people—practical in the ways of making money, using it carefully and striking
a hard bargain, but also kind and considerate of those around them. Their
family turned out to be reasonably middle of the road as far as the village was
concerned, not extreme in the idiosyncratic nature of their behavior or in
the material wealth of their surroundings. Like many other families in
Wusta, they were still going through an economic transition that could be
measured year to year by the additions to their home and accumulations of
material goods. In this respect, they were also not unlike others in the village who, despite a strong consciousness of spending money carefully, were
inveterate consumers. At one time or another, most adult villagers had experienced difficult economic times, and the lingering anxiety over their economic futures predisposed them to accumulate tangible assets as rapidly as
possible rather than to save their earnings. Their standard of living seemed
to suggest, however, that the hard times were over for most of them.

In the beginning when I lived in Wusta, many things puzzled me. But it
soon became clear by the way Um Abdalla and Abu Abdalla drew into them-

selves or changed the subject that asking direct questions beyond what was necessary to identify a person's family status was not an acceptable way to behave. At first, I found it difficult to know what they were thinking or to understand behaviors that at close range seemed to have implications beyond my grasp. "Why," I would ask myself, "is this happening this way?" and often there seemed no explanation that satisfied my own logical framework. For the time being, however, it was unreasonable to ask Um Abdalla and Abu Abdalla to step back and think analytically about behavior they took for granted. Consumed as they were with everyday living, they were not interested in "examining their lives," even as a favor to a foreigner who was a guest in their house. Rather than irritate them, I began to search on my own for tangible clues that would help me understand how they and their children conceptualized the world. I assumed there were logical reasons for their behavior and rationalized that to know how parents conceived the world was also to know how their children would eventually come to conceive it. I assumed also that I would have to understand the larger context in which they lived in order to discover what restricted and what motivated their behavior.

As often happens, many of the useful insights I gained in the first few weeks I lived in the village came unexpectedly while I was trying to fit in and the villagers were adjusting to me as a stranger and the only foreigner in their midst. What helped in those early days was my recent arrival from five years of residence and research in Egypt and, before Egypt, the years I had spent in Saudi Arabia and Lebanon. From these experiences, I had developed expectations of how Arabs were likely to behave. The Egyptian experiences were particularly fresh in my mind, which was both good and bad. I tended to take little notice when Syrian villagers met my expectations for "Arab behavior" and focused single-mindedly on situations in which they did not.

A few days after arriving in Wusta and before becoming aware that women in the village did not go to isolated spots alone, I climbed the hill behind the village where my husband and I had stood on my first day. From the vantage point on the hill, I could make out the plan of the village with its one asphalted street and strings of subsidiary lanes. The houses on these roads were clustered in small groups with enough distance between them to give the illusion of separated enclaves. Many houses appeared empty or at least not fully occupied.

From the hill, it was impossible to locate shops, even though I knew some existed, despite being so informal as to make them all but invisible. This was for the practical reason that the residents already knew where they were and few strangers ventured into the village long enough for shopping. Another reason was to avoid identifying sources of income to government officials who might see them as potentially taxable assets. Knowing where goods and services could be obtained therefore required an insider's knowledge of the village, and choosing where to shop was the way people supported selected families in order to maintain friendly relations. To locals, buying in these stores was more a matter of connections than the quality or cost of the product. Um Abdalla recommended one such "kitchen grocery" to me, but its produce was usually wilted and without much variety, and so I distributed my purchases more widely among all the shops as I searched for the freshest and tastiest goods. I never found out whether my failure to use Um Abdalla's preferred shop reflected poorly on her or, worse, whether I was inadvertently patronizing shops of families with whom she had some lingering animosity. She had every opportunity to comment on these matters when I reported the details of my shopping trips in the reciprocal spirit of telling her as much about my routine housekeeping as she told me about hers, but she never did.

The spacious, solidly built original stone houses visible in the foreground were set in a helter-skelter pattern unrelated to the adjacent road. It took me time to realize that each was positioned to take advantage of summer breezes and winter sun and therefore that in relation to one another, they all were located at the same angle. These older houses commonly contained multiarched verandas with wrought iron balustrades extending the full length of the second floor, allowing the inhabitants to enjoy shade on warm afternoons while they watched neighbors passing by or sun in the winter when the angle of the sun's rays changed. Little children, unaware of their confinement, would peer between the balustrades to greet passersby. Behind them, large arched window-doors opened onto spacious living rooms. In the winter, when the curtains were open, light streamed into the interior through windows at both the front and the rear of the house, indicating how natural ventilation and illumination took precedence over the convenience of interior design.

Most of the houses in Wusta had two stories, in keeping with local building codes prohibiting the construction of more stories unless provision was made for shops or an empty area on the ground floor. In the older houses, the upper floors contained the main living areas, and the ground-level rooms provided a utilitarian underskirt for stores, work rooms, and sometimes kitchens. Newer houses, by contrast, often had the living areas on the ground floor and the sleeping areas on the second floor, if there was a second floor. The very oldest houses had their kitchens in a separate building at the corner of the cleared yard. They also had water runoff channels in their courtyards that predated piped water, suggesting that at one time there had been greater use of kitchen gardens. Now most courtyards were bare of greenery except for an occasional pot of basil. Each day, the women of the households swept the courtyards clean, a fact that could be noticed because, unlike traditional city houses, the outdoor privacy of rural occupants was not usually protected with walls.

From my hill, I could see two gleaming washing machines protected from the elements by the overhang of one veranda. These, the Doctora had told me on our walk, had been gifts of a relative coming from abroad. Since they were not suitable to either the water pressure or the electrical voltage of Syria, they had quickly been abandoned in favor of the sturdier Syrian-made machines that churn energetically before disgorging clothes that are hung on lines for a sweet-smelling effect. The presence of the machines in full public view was a not-so-subtle reminder that the inhabitants had relatives abroad who "spent on them."

On the far edge of town, attached to the entrance road to Wusta at the nearest point of intersection with the highway to Damascus, were the homes of summer visitors—some almost palaces. The houses and their inhabitants were psychologically and physically removed to the periphery of the village, apart from and minimally involved in its affairs. Because time is an important commodity for the working husbands, the location of their houses gives them a small advantage in commuting time.

Summer visitors' homes differed from villagers' homes in important respects. Many had massive grillwork fences for protection during most of the year when no one was present except perhaps a hired caretaker living in a small room at the back. The fences protected them from the paths the neighbors made crisscrossing one another's courtyards on their way to shop in the center of the village. Though visibly pretentious in their cantilevered styles, the summer visitors' houses were usually constructed of cheaper and less permanent cement materials that, in the eyes of the villagers, compared unfavorably with the chiseled, solid stone blocks they preferred to use when they could afford them. Also, instead of long arcaded porches, the visitors built tiny "Romeo and Juliet" balconies leading off every room, upstairs and down, that looked impressive but were decorative rather than functional.

The more imposing the houses were, the more likely they were to be set back at some distance from the roadway, behind the iron grill fences that let passersby see but not touch their impressive gardens. The villagers might plant an occasional kitchen garden with vegetables and fruits, but they were not foolish enough to use precious water on flower gardens. In addition, whereas the village houses turned to the sun for their location, the visitors' homes took the roads as their cue and were built parallel to them, regardless of weather or sun. The villagers located their roads to accommodate their houses, not the other way around.

Directly opposite the hillside, on a far side of the village, I could see a small mosque and, scattered near it, a few homes belonging to local Muslims. When I first asked about the Muslims, no one remembered that there were any Muslims in Wusta, and I had to ask specifically about the mosque to get an answer. These Muslims, the villagers finally told me, had come to Wusta several decades ago in the days when there was political union between Syria and Egypt.[1] Now, most had married outside the village or had left to find jobs elsewhere. Life in a predominantly Christian village was unlikely to have been very congenial for them, especially when the local people had a difficult time remembering that the Muslims even existed. As time went on, I discovered many more of these "invisible Muslims" in the village.

North of the hill where I stood and across a small valley split by a road, I could see an orchard and a large walled cemetery with a few graves outside the wall. All the Christian graves were contained within the walls of the cemetery, while the simple Muslim tombs painted the green of Islam and facing Mecca stood on the hillside outside—another indication of Muslim isolation in the village. On another day, my husband and I climbed to the cemetery and found written in the progression of Christian tombstones, from simple to pretentious, the complete economic history of Wusta and its families.

Wusta's two churches, side by side, occupied the land to the right in my view just before the northern arm of the road exited from the village. Behind the churches, another branch of the road veered off down the valley until the asphalt stopped four kilometers away outside a less prosperous Muslim village that was Wusta's closest northern neighbor.

Behind the hill on which I stood, one of the intersecting dirt roads forming the core of the village looped through the main road and headed down separate valleys. Someone traveling along the more important branch would first encounter a stone-cutting establishment, then a poultry farm, and finally at the end, a spectacular saint's shrine on the brink of a deep valley.

What caught my eye looking down the main valley—north, west, and south of Wusta—were poultry houses scattered at intervals across the landscape, their corrugated roofs twinkling in the late afternoon sun. One of the closer ones, about a mile away, belonged to Abu Abdalla.

I descended the hill through sparse grasses and flowering thistles to dirt paths that wound between the houses in the direction of the main village. Children were taking advantage of the last rays of sun to play tag on the hillside, and their mother, wiping her hands on her apron, came frowning to the doorway to see the unusual sight of a stranger woman coming on foot down their hillside. When I greeted her, she answered hesitantly and stood quietly staring. I felt a pang of homesickness for the lighthearted, voluble Egyptians who would have made conversation easy and wondered whether I could ever talk easily with these intense people.

When the villagers ventured out of their homes, they learned very quickly that they were different from other categories of Syrians. They never spoke openly of these differences, but their tone of voice and the way they talked about their experiences clearly indicated how they felt. During the summer holidays, for example, when emigrants visited from overseas, Um Abdalla and Abu Abdalla felt the differences between themselves as "real" Syrians and the visiting Syrian Americans with second-generation children who were unable to speak Arabic. These visitors indicated that Wusta was a fine place to visit, a place they remembered nostalgically but one where they could no longer live happily for a long time because so much of what they required for a good life could be found only abroad.

When Um Abdalla and Abu Abdalla visited Damascus for shopping or medical care, they also felt different from the people there, who ridiculed their rural tastes or kept them waiting while more important city people were served. Or when they visited doctors, their appointments were broken arbitrarily without concern for the inconvenience it caused them. Even though they dressed in their finest clothes, it was not enough to disguise their country origins.

Religion and influence were other important categories of difference. As Christians, the villagers were aware that the vast majority of people surrounding them in the countryside were Muslim. Within the village, there also were other Christian denominations vying for importance with their own denomination. They saw neighbors in the community, most conspicuously the summer people, who were better off economically or wielded more influence in government. They knew they had few of the personal connections that urban people used in order to get things done in the city.

All these categories of difference carried potential for inclusion or exclusion: Syrian versus foreigner, rural versus urban, Christian versus Muslim, Greek Orthodox versus Greek Catholic, year round resident versus summer resident, rich versus poor, family members versus other families' members. Um Abdalla and Abu Abdalla had little power, or even inclination, to change their identities: people were born in a certain family, a certain religion, a certain location, and a certain nation. What they were born with they lived with and convinced themselves that it was superior.

The more they restricted their activities to their own family affairs, the fewer opportunities others would have to raise invidious comparisons. By drawing into themselves, they could protect their sense of dignity and feel that the world encompassed only the familiar categories they themselves occupied. This was one reason they limited their forays into the outside world and kept a protective line drawn closely around the children. Accordingly, Abu Abdalla usually came back from his trips to the city in a black mood, with complaints about how this or that person had dealt badly with him.

As an outsider, these comparisons also affected me; I must have reminded them of distinctions that they otherwise might not have made every day. The saving grace for me was that I was a new, largely unfathomable category to which it was not easy to apply all the normal distinctions. I had chosen Wusta myself and therefore must have accepted the idea of rural living. I was Christian but of an unknown variety that didn't require them to feel defensive. Although I was an American, I had lived for many years in Arab countries more "primitive" to their eye than Syria, and therefore I must not be as concerned with the creature comforts that Americans "normally" needed. Perhaps, most important, I was alone and dependent on them. They possessed the things in life I needed while in Wusta: shelter, food, and the warmth of human companionship. This put them in a stronger position than would have been the case had we met in "my territory" of Damascus.

The first few weeks I felt them watching me and waiting to see whether I might revive the comparisons they anticipated. As a foreigner, for example, would I dislike their food and refuse to eat it? Would I be impressed if they talked a lot about appliances and spending? Why didn't I show more signs of being Christian—perhaps I was something else? What was the real reason I was there? Perhaps I was secretly laughing at their "primitive" rural ways. A defensiveness crept into Um George's voice when she told me defiantly, "We cook all our food fresh from scratch here because it's more healthy—we don't believe in canned or frozen foods like you people in America." This was only partly true, of course, because in the village people were inveterate consumers of the preserved, the dried, and even the frozen (meats). But I didn't challenge her sense of superiority—and how could I possibly not like her food?

The first time I felt the defenses drop was when visitors from Damascus dropped in for consultations with Abu Abdalla. On a scale of close to distant, it was natural for me to feel closer to a simple person like Abu Abdalla than to the supercilious Damascenes that visited. They tried everything to build commonalities with me against the "primitiveness" of Wusta. But within the limits that politeness required, I rejected their overtures, and Um and Abu Abdalla couldn't help but notice.

I was still a foreign presence, however, that could not be ignored, as much for the negative reminders of their own society as for the fact that it was unusual to have any stranger so intimately involved in a household. What made it possible for them to accept me into their family life so easily? Why didn't they erect the same formidable barriers against intimacy with me that they did with others, both inside and outside their village? I asked myself these questions and decided that my foreignness and being a woman may have helped. On the one hand, even though my foreignness was a barrier to close intimacy with them, it also kept me from threatening their personal interests in any significant way. "How do we know what she is writing about us," sniffed Um George in a bad mood one day. "She wouldn't say anything bad," said the trusting Um Abdalla, confident in the amount of "salt" we had eaten together. Both believed deep down that I was so completely removed from their world that I could do little harm.

Because I was recognizably foreign, I caused a stir when I walked through the village. Villagers were used to strangers who were Damascenes or Syrian Americans but not to people who had no clear connection at all to the village. Most people treated me respectfully though with reserve, but sometimes young men verged on rudeness, especially if they thought I didn't understand what they were saying. I tried to establish credentials for respectful treatment as quickly as possible.

"Hello . . . beautiful morning! Can you tell me where I can find the bakery?" I shouted out to a road crew of young men resting on their shovels. As outsiders themselves, they felt no compunction about giving the village a bad name with their poor manners. But this request for assistance accompanied by polite greetings abruptly changed their leers and snickers to respectful replies and then questions, as they took advantage of a welcome distraction from their work. My request for help activated the compulsion common to most Arabs to treat a stranger hospitably.

Hostile, suspicious eyes peered at me from under the head scarves of the older women as I took my daily walk around the village and ended at the main store. "Good morning," I would call out, and they would come closer to have a better look. If they did more than greet me, there would be no holding back the questions. They came right to the point: "Who are you?" "What is your name?" "What country are you from?" "Why are you here in the village?" "How many children do you have?" "Boys or girls?" "Where are they?" "Where is your husband?" "Why isn't he here?"

I would run through my list of answers, shading the truth a bit to make them more respectable: "My name is Um Dawud." "I am here in the village to escape the noise and bustle of Damascus." (They understood that part.) "My husband works in Damascus." "I am an American." (They recounted the names of relatives who had gone to live in America and couldn't understand why I didn't know cousin Nabil who lived in Wethersfield, Connecticut.) "I have three boys" (a big plus). "It is unavoidable that I be away from the boys, since they are studying and living away from home at universities in America." (They sigh with heartfelt sympathy.) "My husband comes on the weekends when he doesn't have work" (a strange situation to them but possibly acceptable to foreigners). "There is someone who takes care of his food and cleans the house during the week so he lacks for nothing but my company." (That raises a few eyebrows.) I end with "I'm the one living with Abu Abdalla's family." "Oh yes," they would reply when they recognized his name and a slow nod of the head. "My husband has charged Abu Abdalla with taking care of me during the week when he is at work." "Yes, I am very happy living here in the village." It surprised me that in so small a village it took so long for the information about my presence to become known. Perhaps this bears out what I saw at other levels, that families kept very much to themselves.

Even though I was freer with information than they would have been in a similar situation, I felt I passed inspection on all counts but the one concerning my irresponsibility with regard to my husband. I looked gratefully back on the first day in Um George's kitchen slitting olives when the family asked me the same questions. I had had plenty of time to get my story straight. Now each time I told the details, I framed them in an increasingly better light—no untruths, just better management of the information. Their frowns and hesitations told me unequivocally which answers they had difficulty digesting.

Young girls on their way home from school were curious and more open to the idea of my foreignness. At first, they would giggle rudely as if my strangeness preserved me from being offended. "Hello," I would say politely. "Oh, you speak Arabic?" they replied, their schooling giving them an appreciation for the difficulty of learning languages. "Half and half," I answered modestly but accurately. By then, their demeanor would have changed to exaggerated politeness, in the same way as did that of the construction crew. "What is your name?" Trying to give these young people an appropriate name to address me, I answered, "Doctora Andrea." Thinking that opportunity had landed at their doorstep, one would ask, "Doctor of what?" And I had to explain the difference between a doctor of medicine and a doctor of philosophy. They looked disappointed but, still friendly, continued with questions, similar to those of the older women, only modifying them to indicate their respect for me as an older woman. In the end, they politely invited me to their homes. It was tempting—a possible breakthrough in meeting other villagers—but since it usually was time for the noonday meal, I refused, wondering how their mothers would have reacted if I had appeared at their door for lunch.

I began taking daily shopping walks into the village, trying to purchase small quantities of food to make my trips seem legitimate. I knew by then that it was unacceptable for women to wander "aimlessly," that is, to "take walks." "Where are you going, neighbor? Don't tire yourself. Come sit with us. We have everything you might want, or if not, we can send Boulos for what you need," they would say, as I tried to justify my excursions. I learned that the best way to take walks was to decide on a definite mission—bread was the best excuse, since people understood the importance of buying it fresh every day. Then, as long as I carried my shopping bag, assumed an intent look on my face, and moved forward with a purposeful stride, I could range widely through the village. The only condition was that I end at a store and return with my basket full of purchases. By making the rounds of the bakery, the main store, and the out-of-the-kitchen vegetable stands, I soon extended my excursions into longer walks.

One problem with these trips was that it was difficult to look like a person with a mission when I bought such pitifully small quantities. I would buy matches for my stove, one box at a time and since they didn't work well, always breaking before they lit, it was a convenient though not a visually obvious excuse on many days. At the bakery where the wares were cheap and always bought in plentiful supply, I was the only one who wanted to buy a loaf at a time! We stood in long lines for hot bread, and on many days, out of embarrassment, I would buy four of the flat loaves at 25p each to make the money come out even at one Syrian pound. My four loaves were perhaps the smallest quantity ever purchased in this village, even though it was enough to take care of me for half the week, and I knew full well that most of the loaves would go stale before I had a chance to use them. Um Abdalla's goat and I developed a warm relationship through the extras I purchased.

Perhaps because of our common purpose, people were more willing to talk in the bread line. Some would just stare; some would offer brief "hellos"; but still others would respond enthusiastically to my greetings and converse with me at length. I was grateful they did not rush me to the front of the line in a burst of hospitality, as Egyptians always did out of courtesy to a stranger. Waiting for the bread to finish baking gave time to those who had seen me around the village to satisfy their curiosity with the standard set of questions. After responding the first time, I would hear my story repeated over and over like a verbal résumé to each new arrival in the line.

One day in particular, the line was especially long because the electricity had been going on and off all over the village for reasons not clear to anyone, and the baker was forced to stoke up his diesel oven to complete the baking. Before long, my story had been relayed to what seemed half the village, that is, anyone who had missed it before. The electricity cutoffs had also had the serious effect of making us miss an important part of the soap opera serial the night before on TV, and in the bread line, when they tired of me, people began speculating about what had happened in the episode they missed. That night we all would have to piece together what had happened from the current episode. When the fiery loaves finally came out of the oven, my acquaintances helped me shovel four of them into my bag, their hands much tougher than mine when dealing with the hot loaves.

The night before, it had been difficult to find my way around my room in the dark, and so a major item on my shopping list that day was candles. I went to the general store to find candles, but it was out of them and the store owner assured me they would get me some by tomorrow, since they already were planning a trip to Damascus that afternoon. Um Abdalla had also asked me to get her a kilo of something called *yukana*—I didn't recognize the word, so I had carefully copied it down. "Do you have *yukana*?" I asked the grocer. "Yes, of course," he answered, looking puzzled—no one ever fully understood a foreigner's ignorance—"It's right at your feet." I looked down at a box of cabbages, amazed to realize that none of five different words in Arabic I knew for cabbage was used in this village. Perhaps *yukana* was a version of *yukni*, a kind of stew popular in Syria and Lebanon. Later, someone told me that *yukana* was a Turkish word used by these villagers rather than the alternative Arabic terms used in Damascus or Beirut. Why, I wondered, had this Turkish vestige lingered in Wusta: Was it from earlier occupations or migrations or because the vegetable was introduced through Turkey? It was a mystery that if solved would most certainly have given me a clue to the village's history.

I passed Um Yusef, our deaf neighbor, on my way home. She was out buying bread, too, and greeted me warmly. We conversed in sign language for a while. Um Abdalla had explained that her deafness came from the beatings her husband had given her while he was alive. Unlike the mostly confident stolid women of the village, she seemed childlike in her fragility and apologetic manner. I passed others I knew, glad to have my shopping bag by my side, this time visibly full of cabbages and bread.

I quickly learned the importance of doors in expressing social distinctions in the village. It first became noticeable as I watched the intricacies of Um and Abu Abdalla's "door behavior" with me. Despite the totally new experience of having a foreigner in the house, they immediately seemed to know how to handle with skill and delicacy the matter of doors, much as if a foreign word had been introduced into their vocabularies and they had known exactly how to fit it into a linguistic grammar with proper gender and form. I had noticed that Um Abdalla and the children always came to my "semiofficial" backdoor instead of to the "informal" door that opened from their inside hallway into my room or to my "official" door that opened into the street. It was a polite reminder that I was neither a total stranger, obligating them to use the official door, nor a family member, enabling them to use the intimate hallway door.

I decided to follow their example by selecting an in-between door when I visited them. They had four gradations of door to their quarters: the formal front door, the semiformal backdoor, the walk-right-in-without-knocking kitchen door, and the intimate inside hallway door. I decided when I appeared for the first time each day to take the semiformal option, as they did with me. This outside backdoor had to be opened by someone from inside and therefore gave a few minutes for that person to make herself presentable before appearing in front of a visitor.

Um George let herself into her sister's house through the kitchen door, which in good weather stood open most of the time. Um Abdalla would tell me to use this door if we were going between her house and her sister's house, since the kitchen was the closest room to Um George's house. It was an informality, I sensed, that was extended to me by invitation or when we were all together and moving from one house to the other after the first, more formal appearance of the day. The only time we used our common private door into the hall was late at night. After we had finished watching the serial, Um Abdalla would say, "Neighbor, wouldn't you like to go home this way? It's easier." Even on rainy days, we kept up the formalities of the outside door. It was a delicate way to protect a modesty that might have been compromised by using a door that opened directly into a bedroom (mine) or a corridor that opened into bedrooms (theirs) and so was as convenient for me as for them. Um George's house also had a series of doors with similar connotations, and depending on the formality of our visit to her, we respected the distinctions.

Over time, I came to know which persons used the front door, the backdoor, and the kitchen door. This, of course, varied for males and females because of the modesty factor. Women's modesty, it seemed, could easily be compromised, and therefore men—even related men such as Um Abdalla's brother and brother-in-law—would make a more formal entrance than would a woman of equivalent relationship. From the start, women behaved more informally with one another than did men with women of similar relationship. Men's modesty was a matter of seemingly little consequence. It was assumed that women would avoid situations in which they might see men in a compromising state of dress and also that women by their very nature would not take advantage of such an untoward situation.

Perhaps from their own understanding of husbands' demands, women would refrain from visiting woman friends when their husbands were at home. If the man of the house appeared during a visit, the women would usually get up and leave unless the woman of the house begged them to stay or the men were relatives whom the visitor felt she should see.

By watching this "door etiquette," I soon came to recognize the tensions between Um Abdalla and Um George and their mother: She used the formal front door when she came to visit, a behavior that was out of place for a closely related female.

Children absorb these patterns early, and although I doubt that they are ever consciously informed of the distinctions, they nonetheless follow them and in the process learn to identify important social categories. Um Abdalla would direct Lisa to take me some food, or Um George would tell the little children to help me carry something "to her backdoor."

Doors were only one way the families marked distinctions with others. Another was the way they offered food.

They argued with me as a guest about food. "You must eat with us," they would insist. "No, it would be shameful of me to eat always at your house like this," I would protest. They would thrust food at me. I would adamantly refuse and would try to leave before they started to eat. Later, a child would come knocking at my door with a plate heaped high with more food than I would have eaten if I had remained with them. How could I refuse? Sadly, I would accept the heaping plate, bothered by the food that would be wasted. The next time when I came from Damascus, I would bring special kinds of coffee or tea or chocolates or something they liked but didn't have available to them. Finding the right gifts took a lot of time, and I was always worried that they were not right or not enough or had some flaw of which I was not aware. Since they accepted the gifts without comment, the task never became easier.

Strictly speaking, I knew my gifts were not absolutely necessary, as hospitality of the highest form to a stranger was supposed to be offered without expectation of return. But by giving reciprocal gifts, I felt I was able to participate on a more equal footing (as I felt they would have done) to maintain my self-respect. Still, I was never quite sure if my view was the same as theirs or if I was responding correctly.

Although food was offered unstintingly to me, it was not exchanged in the same way between the two families. Um Abdalla and Um George kept careful track of how food was shared and paid for in their families, and they evened up their debts whenever they cooked together. This they did despite repeated rhetoric about food's being given without accounting and insisting that it would be ungenerous to offer food in expectation of something in return. Despite their words to the contrary, I watched them counting their pennies carefully, presumably to prevent misunderstandings that might interfere with the close relationship between the two families.

Who offered food, what was offered, and how it was offered were important ways for women to demonstrate their feminine skills. It was a given—not open to debate—that women were in charge of food in the household. This expectation was so strong that when a boy was thirsty, he was likely to turn to his sister to ask her to bring him a glass of water. When no women were present, there was a great deal of embarrassment about how hospitality might be offered to guests—the absence of females from the house was probably the only excuse for not providing proper hospitality to guests. To prevent this embarrassing situation from happening when she went out, Um Abdalla would arrange to have one of the girls at home to cover the unexpected appearance of guests.

Food marked the formality of occasions and the importance of guests. It was not long before I could judge the importance of guests at Um Abdalla's by the kinds of food she offered them. Um George or the deaf Um Yusef, for example, were given a single cup of tea or coffee and some nuts. Less frequent and unexpected afternoon visitors were given nuts, seeds, and fruit with drinks, with Um Abdalla carefully peeling the fruit before placing it in front of the guests on individual plates. An important guest might receive a cold drink first, before the nuts and fruits, as well as tea or coffee afterward. If there had been warning of an impending visit, cookies or other sweets might be prepared or bought. The more important the visitor was, the greater the fuss would be, including ushering the guests into a more formal sitting room, rearranging the cushions for their comfort, placing trays of food directly in front of each person, continuously replenishing foods, and so on.

The way people addressed one another also established the character of their relationships. When I first met Um Abdalla, she told me her first name and I told her mine, and for a while we went back and forth trying to call each other by those names, but to her the word *Andrea* was difficult, and first names just didn't feel right to express our relationship. First names were something used by girls and not by grown women who were married and had children. She soon lapsed into *jarti* (my neighbor) or, more frequently, *jaritna* (our neighbor). To me, this term seemed cold in contrast to the way

I was addressed by the more sociable Egyptians, who immediately sought a term of close intimacy, such as *uxti* (sister), or if they were young and wanted to show more respect, *khalti* (mother's sister). Egyptians were not content until we were bound in an imaginary kin-like relationship on the side of the most affectionate female relative, the mother.

The Syrians were more reserved, and for a long while I felt that Um Abdalla used *neighbor* as a way of preserving a distance between herself and me. It was only later when I was reading a linguistic study assessing the degrees of emotional closeness in Lebanese terms of address that I became aware of how this term, *neighbor*, might be used by Syrians as the equivalent of the Egyptian *sister* or *aunt* to denote closeness. According to this study, the word for *neighbor* in Lebanese, a dialect of Arabic much like that spoken in Syria, is quite similar in value to the term *garayib* (relative or kinsman).[2]

Abu Abdalla found it more convenient to call me Um Dawud, "mother of David." For him, this more respectful way of addressing me, which connoted marriage and motherhood, established the appropriate tone for the relationship between an unrelated male and female. This way of addressing me was more distancing than those required between women but not as distancing as Madame or some such other citified Syrian usage.

A curious way of addressing relatives, peculiar to Syrians and Lebanese, was calling a person by one's own name. For example, a mother might call her child Mama, and a father his child Baba. It seemed a confusing and circuitous way for children to learn how to connect terms of address with the appropriate people. They first learned a number of different names for themselves that they later sorted out to refer to specific relatives. One appealing explanation for this practice was that by using these terms, children more quickly learned the inseparable relationship between themselves and their relatives. There was no separate sense of "me" but, rather, a sense of self connected in important ways to significant others.

The Syrians have other endearing ways of expressing closeness in family relations, including the common expression of endearment *tikbirni*, which means "may you bury me" or, in a more accurate translation, "my life isn't worth living if you should die before me, so I hope you bury me first."

More than do the Arabs of Arabia, Syrians demonstrate an egalitarian sense of connection to both parents in the way they address strangers. A young person, for example, wanting to ask a question on the street approaches older persons respectfully with *ammi*, or "uncle" (father's brother), or *khalti*, "aunt" (mother's sister). By selecting words that connect the stranger with the "closest" relatives—the same-sex siblings of mother and father—they show their recognition of the importance of both branches of the family. The Saudis, who are a more tribal, patrilineal society, emphasize the male side with *ammi*, or "uncle" (father's brother), and *ammiti*, or "aunt" (father's sister), as terms of respectful address to strangers. In both countries, people call strangers by names "closest to their hearts": the Syrians by names for a "substitute mother" and "substitute father" and the Saudis with exclusively paternal names taken from the "respected" side of the family.

Um Abdalla took seriously the Doctora's admonition to look out for my welfare. Part of that responsibility, it seemed, was providing me with companionship during the day so I wouldn't feel lonely. What I was doing—writing—was not "work," in Um Abdalla's view, so she felt no qualms about "disturbing" what I was doing, and on my side, I was enjoying the relaxed companionship of my neighbors too much to feel guilty that the book was not progressing very quickly. More important from Um Abdalla's perspective than my work was the fact that I was alone. This made me an object of pity to her, and she feared I might become depressed if they left me too much to myself. All day, she and her sister seemed to be thinking of ways to keep me occupied. When they were indispensably involved in early morning cleanup, they sent the children to distract me from my "loneliness." When they finished their housework, they immediately called me to do whatever they were doing. "Being with" was the essential feature, not doing something special. And I always went when I was summoned. "It's time for a nice cup of tea," Um Abdalla would say kindly, knocking on my backdoor. Or Lisa would come over after she came home from school with a brief, "My mother wants you to come." Or there would be a tug on the hand by little Miriam as she pulled me back to her mother's house. At first, I thought the summonses were for some special event, and I would go quickly to see what was happening. Instead, I invariably heard the friendly complaint, "What are you doing, Um Dawud, sitting there all by yourself? Come join us by the stove." Sometimes they organized entertainment for me: a walk up into the hills to the chicken farm to take tea with the bedouin caretaker's wife, Um Mohammed, or a family excursion so Abu Dawud (as Um Abdalla called my husband) and I could see the saints' shrine on the edge of Wusta or, more often, visits to the homes of other villagers.

Much as I recognized these moments as valuable for learning about their lives, the hours of sitting together "doing nothing" made me fidgety. I couldn't rid myself of the feeling that I should be spending my time more productively "accomplishing things"—completing chapters of the book, writing letters, doing dishes, or whatever. It wasn't productive enough, as far as I was concerned, simply to be with people. Before long, I found myself the center of attention, directing the activities and conversations too much or creating learning experiences for the children so they wouldn't be "wasting their time" either. When I realized what was happening, I knew I would somehow have to solve the problem.

This raised a question that always bothered me in fieldwork: how much to remain a distanced observer and how much to hold up my end of the social interaction. In certain respects, a participant in a social gathering owes it to the others in the group to be interesting and not just a passive observer. One time I watched another foreign researcher in "her" village coping with this problem. She was a lively, active person who took seriously the need to be interesting to those around her. As a result, she continuously played the part of a clown, at least partly to compensate for her lack of the local language. Villagers gathered around her night and day to watch her antics, which, though totally unlike the approved modesty behaviors of local women, did not seem to be construed by them as a sign of her "immorality." People seemed genuinely to like her and responded well to the emotional atmosphere she created around herself. The main problem with this approach, from a researcher's perspective, was that she was always the center of attention, and so almost nothing was "normal" about the activities in which she took part.

Did I want to provide the same kind of entertainment for the villagers in Wusta? Decidedly not, but I needed an excuse for both my sake and theirs to withdraw from the central position I was beginning to occupy. On my next visit to the village, I brought some intricate embroidery with me that took a great deal of my time and attention, and once I was busy with that, I was able to fade more easily into the background. With heavy concentration on a difficult row of stitches, I could listen to the banter between parents and children or a family quarrel and become more like the proverbial "fly on the wall" that by personal inclination I preferred to be. Besides, the embroidery also satisfied my need to do something productive.

There was the other question, too, of how much I should be telling them about my research intentions. After my initial weeks in the village, when I sought no more from them than their company in the hours when I was not working on my book, I gradually came to have a more focused interest in observing their lives and particularly their relationships. I felt guilty not telling them of my newfound interest, yet at the same time it was difficult to bring up the subject in a tactful way. The compromise I settled on was to answer, when asked why I had come to stay in the village, that I wanted to learn about the way people in the countryside lived. This was consistent with the many questions I asked but nevertheless did not seem wholly truthful to me. I still felt guilty when, in a bad mood, Um George would express reservations about me and what I was learning.

It amused Um George and Um Abdalla that I wore two gold bracelets. One day they brought up the subject and explained gently that it would look much nicer if I wore at least three or six, or some larger number. "Two isn't enough," they said, "because it makes you look as though your husband can't afford to give you any more, and we know that isn't true." They themselves collected quantities of gold jewelry, though they wore it only on special occasions. They saw buying gold as purchasing something concrete with their money that would only increase in value. "A woman needs this security because she never can tell what may happen to her," they told me. "She may lose her husband or be in a position where she needs money. It is better for her to have gold, so she won't have to ask her husband for money if she needs it." "But aren't you afraid to have gold around the house?" I asked. "No, it's perfectly safe—who would steal it in the village? As soon as they wore it, someone would know where it came from." The reason for acquiring jewelry was at least partly to display it at "events," and a thief who could not display a stolen piece would lose an important reason for acquiring it. Perhaps there were security reasons for inviting people to see the gold of an engaged woman.

"When do you wear your jewelry?" I asked, never having seen either Um Abdalla or Um George wear much jewelry. "We wear it mainly at weddings," they replied and asked if I would like to see what they owned. Um Abdalla brought out her gold: necklaces, chains, earrings, and bracelets—more than I would ever own in a lifetime. She explained that they liked to see how much jewelry a bride received because then they knew the length to which families were willing to go to connect themselves permanently with other families. "We are Christian and therefore don't take as much interest in gold as Muslim women do. They need it more than we do in case their husbands divorce them. We Christians don't divorce," they said somewhat smugly.

After a time, I became aware of how important clothing was in identifying certain things about people in the village. From a distance, for example, it was possible to know immediately from the dress that a person was male or female, young or old, educated or uneducated, modern or traditional. Old men in the village wore the traditional Syrian costume of full-sleeved white shirt and baggy black pants with tight leggings that gave them a bandy-legged look. On the heads of the most traditional men, white scarves were wound tightly over fez-like hats, giving the effect of an elongated pill box set in a ring. With their full white beards and stout walking canes, these men had the same dignified appearance of those depicted in older books about the region. Younger men were more likely to wear the "Western" dress of pants, shirt, and suit jacket that indicated modern educated status.

All older women wore black dresses, symbolic of their perpetual mourning for husbands, fathers, and other deceased family members. These dresses were waisted but made to fit loosely to accommodate the inevitably stouter figures of women in this age group. Some wore scarves on their heads, but not in the way that Muslims did so that no hair was visible. The wisps of hair escaping from the scarves were usually gray, very different from the uniformly dark-haired city women in the same age group. Most Wusta women of middle and older age wore dresses or skirts; occasionally a younger married woman wore pants. The younger the woman was, the more likely she would wear bright colors. Trying to think of a practical reason for wearing skirts, Um Abdalla noted, "Most women wear skirts instead of pants around here after they marry because they are fat like me and skirts are more comfortable. Um George wears jeans because she's not fat." Um George, who was really rather stocky, was the only matronly person I saw wearing pants. I guessed that the sisters dressed differently because Um Abdalla was just enough older than Um George to have missed the beginning of the pants fashion in Wusta. I was so used to seeing reasonably long dresses worn in rural areas of other Arab countries that it surprised me at first to see Um George's pants and Um Abdalla's knee-length skirt.

When we went to call on people, Um Abdalla seemed much relieved if I changed from the wool pants I sometimes wore around the house—I think she felt I was too old for pants—into something more appropriate. People dressed up for two occasions, to go to church and to visit people, even including friends and relatives. In the cold of winter I used to wear long ankle-length wool skirts covering layers of long underwear. The women considered my long skirts laughably quaint, something only lower class, illiterate, or conservative Muslim peasants might wear. Um Abdalla's outfit for visiting consisted of a tight knee-length skirt and bare legs with little lace-edged socks that barely poked out of her pumps or, on especially fancy occasions, nylon stockings. In the winter, her bare legs became chapped from the cold. I pointed out the advantages of long skirts when sitting on the floor, but as usual, logic held little weight against what she thought was appropriate to keep up appearances. In the interest of fashion, she preferred to clench her knees together and tug at her skirts.

Clothing was a major concern to the teenagers Lisa and Muna. At school, they had to wear their military uniforms, but as soon as school was over, they would change into casual pants, Lisa into jeans and Muna into cords. Muna's favorite after-school shirt had written on it the words HOCKEY TEAM in English. The actual meaning of the words was not as important as the fact that they were written in English. Similar shirts were sold everywhere in the *suq*, more often than not with words that were neither relevant to the context (Kiss Me Baby) nor to anything real (California University). I tried to explain to Muna what a hockey team was, but since she had never seen people skating on ice, I ended by comparing the game with soccer, except that the players used special shoes that helped them move quickly over the ice. This obscure treatise on the game of hockey neither added to nor detracted from her appreciation of the modish shirt.

Lisa told me that at a wedding in the village, all the young girls had worn pants, and all the married women had worn dresses. The change in fashion from skirts to pants in the space of a generation seemed momentous to me, given the strong prohibitions in the Arab world against exposing a woman's shape. I assumed it was brought about by the government's suddenly requiring compulsory military-style school uniforms for both sexes. The government's purpose was to produce a revolutionary frame of mind in young people, much in the spirit that Atatürk tried to modernize Turkey by decreeing the end of the veil. In Syria, the change of dress was accompanied by military training for both boys and girls. Once while I was staying in Damascus, a group of young women returning from such a training exercise began shouting insults at veiled women in Damascus and, in some cases, trying to rip off their veils. In their training lectures, they had been urged to rid the society of reactionary symbols such as veils that slowed the development of the modern state. Although the girls in our household did not make the change to pants because of revolutionary zeal, they took advantage of the new climate to prevail against their mother as often as possible about wearing skirts.

Another reason that pants found greater acceptance in Wusta was, of course, the fact that it was a Christian village. Christians are generally more broad-minded about adopting styles that reveal the feminine form. The growing "fundamentalist" movement in Syria, as elsewhere in the Middle East, is causing Muslim girls to abandon the pants and jackets of the current school uniform in favor of skirts. Many urban girls are also rejecting the military caps and are concealing their hair with scarves, some using this practice to denote resistance to the government's secularist policies. Eventually pants may be seen as a way of identifying Christians, if Christians do not also adopt more conservative attire.

Although dress styles varied widely in Syria, similar distinctions of sex, age, and modernity appeared everywhere. For example, the women in Muslim villages near Wusta covered themselves more completely so that their shape and hair were not visible. In these villages, girls were not as likely to go to school and therefore had not become accustomed to the form-revealing uniforms. In addition, younger women wore the same styles as older women, though in more colorful and lighter-weight fabrics.

The insights I gained in my first weeks in Wusta, though not particularly profound, nevertheless sketched some general outlines of what was important to people. Most surprising from my experiences elsewhere in the Middle East was the absence of a strong connection between the families of the village. Each family kept to itself except when, in a deliberate move for some conscious reason, they made a formal visit to another household. Although I never suffered the illusion I could become "one of them," my newly acquired insights immediately became useful in understanding people's expectations about themselves and in helping me fit into their lives more inconspicuously.

FOUR

The Inner Circle

Many of us [Americans] get our greatest sustenance from home life and yet raise our own children to leave home. Often we live in families counting on each other for support and yet teach our children "the importance of self-reliance as the cardinal virtue of individuals."

— Ellen Goodman, "Our Finding Fathers"

As women, most of our days were spent within the four walls of the two houses, and our concerns revolved around taking care of the other members of the household: cleaning for them, preparing for them, and, in the evening, being with them. Although we stayed home most of the time, Abu Abdalla and the children spent a good part of the day on business outside the house. When it finally was time for them to return home, it was obvious they did so with a sense of relief and pleasure. Being at home was the better part of their day.

As the days became cooler in the fall, Abu Abdalla, true to his promise to the Doctora, bought me a secondhand stove to install before the days became really cold. He and Hanna came knocking at my outside door one day—the only time in my stay, other than my first day in Wusta, that a male member of the household older than the toddlers came to my door or entered my room. Abu Abdalla hastened to explain his errand, telling me that Hanna, who was the most talented of the boys at installing stoves, was ready to install mine. It was his customary job, his father explained, to remove the stoves from the rooms in the spring and return them to their places in the fall, so he had had considerable experience in his not very long life of eleven years.

Abu Abdalla left the quiet Hanna with me to begin the work. "Where do you want it?" he asked, monosyllabically. I thought a minute and decided I wanted it in the corner of my room nearest the vent hole where it would be out of the way. He looked at me strangely but, used to taking orders from adults, did not question the wisdom of what I requested. He started to work and in a very short time had installed the stove and erected the pipe to follow the line of the wall and exit at the vent hole near the ceiling.

A few weeks later, Um Abdalla and I were having tea in my room and huddling close to the stove. I apologized for how cold it was. I had diagnosed my room as particularly cold because of its northern exposure and the fact that I left it unheated during the part of the day I spent at Um Abdalla's or Um George's. Um Abdalla asked casually why I had decided to put the stove in the corner of the room. Only then did I discover that stoves were traditionally located in the middle of the room where they could evenly distribute the heat on all sides. Moreover, from a central location the piping could travel a maximum distance within the room before venting to the outside, in effect, making the piping an important auxiliary heater. Um Abdalla commented that they all had been surprised to hear that I had asked for my stove to be located in the corner of the room but felt that perhaps I knew something they didn't. She looked pleased to discover that they had been right all along and that my method didn't work. But out of politeness, they had said nothing.

Stung by my ignorance of thermodynamics, I asked engineers in Damascus about the efficiency of heating stoves. Studies had been conducted, I learned, showing that heat could be more effectively conserved if the pipes coming out of the stove were bent stepwise a couple of times before proceeding upward to the ceiling. This caused the heated air to slow on its way to the ceiling at a point in the lower part of the room where it could be most efficiently utilized. The only disadvantage with this method was that uncombusted materials might build up in the pipe and create a fire hazard. But I was convinced that the regular removal and cleaning of the pipes every spring would eliminate this problem.

Armed with this information, I returned to the village and presented my findings to Abu Abdalla. He politely poured over drawings with me. "It could save you maybe 25 to 50 percent of your fuel costs," I said triumphantly. He thought about it for a while and observed, "If this method is so good, why hasn't anybody in the village used it before?" And that was the end of the idea. Partly, I suppose, my idea was rejected because of my failure to locate my stove correctly the first time. But partly it was also a general reluctance among the villagers to try anything new that they had not seen in actual operation. They were unwilling to experiment with anything requiring money or effort that was not instantly assured of results.

"Mama says come," commanded the two little girls at my backdoor one day. It was eleven-thirty in the morning. Mama and Um Abdalla were in the kitchen with pots piled all around them. Abu Adil was about to start out on his next trip to Saudi Arabia, and Um George was making the food for his journey. "Come sit with me, neighbor, while I cook," she urged cheerfully. "No, let me help!" I begged. "I can't let you do that," she declared. But I continued to insist, and finally she gave in. Since I was the inept one, she gave me the unskilled task of peeling and cutting potatoes and eggplant. Um George took charge of the pots on the burner, and Um Abdalla relieved her when she was called away by the children to do something else. Each knew exactly what to do. It was Um George's task, so she took the initiative in deciding what foods would be prepared and how they would be cooked, and Um Abdalla and I worked as assistants. Um Abdalla knew when something needed to be done that would help, but I needed directions on everything, down to how big to cut the potatoes and eggplant. Occasionally, they claimed again that I was a "guest" and should simply sit and watch.

Um George's kitchen was amazingly well equipped with most of the conveniences I had in my own kitchen in the United States. There were two refrigerators, a large cupboard for china, and assorted cupboards for pots, pans, and hand appliances that included a blender, mixer, and coffee grinder. To my mind, only two major appliances were lacking—an oven and a dishwasher. When asked about baking, Um George said she used a domed cover that fit over the item to be baked, which in turn sat on the gas burner. She rarely needed the dome because almost all their foods were boiled or fried. When I tried to make a cake with this cover, I found it didn't work very well—the cake rose unevenly, cooking too much in some places and not enough in others. This failure in cake baking confirmed her notion that Americans didn't know how to cook.

The table where we worked stood next to a window with a view over a little-used back lane leading to the main village. A two-burner propane hot plate sat on a counter near the sink and, on the floor in the center of the room, whooshing like a blow torch, stood the kerosene burner that acted as an auxiliary cooker. Um George found this cooker more convenient for heavy work because of its powerful flame that made the cooking—especially frying—go faster. Another convenience of the cooker was that when the oil spattered all over the floor from frying, it was easier to clean up. The three burners together, all turned to the highest fire, were a happy mixture of modern and old-fashioned.

Um George rotated between tending the burners and washing the dirty pots. Um Abdalla stepped in to turn a slice of eggplant or pull the potatoes out of the oil when they were the correct shade of golden yellow. The two women were a well-practiced team in the kitchen, and the subtle shift in who was responsible for what activity was made easy by their sensitivity to each other's needs. In her own home, Um George had an edge over Um Abdalla, who in more neutral territory would have been deferred to more frequently as the older sister.

The food for a twelve-day trip for a trucker and the three or four others who drove in the convoy with him—who also brought food of their own, with extra to share—consisted of large quantities of fried potatoes and pressure-cooked meat with a small amount of cinnamon added to remove the raw meat smell; fried slices of eggplant previously soaked in salted water to remove the bitter taste; fried cauliflower softened first by boiling; boiled spinach and fried onions with lemon squeezed over the top; meat ground with fat, salt, pepper, and bread crumbs and pressed into a flat pan for cooking; and fava beans cooked in the same manner as the spinach. All the frying used up a large canister of ghee. Um George explained that the frying, salt, and lemon would preserve the food for most of the trip. As each item was finished, she packed it neatly in plastic containers while still hot, which also probably served as a form of sterilization.

While we were cooking, the children played outside, and occasionally their screams drifted in to us. Even though their problems sometimes sounded serious, Um George ignored them. The small Ilyas in a walker spun down the hall to the kitchen door to stand whimpering for his mother, sporadically at first and then increasing in volume. When his uncle stopped by for a moment and later his father came in from tinkering with the truck, they picked him up and held him until he was quiet again. Then a visitor came to see Abu Adil, and Ilyas was handed over to Um Abdalla. Finally, when a natural pause in the cooking came, Um George found time to give him something to eat, followed by his bottle.

I asked Um George whether she didn't become tired from all the work she did, cooking, taking care of the children, and cleaning. She replied that on the contrary, she loved to be busy from morning to night. She recalled how difficult it had been after her first husband died when she had only George to keep her company and very little to do. Watching her enormous energy, I could only believe she was telling the truth. Again I had the feeling that I had had on the day of slitting olives that these women enjoyed being the hub of their family activities and felt a sense of satisfaction when they could manage problems in the household. "Do you cook when your husband isn't here?" I asked Um George. "Of course, just the same. The children have to eat, and I never buy ready-made food." Again the defensive tone, meant to show the superiority of her ways over my American ones, just in case I might be supposing her ways were inferior. With Um George, it was difficult to know when and how I might offend her.

The children started coming home from school, George first at one o'clock and then Lisa and Muna. We continued to prepare the food for Abu Adil's trip until two, when everything had to be halted for the midday meal. This time we all sat down together to eat from the extras that Um George had prepared. This was one of the few times the two families took their main meal together—Um George's way of compensating us for helping out!

Um George: "When two sisters marry two brothers, everyone says it is a good thing—that these kinds of marriages are better than others. Um Abdalla and I didn't really plan to marry like this—it just happened that we all liked each other. Of course, we had known each other growing up in the village. I married the first time at fourteen, and my sister when she was even younger." (According to Um Abdalla, however, she was married just after she finished the ninth grade.) "Whenever possible, girls and boys prefer to marry someone from their own families; it can be on either side, the daughter or son of their mother's sister or of the father's brother. Both are better than marrying outside the family."

"But don't Muslims prefer their marriages to be with the son or daughter of a father's brother?" "Well, we Christians like that, too. The important thing is to marry a relative if you can."

I was thinking that her examples of marriage between children of same-sex siblings might have been mentioned intentionally as the ideal kind of marriage. People seemed to think that these marriages were also better for the children, since the emotional attachment between children and the aunts and uncles of the same sex as their parents should be greater than with the aunts and uncles of the opposite sex from their parents. The argument was that because a woman should feel closer to her sister and a man to his brothers, this emotional attachment would extend to the next generation so that women would be closer to sisters' children, and men to brothers' children. This was the logic behind these sibling marriages.

When I asked her about this, however, Um George denied that the examples she had given were preferable to other forms of relative marriage. She often became irritated when I asked for detailed explanations, because she knew intuitively what was right and so didn't think explanations were necessary. In reply, she would say, "No, it doesn't mean anything, Jaritna," or "I don't know any more." It was possible that since her own marriage was not a relative marriage, she did not want to talk too much about preferred forms of marriage that, by comparison, would make her own marriage seem less than ideal. In practice, what translated into an advantage in the marriages of Um George and Um Abdalla was the already close relationship between the sisters on the one hand and their husbands, who were brothers, on the other. In theory, according to the principle of cousin marriage, their own children would be considered perfect matches, but it was difficult to imagine how cousins like these who had been brought up almost as sisters and brothers might ever come to see one another romantically as mates. And times may be changing, as well. On another occasion, Um George and Um Abdalla said they heard it was "unhealthy" to marry relatives.

We were nearing the end of the evening homework and were relaxing on cushions around the floor at Um George's. As Um Abdalla's children from the other house finished their homework, they came one by one to join us. Little Miriam and I were working on the fine stitching of my embroidery. First I would take a stitch, and then she would take the next. Progress was slow, but we were enjoying working together. The older boys sat watching and looking as though they wished they could try a stitch or two. I handed the cloth to George to see whether he would like to take a stitch; he rejected my offer with a shrug of his shoulders and an embarrassed grin at his cousin Abdalla sitting next to him, as if to say he wasn't about to be caught doing woman's work.

Miriam took another stitch and returned the embroidery to me. She reached for a cracker from a box sitting on the tray in front of us and took a bite but decided she didn't like it. She licked tentatively at it once again and then, hoping no one noticed, tried to hide it between the cushions. Her sharp-eyed sister, Lisa, saw her and announced to everyone that Miriam was sticking a cracker under the cushion. Miriam removed it and walked guiltily toward the kitchen. "Eat it," her mother encouraged without rancor, but Miriam continued out the door to dispose of it. Um George accepted almost any behavior from the small children as natural—not something to get excited about. But when the children were older, like George, she expected them to be more responsible.

After a while, Abu Abdalla came back on the late bus from Damascus and, finding no one at home, came over to Um George's to see if we were there. Um Abdalla and the older girls jumped up and returned home to heat up a portion of the noonday meal that had been saved for him. Reminded of how late it had become, Um George also got up and went to prepare food for her children before they fell asleep. We all gathered around the main tray and dipped our bread into dishes left over from lunch—meat, fried potatoes, tomatoes, olives, and cheese.

Watching Um George with her small children gathered around, I became aware of how different an experience it is when people sit and eat at floor level. At floor level, everyone participates equally in the eating and talking. Little children move in and out, eating first from this dish and then from another, falling into one lap, crawling out of another, accepting a tidbit from this person, offering it to that one. Adults are not in a position to control the quantities of food, drink, and even affection that the children receive, in the same way that they are when these commodities are kept at a safe distance from the children. Rather, on the floor, children take what is there when they want it. There are no special foods served in limited portions to certain categories of people by those who control the supply. At floor level, there is a kind of necessary egalitarianism.

We finished the meal with a great deal still left over on the tray. Um George and I relaxed against the cushions enjoying our tea. Three-year-old Adil sat near the tray idly playing with a limp piece of fried potato. Four-year-old Lisa next to him dipped her finger into some thick sweet *dips* and licked it appreciatively. Miriam fell asleep between Muna and Hanna, each playing with one of her lifeless hands—holding it up and letting it flop. The food and the oppressive heat from the potbellied stove combined to make us all sleepy. The children sprawled in a mass of entwined bodies, cousin shoulder to shoulder with cousin, sister draped across brother. The littlest, Ilyas, crept into his mother's lap and fell asleep, effectively preventing her from clearing away the plates. She stroked his head, content to put off the time when she would have to wake the others to get them ready for bed. I was reluctant, too, to leave the congenial company for my cold bedroom in the house next door.

Another evening, we were sitting together in Um Abdalla's winter family room. Abu Munir had just brought news of how much bananas cost in the next town. That information prompted everyone to start the routine discussions of how much everything cost this week in various places. Little Miriam sat folded into my side, with her feet stuck out straight in front of her, crossing and uncrossing her hands as she watched me do the same. Her ageless face with its serious expression and penetrating eyes observing everything in the room reminded me of the portraits of children painted by nineteenth-century American painters that made them look like wizened little adults. She became momentarily distracted from her imitations of me by a conversation between two of her siblings, little Lisa and George, and when she turned back, she looked irritated to find that she was out of sync with my hands.

To pass the time, I asked Miriam whether she had seen her grandmother over the holidays, and she said no, that they almost never went to visit her. Um Abdalla, hearing this comment, interrupted to change the subject, "No one visits old Um Yusef next door, either. It's partly because she's so deaf but also because no one wants to take sides in the fight she is having with her family." It was uncharacteristic for Um Abdalla to talk about her neighbors' problems, but since she had brought up the subject herself and I was curious, I asked her to tell me more about it. She related briefly that Um Yusef had taken the side of her grandson when he had disobeyed his father and now the father, Um Yusef's son, refused to have anything to do with her. This was all Um Abdalla was prepared to say about the matter at that time, and so I let the subject drop. She had successfully steered the conversation to the matter of Um Yusef and distracted us from the discussion about her own mother. Um Abdalla did not like negative aspects of the family's private affairs aired in front of outsiders.

In early fall, when dinner was over and the cleaning up finished, Um Abdalla would send Muna to the back porch to shake the chaff from the winter supply of wheat drying in the sun. Um Abdalla bought the fresh wheat from a local farmer because it was cheaper, and she wanted to be sure it dried properly. While Muna was doing that, Lisa might be sent off to buy some staples from the nearby store. Um Abdalla always sent Lisa when she needed a special item because Lisa was more competent at choosing the right thing than the boys were. Otherwise she sent the boys to buy matches or bread or anything else that required their knowing only how many to buy. If Lisa was busy studying for an exam, Um Abdalla would send the boys for complicated items, but only after she had reinforced in their minds that she wanted only a certain variety or only if the item was very fresh. Boulos, however, was an exception to her belief in the greater trustworthiness of girls. Because of his serious, reliable nature, she could also count on him to bring back the right item.

Running errands was only a minor part of what needed to be done in our household. Um Abdalla and Abu Abdalla liked to keep the children busy all the time they were not doing their homework. Daily in winter, besides their homework, the girls ironed their uniforms, brought food to guests, made tea when it was needed, and helped prepare the food and clean up after meals. On their one day off from school, they took on a larger share of the daily food preparation and cleaning chores, usually working for most of the morning before they finished these jobs. Whichever of the older children was around and unoccupied when the task was required filled the stoves with fuel. Most frequently, that task and feeding the chickens fell to Muna, who was more likely than the other children to appear to have nothing of importance to do.

During their summer holidays, Lisa and Muna did most of the housework so that their mother would be free to do other things—visit Damascus to buy clothes for the children or sew clothes for herself, which were less expensive than the ready-made clothes she usually bought for the children. One of her summer tasks was to sew the children's uniforms for the coming school year.

Although the girls were quite capable of doing most of the household jobs on their own, Um Abdalla gave them detailed instructions about what to do and how to do it. They rarely started a major activity on their own before consulting her on how it should be done: "Umi [Mother], what do you want us to clean today?" "Now, Lisa, get the bucket from the kitchen and fill it with soapy water. Take the cleaning rag from the line and start working on the front hall. In the meantime, Muna, you sweep just ahead of her to get most of the dirt up." Their cheerful chatter moved through the house. "But, Umi, the cleaning cloth is not on the line where you said." "Well, look in the bucket; perhaps I put it there." "Should I do the front stoop, too?" There was no irritation in the voices and no need to finish quickly. It was a routine that never failed to take place, and there were no compelling leisure activities to motivate them to finish quickly. As long as she was around, Um Abdalla directed their activities and often worked with them. When she was away, they worked on their own but were quite happy to go back to taking directions when she returned.

The expectation that older people should supervise younger people was not unique to Um Abdalla's family. Once I was cooking with a Syrian neighbor. We had assembled all the ingredients and were about to begin when she realized that her servant, an old family retainer from the time she had been a child, had stepped out for a while and therefore could not be asked for instructions on how to make the *fatet makduus* we had in mind to cook. "Don't you know how to make it yourself?" I asked. "Yes, of course, but I've never done it without asking her. She will be upset to think I can do it on my own without her." My friend contemplated waiting until the servant returned but decided to tell her that she had tried to make it herself but, of course, it didn't taste as good as when the servant directed her. Respect and affection for this older woman made my neighbor reluctant to remove from her the one meaningful thing—her experience—that she still contributed to the household.

Every day, the two older boys filled the water tankers that were pulled by tractor out to the chicken sheds. They also consulted closely with their father on what other tasks needed to be done, and Abu Abdalla made regular trips to the chicken houses to keep track of what they had accomplished. Both parents kept tight control over the children's work and stepped in when necessary to see that their own high standards were met.

Most of the household work was done by the parents and older children, but the two small girls at Um George's were also being eased slowly into assuming responsibilities. They ran errands between the two houses and did small tasks like sweeping the outside cement porch, feeding scraps to the chickens, and keeping the goat away from the drying grain. Some of these jobs they did spontaneously as if already possessing an adult's consciousness of what needed to be done and matter-of-factly going about doing it. However, with the exception of asking them to run errands, Um George did not require that they do anything else. As I knew from watching her refuse the children's requests to help with more complicated tasks, she believed that they should not be involved until they were old enough to do a job properly. This, of course, made the tasks more desirable to the children, who saw in doing them the chance to become part of the serious world of adults.

"We women don't work outside the home like you Americans, and since we don't like prepared food, we take the time to do everything from scratch." It was the third or fourth time I had heard from Um George the refrain about not eating ready-made food. Even though I knew she was partly right, I was beginning to feel defensive. I tried to distinguish for her between canned and frozen foods in terms of freshness, but she believed both were the same. I found myself repeating, "Doctors or researchers say such and such is better . . ." to bolster my case but soon learned that she did not believe doctors were as competent as mothers to make judgments on issues like these, which were outside their strictly medical jobs of curing actual illnesses. Being around Um George made me realize how much I relied on scientific experts and how much she relied on personal intuition, much of which certainly came from information passed along from parents or neighbors. It was a situation similar to the heating stove— she was more confident when depending on the experience of people she trusted than the pronouncements of unknown "experts."

Feeling a little guilty after her remarks about fresh foods, Um George sent me part of their midday meal: chicken soup with rice, onions, and parsley, accompanied by sweet pickled eggplant. I put the food away in the refrigerator, still full from the noonday meal sent over by Um Abdalla. It struck me that I had rarely eaten the exact same midday meal twice, so great was the variety in the two households. Although the ingredients were limited, they knew how to combine them in ways that made each meal seem unique.

It was late afternoon one day, and Lisa summoned me to her mother's house. I came in the backdoor, removed my shoes just inside, and walked through the house until I found the family in the television room. As I walked down the hall between rooms in my stocking feet, Muna pushed forward a pair of house slippers for me to use so my feet wouldn't get cold—a simple courtesy, automatically rendered. I joined the family on the cushions around the stove. The two girls were studying. Two of the boys were playing quietly together; their school had been given a holiday because of the elections, and so they had no homework. The television was on, but the program was so uninteresting that it proved no distraction to the students, and even the adults ignored it.

Abu Abdalla had taken Abdalla to the doctor in Damascus once again, this time to find out why the hand that had been operated on to remove the gunshot pellets was festering and painful. Um Abdalla, a guest, and myself were the only adults in the room. Um Abdalla had moved the guest to the television room and turned on the set in her honor. The children, knowing no "formal" male guests were present, had gravitated from the usual homework room following their mother, even though television was usually banned during study time.

I realized that this time there was a special event that I had been called to witness. Um Abdalla's mother had come to make one of her rare visits. She had an infected eye—perhaps a sty. The discussion lingered on the topic of how painful it was and what she might do to cure it. The doctor in Wusta was not the appropriate kind for eye infections, and the mother didn't feel she wanted to go all the way to Damascus. She hoped her daughter or the "foreigner" might be able to give her advice on curing the eye. Um Abdalla listened with only half an ear to her complaints. She was preoccupied with the problem of Abdalla and worried that Abu Abdalla might not find the doctor in his office. To distract herself, she went to get another pot of olives to split—this time black ones she had bought later in the season. Wanting to divert attention from the talkative mother whom, in any case, I couldn't help, I asked Lisa to get me a knife from the kitchen so I could help Um Abdalla. Um Nabil droned on about the eye as we listened politely.

Suddenly, when listening for the returning bus, Um Abdalla noticed that she could not hear the goat bleating at his tether near the porch. She asked Lisa to go and see where he was. Lisa went out and returned to report that she was unable to find him. Um Abdalla sighed as if to say all her calamities came at the same time and went out to look for him herself. All she found was the end of his frayed tether and decided he must have gone off with the goatherd as he passed by early in the morning. "Never mind," she said on her return, "we'll get him again when the herd comes back this evening."

Um Abdalla was called over to help Muna with a homework problem, and so I took her place before the larger tray holding the remaining olives. Um Nabil turned her full attention to me. "How many children do you have, . . .?" I answered all her questions and then turned my own barrage of questions at her, using the same set I was growing to know so well. She was more than happy to talk about her children. One son was a trucker and one son was in the army. The trucker son, Nabil, hadn't been out on a trip for ten months because, according to her, he had completely exhausted himself from the work and needed a rest.

After a while, Um Nabil decided she had stayed long enough at Um Abdalla's house and should go to see her other daughter, so we all gathered up our work and marched over to Um George's, except the girls, who remained behind to finish their homework. There we were joined by Abu Adil, Um George's husband, and by Ilyas, Um Abdalla's and Um George's brother in the army, who had also been given leave because of the elections. He told me he had no problem getting away any time he wanted because the officers were so lax, but because his camp was one hundred kilometers away on the road to Suwayda, it took too much time and money to come to Wusta very often. Nevertheless, he tried to get home once a week. He was sitting next to me, and when I asked what he planned to do when he finished his compulsory service, he began telling me that he wanted to become a gold-smith by taking an apprenticeship with someone who worked in Damascus, that this profession was one that Christians often took up. I said I guessed that would mean he would have to leave the village, and he agreed that there wouldn't be enough opportunities to support a goldsmith in the village, although the villagers would probably give him some of their business wher-ever he set up shop. The thought of leaving the village didn't seem to make him happy or sad—perhaps he hadn't thought far enough ahead about the implications.

Just after sunset, a hundred hollow-sounding bells tock-tocked by my door as the same number of woolly backs cascaded toward the village. It was the goatherder bringing his charges back from the mountains. Just as Um Abdalla had predicted, their goat had gone off with the goatherd. I heard her tethering him again by the back porch.

Um Abdalla and I came home from visiting some neighbors one evening to find Abu Munir alone with Lisa in the television room listening to her les-son. When he came, she had discreetly removed herself from the intimate family room where the rest of the children were studying to the formal vis-iting room that she knew befit his guest status. Abu Munir had a large lump on his head and a cut with dried blood on the side of his face. Um Abdalla said it was not surprising to see him this way, since frequently when he got drunk, he fell down and injured himself. As usual, he was taking his tutoring responsibilities with the exaggerated seriousness of a person who was barely able to control his thoughts. He obviously wanted to do his best, but his usefulness to Lisa was not much greater than the blank wall to which she usually addressed her memorized phrases. She was polite to her parents' friend but looked relieved when we entered, knowing that he would turn to us for company and she wouldn't have to waste any more study time listening to explanations of French verbs.

When we appeared, Abu Munir lay down the French book he was reading and started to regale us with the bits of information he had collected around the village since we had last seen him. After a while, he fell asleep in his corner, and we all feigned interest in the television program to keep from waking him.

A little later, Lisa was sitting looking off into space, and her mother asked why she was not doing her work. She explained that she was supposed to decorate a paper cover for her schoolbooks and had been leafing through the pages of a design book to see whether she could find anything to copy. Nothing pleased her, and she couldn't think of anywhere else to look for inspiration. She turned to me and asked if I could draw her something that she could repeat over and over to make a border for the book cover. I made a row of stylized flowers, but they were not regular enough to suit her, and she returned to the pattern book for inspiration. It didn't occur to her to create her own border. She and her teachers preferred copied perfection to originals, much like the memorized perfection of all her daily schoolwork.

Abu Adil returned from his trip to Saudi Arabia. Um George had been notified by the trucker's network that he would probably arrive that night, and so she had spent most of the day preparing for him. The house was cleaned to shining perfection with sparkling floors and fresh sheets on every bed. Um George also had put on stiffly clean clothes—her usual jeans and shirt—and had just washed her hair, which was wrapped in a head scarf when Um Abdalla and I came to wait with her. One advantage of the trucker's frequent absences was the real pleasure and excitement of the whole family when he returned.

We were still sitting there around sunset when suddenly she jumped up and rushed to the door. Although I could hear nothing yet, she had picked out the sound of his truck from the rumblings of others that circled the village during daylight hours. In a minute he was there, bringing his giant truck to a standstill, revving the engine a few times, and climbing slowly down from the cab, suppressing the smile on his face to keep from looking too pleased about being home again. Um George had gone quickly inside again when she was sure it was his truck and was delayed in greeting him for a minute while she pulled off the scarf and arranged her hair in more presentable fashion. We wanted to leave and go back to Um Abdalla's, but they both insisted that we stay to hear his news and to tell ours. So we remained to hear the few sentences he had to offer about his uneventful trip, and we added our own news about the generally good health of everyone as well as the state of Abdalla's hand. Meanwhile, Um George brought us all coffee before we left.

The next morning, while Abu Adil was in town seeing to the servicing of his truck, Um George came to our "women's coffee break" for a few minutes to tell us that Abu Adil had brought sacks of potatoes, onions, and garlic from Lebanon for Um George; a can of ghee for me; and cologne for Lisa. Lisa was especially pleased with her gift, which was unexpected and seemed a recognition of the fact that at fifteen, she was suddenly becoming a young lady. She showed us all the attractive bottle and let us sniff it. Even Um Abdalla and Abu Abdalla seemed pleased by Abu Adil's gift to her.

This time, Abu Adil had driven all the way down through Saudi Arabia to Dubai to get higher prices for his produce. It took him the normal two days and one night coming back because it was easier to cross the border when his truck was empty. On his way down full, he sometimes had to wait two days for inspection of the produce from Lebanon when he entered Syria. The regulations changed from trip to trip, but this time things had gone more smoothly than usual—he had been permitted to travel alone across Syria instead of waiting in line for a convoy to Jordan. At the Jordanian border, he had waited for only a day to complete the complicated government formalities, instead of the much longer time he sometimes waited when many trucks from Europe and Lebanon converged on the border.

Um George didn't say anything about it, but later I noticed she had a new machine-made oriental carpet on her floor that Abu Adil most certainly had brought back for her from Saudi Arabia. Perhaps she didn't want to tempt the evil eye by pointing out a new possession, or maybe she didn't completely trust me with the information about his expensive smuggled gifts because, as she sometimes said about me, "Her husband knows people in high places." On my side, I wondered how Abu Adil concealed such a large item in an empty truck but was afraid to ask for fear of confirming her suspicions. He had probably paid something to a border guard. He always said, perhaps out of xenophobia, that the most corrupt guards were found at the Jordanian border.

I went one day with Abu Abdalla to look at an impressive house being built for Damascenes halfway down the road to the chicken shed. He obviously felt uncomfortable walking alone with me—unrelated men and women just don't walk together in the village, and he probably regretted his invitation— extended during one of our conversations about how he had built his own house. He had heard that the workers were doing some expensive interior work and decided to go look at it. Even I immediately noticed the better-quality materials going into the building, though from my standpoint the designers had collected too many colors and patterns in too small an area. Most impressive were the tiles that would cover all the floors of the house. They were of natural stone from a number of regions in Syria and selected for their special hues and fine-grained quality, not like the cruder tiles made locally that most villagers used in their homes. Abu Abdalla had installed his own tile floors and was therefore curious to see how professionals did the work. He had already explained how the floor had to be laid with an almost imperceptible slant that allowed the water during cleaning to run into the side drain. To show me what he meant, he brought out a level and in his meticulous way demonstrated again how these workers had used the same technique as he had used. As always he was amused to be talking about such things with a woman and ended by saying, "But look, Um Dawud, if you want a tile floor, you choose the colors and let your husband install it. This isn't work for women; it needs a strong man."

On those days when Um Abdalla stayed in town shopping until late, at the right time Lisa would go out to the kitchen and prepare scrambled eggs with cinnamon and olives—a common fallback for the evening meal. In addition, she would serve cheese balls in olive oil, a dip of *zatar* (a mixture of thyme, sumac, and sesame seeds) and oil, and green olives. When Um Abdalla came home, she would bring *harissa* (a sweet pastry) or some other delicacy she had bought in Damascus as a treat.

Abu Munir came by during the homework session, and this time he was really quite drunk. The children playfully imitated his gestures to one another so he wouldn't notice. Um Abdalla and Abu Abdalla tried to ignore him, clearly wishing he would go away, but they were unwilling to say anything that might sound like criticism and hurt his feelings. Um Abdalla leaned over to me and whispered disapprovingly, "God help his wife. When he gets like this, it takes several days until he comes out of it." He sat on the cushions with a half liter of *araq* he had brought with him sitting by his side. It was the first time I had seen him display his drink so obviously, and clearly it was an irritation to Um and Abu Abdalla, who feared his condition might worsen. While I was around, he talked continuously about Lisa's homework and his favorite subject—his proficiency with languages—before he slumped into a restless sleep.

One evening we were sitting in the television room when there was a loud knocking at the front door, and Abu Abdalla went out to see who it was. The knocking sounded demanding and not the way a person would knock who was coming for a friendly visit or routine business. We could hear a loud argument going on at the door among several people. It turned out to be three men who had come to see Abu Abdalla. One was Abu Adil from next door, and the second was another of their brothers, Munir, whom I had never met before. I searched my memory for some mention of him—perhaps they had said something in the early days when I was trying to digest so much information. If so, they certainly didn't speak of him often. The third man was a stranger—someone who wanted to buy land. An argument had started over land that, it appeared from the discussion, belonged to the three brothers. Munir wanted to sell the land so he could buy a truck bigger than the one he had been driving. He had already sold his old truck but had then found he didn't have enough money to buy a bigger one. The two other brothers, Abu Adil and Abu Abdalla, did not want to sell the land because, as they argued, "it's land," with the implication that one has security as long as one has land. In addition, this land also brought in a small amount of income in annual rent. They were equally adamant in insisting that they would not lend Munir the money because, as Um Abdalla explained later, he was lazy and they were afraid they would never get their money back. They argued that it would be better if he worked as a driver and earned the money to buy the bigger truck. He was young, they advised him, and shouldn't let himself get in so much debt. The man who wanted the land lent his weight to Munir's side of the argument, albeit hesitantly, and interceded when the discussion became too heated. He had probably instigated the meeting to find out the reactions of the other two brothers.

The argument at the front door seemed to be a continuation of an argument that had started at Abu Adil's house. Munir had expected an easier time with the younger of his two brothers and was incensed by Abu Adil's resistance to his plan. Now he felt he might have an easier time trying to convince his older brother. Abu Abdalla, in his calm way, said nothing at first, noting only that they could discuss the matter better if the men came inside and sat down. Um Abdalla and I had been sitting in the room with Abu Abdalla and were still there when we heard the arguments by the front door. As soon as she heard the voices outside, Um Abdalla rushed to put everything in its place and remove the piles of laundry she had been folding. I continued to work my embroidery while Um Abdalla went to bring tea. Their voices calmed for a while, embarrassed to air their grievances in front of a stranger. When the tea was ready and Um Abdalla had passed around cigarettes, the argument resumed in earnest, and we quietly left the room. Normally, Um Abdalla would have felt obliged to stay and see that these in-laws of hers were served what they needed, but she felt uncomfortable being present during a quarrel between members of her husband's family.

We settled in the girls' room, where Um George soon joined us from the other house, entering through the backdoor where the men could not see her. She filled us in briefly on the part of the argument that had started at her house. When she finished, we sat quietly listening to the discussion going on in the other room. Now and then, when they thought their husbands had made important points, Um Abdalla and Um George would exchange gleeful looks. They both agreed that their husbands shouldn't relent on the question of land, because as they explained to me, land is security against bad times, and they didn't trust this brother who had proved himself unreliable in the past. I left before the argument ended, though even from my part of the house through two solid doors and across a hallway, I could still hear isolated outbursts from the men until late that night.

The next day while the family was still discussing the events of the night before, I learned that just before his death, the father had put some of the land in the younger brother's name, and therefore the brothers could not really stop him if he wanted to sell it. He was simply trying to get agreement from his older brothers for the transaction before he made the sale. Because the land adjoined theirs, he knew he would be reducing what could be a large, jointly farmed area. The buyer was anxious that the sale of the land not irritate the other brothers, since he wanted to have friendly relations with them when he owned the property adjacent to theirs. Although they didn't approve of the transaction, the brothers made clear to the buyer that they wouldn't extend their irritation to him.

By not giving their permission, the brothers forced Munir to decide between acting in the interests of all the brothers and going off on his own to the detriment of the rest. If he decided to follow their advice, they would feel responsible for bailing him out if his business failed later. But if he refused it, they could reject his requests for help in the future. Munir felt let down by his brothers, who were financially in a position to help him, and he was angered by the choices they forced on him. In the end, he bought his new truck, against his brothers' wishes, with money from the sale of the land and, in doing so, lost their support. As far as I knew, he never came back to visit during the time I was in Wusta, nor did Abu Abdalla ever speak of him after that visit. In typical fashion, he kept the details of his personal and financial dealings to himself, and it was only by accident, or through Um Abdalla, that I came to know of them.

I had trouble reconciling the rhetoric about the oppressiveness of women's lives in the Arab world with what I saw in our household. Were Um and Abu Abdalla an atypical couple, or were the cases described in articles and books exaggerated examples to make an author's point? It would have been pointless in our household, for example, to determine whether Abu Abdalla or Um Abdalla, as male and female, measured up differently on a scale of power or productivity. From the perspective of family life, both made meaningful contributions to the household: the domestic aspects that were her responsibility and the income-producing activities that were his. It was true that Um Abdalla worked almost every waking hour of the day to maintain her own standards of household organization and cleanliness, but to large extent those were her own self-imposed standards, and she took pride in meeting them. There was no doubt that she was the center of household arrangements, and because they were so much a part of everyone's day, she was also the core around which the rest of the household rotated. It was Um Abdalla who decided what everyone would eat and when, who determined what they would wear, and what they would do to contribute to the work of the household. She was the one who decided on major purchases or projects inside the house—such as an expensive plastering of the interior walls of the house or the addition of a more presentable porch where they could sit on summer evenings.

In these household arrangements, Abu Abdalla was the facilitator who brought provisions from distant shops, who provided money for shopping trips to the city, and who negotiated contracts for workers to carry out Um Abdalla's schemes. Within the family, he was a quiet presence who could be galvanized into action when discipline was needed for the children but who, for the most part, left the business of the household to Um Abdalla, just as she left the income-producing businesses to him. The times when he assumed a role of public authority was when visitors came to negotiate business, and then his authority came mainly from his position in the local *baladiyya* office.

Um Abdalla would have scornfully rejected the idea that she might want to switch places with Abu Abdalla. The anxieties and problems connected with his work were not especially appealing to her, and his authority in the household was so benign that she had little reason to covet his position.

———

Livelihood

For you Americans the task is the important thing. You get your status from
being good at doing things. For us [Arabs], it is people who are important,
since it is through them that we get things done in life. We already have our
social position through our family and that won't change no matter what kind
of work we do.

—An Arab observer

"What do you want to be when you grow up, Abdalla?" I asked the question
routinely asked of American children. He shrugged and didn't answer. I
pressed him, and he replied that he didn't know. Did he really not know?
Was it possible that he had not thought about his future occupation? I asked
him again, and not wanting to be impolite, he finally answered, "Whatever
my father wants me to be." The girls were generally more talkative, so I
approached them, "What do you want to be when you grow up?" I knew
villagers were reluctant to speculate about future events, but still, I at least
expected them to tell me that they hoped to marry. Lisa immediately replied
that she wanted to be a doctor, and the domestic Muna said hesitantly that
she might want to become a teacher. Neither wanted to talk about marriage.
Revising my expectations, I assumed that they didn't want to appear overly
eager—boys sought out girls, not the other way around.

Why, I thought to myself, were the girls' reactions so different from the
boys'? Both parents had told me they wanted the boys and girls to continue
on in school as far as they could go, even to finishing university if their grades
were good enough. Perhaps the differences could be explained by the fact
that the boys had a clear and consistent role model in their father, whereas

the girls had a more ambiguous one in examples from the village, as well as from what they were implicitly learning in school about working women.

The children's ideas about their futures were undoubtedly colored by the experiences of village people in recent decades. They had heard stories about how difficult it had been for their parents when they started their married lives, and every summer they saw well-to-do emigrants returning from America with stories of the early hardships and loneliness of making a new life in another country. They watched neighbors pursuing various paths in search of financial security, and they had no difficulty deciding who had been successful. They also saw wealthy Damascenes, almost all professionals, who built expensive houses in Wusta.

A Syrian sociologist, Safouh al-Akhras, once divided the villages in modern Syria into three types based on the way the majority of residents earned a living. The first type was those villages whose residents had developed income-producing businesses, not necessarily in agriculture, that could be operated from a base in the village. The second type was those villages in which most of the able-bodied men had either migrated or were commuting long distances to work. The final type was those villages where nomadic bedouin had settled and were engaged primarily in sheep raising. What this classification suggested was that in large parts of Syria's countryside, it was difficult, if not impossible, to earn a living from agriculture alone. As a village that had developed home-based businesses, Wusta fell into the first category. Villages of the other two types lay not far away, victims, to a certain extent, of historical circumstances and more limited resources to invest in the transition to a modern economy. People in Wusta used to say that those villagers lacked "guts," the capacity to take risks when the future looked uncertain.

Most of the adults who supported the eight hundred to one thousand inhabitants of Wusta[1] had come from families that in the living memory of the older generation had relied almost entirely on agriculture for a living. By the time of my visit, however, few people supported themselves from this source alone. Official Syrian statistics show that between 1971 and 1982, the total area of arable land dropped from almost 9 million hectares to around 6 million hectares. Of the latter figure, more than one-third was left uncultivated, and an additional half was not irrigated and thus vulnerable to periodic droughts.

By 1981, the land cultivated by local residents was almost entirely used for their household consumption or as a supplement to a main income derived from other sources. As a matter of course, families planted small kitchen gardens with a grapevine trained to shade a sitting area near the house. What limited land they planted besides these kitchen gardens was devoted to fruit trees. Fruit produces a relatively greater income than other crops, and the care of trees is usually minimal and seasonal. The ethic of self-sufficiency was especially strong among those residents who grew up during the days of agricultural dependence. And what they didn't produce themselves, they bought locally from farmers whom they trusted.

The villagers were surprisingly affluent, considering the difficult times preceding this period when drought and falling water tables threatened to obliterate the agricultural base altogether. They were able to adapt well to these and other periods of marginal agriculture largely because young men supported by their families were able to take advantage of opportunities that materialized at crucial moments.

One opportunity in Wusta was the early emigration of young men to work abroad. At about the turn of the century, the first such enterprising young man, with the help of a Lebanese acquaintance, found work selling dry goods in Woonsocket, Rhode Island. When he proved successful, others followed, first to Rhode Island and later to areas as far west as California. In the first waves of emigration, most of the young men were intent only on saving enough money to return and live comfortably in the village. A common pattern was for the emigrant to visit the village during the holidays, prepare building plans, and put a relative in charge of overseeing the construction of an impressive stone house. At the end of the holidays, the emigrant returned to America to earn enough to complete the house and accumulate enough savings for a comfortable retirement. In the early years of emigration, young men came back on holidays to marry young women from the village. Relatives encouraged these marriages because they wanted the emigrants to form closer ties with the village and eventually return there. Although the motivation was mainly sentimental, it was probably also reinforced by the expectation that emigrants who felt strongly about their roots in the village would be more likely to help support those left behind. By the 1970s, however, the pattern had changed. Emigrants were less willing to return to the village. More of them either had taken younger wives who adapted to life abroad or had married foreign women and were raising children who were rapidly assimilating into the new culture. Those emigrants who felt nostalgic about the village brought their children back on visits in the summer to acquaint them with the local language and customs but then found that the gulf of experience and resources separating them from the villagers was too profound to make feasible a full return to village life. Their second-generation children could not live permanently in the village, and the emigrant parents preferred to live where their children were.

Emigration to the United States resolved the early economic problems of some village families but eventually proved too difficult a route for others to follow. At one time, the villagers said, every household had a relative in the United States. But then the United States enacted more stringent immigration laws, and although some of the relatives of the earlier migrants were still eligible for immigrant status, others who wanted to go could not qualify. As an alternative, young men started emigrating to South America—primarily to Argentina—where the laws were not so rigorous. Their financial successes were usually not so great as they were for those who emigrated to North America, and they found it more expensive to maintain close connections with the village from such long distances. The villagers thus began weighing the costs of going abroad, including the almost certain estrangement from their families, against new opportunities that were opening up at home. By the late 1960s and early 1970s, a few young men were discovering ways to earn a good living without ever leaving the village.

Abu Abdalla's experience, put together from a series of conversations I had with him about his income-producing activities, illustrates some of the influences that affected the prospects of young men in Wusta:

> Until about fifteen years ago, the entire village worked in agriculture, but then several things happened at once. First we had a drought that lasted for several years, and because most of our fields depended on rainfall, we harvested almost no crops. All that time, the water table had been dropping so that even when we did have some rain, it was difficult to keep the crops going during the growing season. Sometimes we were forced to plant only on the land close enough to a well to be irrigated. But this wasn't a good long-term solution for us because the wells also were going dry and it was too expensive to dig them deep enough to maintain a steady supply of water.
>
> It's probably hard for you to understand the difficulties we faced. We couldn't just neglect the fields for one year, since our best income came from fruit trees and vineyards that take years to produce a substantial crop. You can still see the remains of these fields that slowly withered and died[2] as the water disappeared and the costs of fertilizer, seeds, and insecticides rose. We had no way out because the government kept farm produce prices so low. I, and

others like me, struggled for a couple of years to try to make ends meet, but eventually we realized that we could no longer earn a living through farming alone. I was a young man then, just married, and soon with our first child on the way.

Then in 1967, when we were becoming desperate, a man from Qamishli who had lived in Lebanon for a while came to the village six kilometers down the road and started a chicken and egg farm. At that time, Syria was importing many of its chickens, so there was a good market for both the birds and their eggs. That was a new idea for us, but we saw immediately how well suited it might be to our situation. I was not eager to go out on the road trucking as others were starting to do then. We had plenty of land, enough well water for the requirements of poultry, nearby sources for chicken food, and markets for our products not too far away. Syria then was importing large quantities of eggs, and the government was therefore glad to support efforts to increase local production. They did this by providing cheap subsidized feed.

For me, egg production seemed a better idea than broiler production. I could use my marginal land for the sheds and keep the better land for farming if we ever got back to that, and I could build the business slowly by adding facilities as money became available. I started with two hundred chickens at my house before the sheds were built, but it was my bad fortune that this first lot of chickens died. I hadn't realized how complicated it was to produce large numbers of chickens and keep them healthy. I didn't feed the first lot correctly, and so I had to start all over again. Slowly, by asking for advice and observing how the man from Qamishli organized his farm, I built these two chicken houses down the road with my own hands and eventually added mechanized feeding and drinking troughs so that now I can accommodate six thousand chickens at a time. Later, I added an automated grinding machine so that I could buy the raw ingredients for the feed and not have to pay to process them.

I've concentrated on egg production because it requires the kind of supervision that one man can handle on his own. Remember, I had small children at the time and no one to help me. Once everything is set up for egg production, the work is fairly routine and doesn't require the frequent turnover of the flock, as is the case in broiler production. It is this turnover that takes the most work because it means selling all the chickens at once, cleaning out the sheds, and buying a new lot of birds. But the eggs are sold to wholesalers who take the eggs either to Damascus or to areas farther away in Syria like Qamishli where they can get better prices than in Damascus. It's easiest to use a wholesaler, because after he takes the eggs from the farm, he bears the risk and I no longer have any responsibility.

Until the 1980s, business was very good. The government restricted the import of birds and eggs, and even though it controlled market prices, demand was high. Now the government is getting involved in a way that makes it difficult for us to make the profits we once did. It sets the prices on feed and the quantity of some of the essential ingredients that are imported, so it has become difficult to get enough of the right kind of food for the birds. Other costs, such as those for the diesel fuel that runs the electric generators needed for the machines, also are rising and eating into our profits. Another problem is that many others have started chicken businesses, including large investors from the city, and consequently the competition makes it harder for us to find markets—wholesalers prefer the mass producers.

The way I make ends meet—to protect myself against fluctuations in the poultry business—is to work at a government clerical job, which gives us a small but still steady income and occupies my time only from eight to two. My sons are old enough now to take care of most of the routine hauling of water for the chicken houses, and I hire a family of settled bedouin to do the rest of the work. I also supervise construction workers building houses for the Damascene summer visitors. This last way of earning income gives me a headache. Negotiating construction work takes a lot of my time and gets me involved in controversies between workers and owners. I can't really give up any of this work, though, because times are uncertain and I need to be able to move in whatever direction offers the best opportunities. Also, none of these ways of bringing in money is sufficient by itself to let us live the way we are used to living now. We will see in the future which directions will be best for the boys, and that may decide where our investments will go. For now, all the children are in school, and it's too early to tell.

Abu Abdalla's advances toward economic solvency could be measured visibly by the three dwellings he lived in during his lifetime: the tiny run-down home that was abandoned after his parents died, the simple rooms I occupied that served as Um and Abu Abdalla's first home when they married, and the enlarged house with several more rooms and modern plumbing where they were currently living. In addition, I saw impressive amounts of money go into improving this home while I was there.

Another villager, Abu Ilyas, who was born and raised as a farmer in a prominent local family, took a different direction when agriculture no longer provided sufficient income for his family. Abu Ilyas's was one of the impressive success stories in the village. In 1971, he sold some of his land to Damascenes to start a trucking business, and now, a little more than a decade later, he owned a fleet of ten stake and refrigerated trucks whose income made him probably the richest man in the village. When he started out, there were no refrigerated trucks, and so in order to make a profit, getting the goods down to Saudi Arabia during the hot season depended on speed.

According to Abu Ilyas, as recently as 1978, a person could buy a refrigerated truck for S£400,000, but by 1982 a stake truck cost about S£600,000 (approximately $150,000), and a refrigerated truck about S£850,000 ($212,500). The latter could earn up to S£25,000 ($6,250) per trip for legitimate business during the hot summer months and S£6,000 ($1,500) in the winter. The stake truck earned a more consistent, though less spectacular, amount throughout the year. Abu Ilyas used to buy his trucks in Beirut, but recently he had found a better deal in Jordan. Most truckers were careful not to register their vehicles in Syria, where they would be subject to tax and other restrictions placed on Syrian trucks. Abu Ilyas's trucks moved continuously from Wusta to Lebanon (where the goods were loaded), back through Syria and Jordan, and down to Saudi Arabia, Kuwait, or another of the Gulf States before returning to the village. Each truck could make two trips a month. When work was good in the summer, truckers might stop only long enough for a night's sleep in the village and then go out on the road again.

Two of Abu Ilyas's sons drove for him, and he had eight other drivers who worked at a monthly salary of S£3,000 each. Three of them came from Wusta, a couple from the neighboring town, and the rest from different villages farther away. While I was in the village, he had stopped buying new trucks so he could put his money into the construction of a palatial house which, he said, had already cost more than a million Syrian pounds. "Every kid in the village wants to be a driver," he said shaking his head.

> I would say that more than 90 percent of the young men in the village who are old enough are drivers and that probably all but ten to fifteen families are into trucking in one way or another. Our boys here in town are *abadai*— aggressive go-getters, and when they see something that looks good, they go for it. The people here are different from those in the village down the road, who don't have so much initiative. There they're not interested in trucking because of the initial costs and risks and prefer to stick to raising livestock or doing wage labor.
>
> My son Ilyas is one of my drivers. He went to school and got his high school certificate and then served in the army for three years before starting out on the road when he was twenty-one. My next son, George, dropped out

of school in the seventh grade, and we paid a *mukaffe* (fee) to the government so he could avoid military service. In five more years, we'll pay another S£10,000 so he won't get drafted.

Although trucking can eventually become a lucrative business, getting established requires a great deal of investment and patience. When I lived in Wusta, it was common for a villager to pay monthly installments as high as S£25,000 in the first three years after buying his truck, making it difficult to earn a profit until the truck was paid off. Making payments frequently required creative financing. Young men might drive trucks for other owners for a number of years to save enough money for a down payment. They could earn S£3,000 to S£4,000 a month, plus in earlier years a bonus of S£600 if the cargo arrived safely. Or they might ask relatives to buy a share in a truck that they would eventually pay off. It was a temptation for young drivers to enhance their earnings through various means, including false accounting to owners, extra work contracted on the side when they were in the Gulf States, or smuggling goods like pistachios, cloth, inlaid woodwork, and other handicrafts out of Syria to Saudi Arabia, and goods like videos and radios that were tax free in Dubai back across the border. All these activities carried risks for the drivers as well as for the owners, and so the latter tried to invest in people they felt they could trust.

For Abu Ilyas, trucking was convenient because he had a number of brothers and sons who could act as drivers. Family members were generally considered more reliable when accounting for expenses and earnings. After Abu Ilyas set up his business, the profits from his fully owned trucks helped offset the costs of bringing new trucks into the fleet, and he kept the costs low by using family members as drivers. This family's success was demonstrated—advertised, one might say—in their visibly expensive residence under construction on the hillside overlooking the village. Despite various problems, this family had achieved the kind of cohesiveness that adults in the village found highly desirable. The new residence would house, under the same roof, all the sons and their families, along with members of the older generation. Their example tended to reinforce the idea that "family cooperatives" were not only an emotionally pleasing arrangement but also economically viable.

Much of Abu Ilyas's success was a consequence of his own hard work. Showing prudence from his experiences with the fluctuating Wusta economy, he went out on most days to farm what remained of his own land and the land he had sold to Damascenes to finance his trucks. His instincts made him unwilling to give up a livelihood that he could "touch with his own hands."

As the independent owner of a single truck, Abu Adil, our neighbor, was a more common example. He was still a young man with small children who were too young to help him build a business rapidly. For the immediate future, trucking was a way to support his family and finance the completion of his house. In the future, he planned to build a small shop that his wife could run while he was away on trips. His plan was for the children to help out in the store during school holidays and after school. Then, when he could afford it, he would hire a driver so that he could spend all his time in the shop. Other truckers in Wusta used their money to make similar investments or to construct a house for their families or for renting during the summer season.

All but the very young men expressed a desire to leave trucking as quickly as possible or at least to find drivers to take over the trips to the south. "The work is hard and only for young men," they would say. "After thirty-five, most of the drivers have had enough of the road."

Nabil, Um Abdalla's brother, was one of those most tired of driving. He also had his own truck and was doing well, it appeared, from his substantial modern stone house, but he wanted to do something else. For a period of many months, he sat at home depressed, trying to decide what he would do next. "How can we manage if I stop? What kind of work could I do?" he would ask. Alternative work in the village earned comparatively less money, and he had no skills besides driving that could translate quickly into lucrative possibilities, even if he moved to Damascus. Nabil's young children would not be able to help him for a decade or more. And like most truckers, he felt strongly that his children should go into other work because of the dangers on the road.

Nabil's younger brother, then in the army, had already made up his mind, he said, to leave Wusta and live in Damascus where he could become a goldsmith. Perhaps he would be more typical of the younger generation who could either not find jobs in Wusta or felt themselves "too educated" for trucking or agriculture.

The final major industry, besides chicken farming and trucking, that flourished in Wusta was the construction business. Although not, strictly speaking, a new industry for the village, modern construction had many innovations that required specially trained workers: to install plumbing and electricity and to complete interiors with a smooth plaster finish. Expansion in the industry was fed by two sources, the excess cash of those villagers working in other high-earning sectors and the desire of affluent visitors to build summer homes in Wusta.

Investment in home construction followed the tradition established fifty or sixty years earlier by emigrants building the substantial older stone houses in Wusta. The villagers took pride in the fact that most of the stone houses belonged to permanent residents, whereas the cheaper concrete block and stucco houses usually belonged to vacationing Damascenes. In 1982, about two-thirds of the approximately 150 houses in the village showed signs of recent construction, some awaiting more funds before completion and a considerable number unoccupied even though substantially complete.

Home construction was viewed as a satisfactory investment both for personal reasons and because villagers expected a long-term demand for solidly constructed houses. When their incomes allowed it, parents built housing for their married sons, under the same roof or in a separate building nearby. Spacious housing was a powerful incentive for children to settle down in the village near doting grandparents, rather than move away to cramped and expensive urban apartments. Because of these hopes for expansion in their families, because quality stonework took time and much money to construct, and because the villagers' housing needs changed over time, many families found themselves supporting construction projects for many years. They rationalized that if their children were not ready to marry soon, the buildings or rooms could stand empty for a time or could be used temporarily for storage or rented to urbanites as vacation homes.

Contrary to that dream, however, it was becoming more and more difficult to keep the generations together under the same roof or even in the same village. But dreams die slowly, and many people continued to build beyond the time when there was a practical reason for doing so. Attractive housing offered the villagers a standard of living they could justifiably point to as making village life equal to, if not better than, urban living.

Other reasons to put money into construction were economic, the villagers' fear of inflation and future instability coming from the government's arbitrary actions affecting their livelihoods. When they had money, therefore, they wanted to convert it as quickly as possible into something tangible. Housing was ideal for these purposes, since it secured a high standard of living for years to come and in the meantime consumed large sums of money quickly. Impressive construction also had a more immediate purpose. Other families were more likely to establish and maintain ties of business or marriage with families who appeared to be prosperous.

Villagers working in the construction industry specialized in either skilled work or the supervision and direction of building for outsider owners. They were not interested in unskilled work. When local people built, they made contracts directly with skilled workers or performed the simpler building tasks themselves, much as Abu Abdalla did when constructing his own house and chicken sheds. Their continuous presence in the village allowed them to supervise the construction work carefully and avoid what they always seemed wary of, being cheated in a business transaction. By contrast, the summer residents had to hire supervisors, who in turn made subcontracts with the workers. Thus construction for summer residents produced a middleman layer in the industry that proved profitable for entrepreneurs like Abu Abdalla.

The master craftsmen who were hired to lay tiles and install plumbing and electrical lines earned substantial wages. Even the work of finishing houses' interior walls, with the many-layered plastering that villagers preferred, might earn a plasterer and his helper the equivalent of a thousand dollars for a couple of weeks' work. One reason that the houses seemed to be continually under construction was that families lived in their unfinished houses while saving up to pay for the next expensive step in the construction. In Abu Abdalla's house when I arrived, the walls of the new part of the house were unfinished, but by the time I left, they had undergone the expensive, time-consuming finishing process.

Villagers who worked in skilled labor came from families who for some reason had been unable to afford either the extended time required for their children to continue academic studies or the capital to invest in more lucrative livelihoods like trucking. Becoming a skilled craftsman required only that a person serve an apprenticeship for a time with an already skilled master. The training could be started at a relatively young age with no loss of income, unlike trucking, which needed a minimum age for a license and the completion of compulsory military service as well as a considerable outlay of funds. Abu Munir's son became a skilled worker for these reasons. Abu Munir's alcoholism made it impossible for him to hold down a stable job, and what money the family did have was mostly squandered on wine. As a consequence, the son, Munir, had to go to work at an early age to support his mother. He chose plastering as a way to earn a substantial wage without spending a great deal of time in training. The villagers kept him busy partly out of sympathy for the innocent family victims of Abu Munir's addiction but also because he was a competent worker.

Abu Antoine's son also was a finisher of interiors. Abu Antoine was an elderly farmer who was too old to change his livelihood at the time when people were making the transition to more profitable occupations. When Abu Antoine's health was good, he planted his land with enough fruits and vegetables for household use and then depended on his son's wages to pay his other expenses.

Another of the construction-related businesses in Wusta was the small family-owned quarries that cut and finished tiles for household interiors. These businesses had existed for some time in Wusta and were now flourishing because of the boom in the construction industry.

There were few adult income earners who did not engage in one of the three major occupations: trucking, chicken farming, or construction. These few included the priests of the two churches in town, Greek Catholic and Greek Orthodox, and the nuns who lived in the convent of one. There also was a nurse in the village who gave injections for minor illnesses. She came from a family left destitute by the father's death at a young age. There was also the doctor to whom people went for simple problems. A few families owned small shops, selling produce from their gardens, and one man owned a more substantial shop. There was also the baker and the man who sold fuel for heating stoves and trucks out of his backyard. One family ran a "boutique" with sewing supplies and female accessories. On special holidays and in the summer, another family ran a restaurant for the summer residents, serving roast chicken with side dishes. Other older couples like Abu Antoine and his wife relied principally on agriculture and the support of their grown sons. A few younger adults commuted to work in Damascus, and some, though technically perhaps no longer villagers, made their permanent homes there. One man from Wusta owned a shop in neighboring Mafraq. Several young men worked as mechanics, informally out of their homes in Wusta or as employees in workshops along the Damascus road.

One source of income for the village that had not been fully exploited when I lived there was the "summer trade." Villagers could earn money from this source through land sales, summer rentals, and wages paid for the construction of new homes and from small amounts garnered from services and commodities provided during the summer season. On their side, the Damascene professionals found Wusta an attractive and more reasonably priced alternative to going abroad or summering in the popular but expensive communities of Bludan and Zebdani in the Anti-Lebanon range. But with the exception of construction and land sales, the summer trade dried up for the villagers in the winter months, when the summer visitors shuttered their houses and returned to the city. It was therefore not a stable source of year-round income.

Fortunately for the landowners in Wusta, the demand for vacation homes kept land prices high despite their diminishing agricultural value. The villagers thus could use land to bank credit with a guaranteed high interest that increased as land prices rose. They usually sold the land only as a last resort when capital was needed for critical immediate needs or to secure a long-term income with a project like trucking, as was the case with Abu Ilyas and Abu Abdalla's brother. There were enough examples of hard times for people to want to secure some means of future livelihood, and land was the kind of tangible asset that ensured future options.

One consequence of the villagers' changing to more lucrative livelihoods was that opportunities opened up in Wusta for the residents of the nearby poorer villages. Wusta's residents were not willing to work in areas of low prestige and poor pay, and so when their growing affluence permitted it, they preferred to pay for services they had previously performed themselves. Similarly, those residents of Wusta who still did occasional farming tended to use the well-watered and more reliable fields close to home and to abandon the distant fields where grain and grapes once grew. This limited home consumption required only a small portion of the acreage available in Wusta.

Seeing an opportunity in the unused lands of Wusta, farmers from the nearby less well-off villages rented Wusta's productive lands. By expanding their own acreage of crops that did not need extensive watering, these farmers could survive in agriculture by using mechanical means of farming without costly wage labor.

Chicken farming also attracted cheap laborers from outside Wusta who came to care for the chickens. Their tasks included grinding the feed, watering the chickens, collecting and boxing the eggs, and cleaning out the sheds when new birds were brought in to replace the birds sent to market. In Wusta, it was mostly poor settled bedouin coming from the environs of the city of Homs who agreed to work in these unskilled positions. The head of the bedouin family would be given a monthly salary, and it was assumed that his wife and children would also help out around the chicken sheds at no extra cost to the owner. The bedouin would live in a primitive dwelling that the owner provided and would eat the cracked eggs and defective chickens from the sheds. The village owner and his sons—as was the case in Abu Abdalla's family—would supervise the business on a daily basis and see that water and feed were delivered to the sheds.

The construction industry also hired outside workers who performed the skilled and unskilled tasks the villagers refused to do. The most important of these were the stonecutters, who chipped blocks of stone with chisel and hammer into rectangular shapes suitable for the finished outside walls of homes. The village used Christian stonecutters from the city of Hama who traditionally did such work. Other manual laborers with no special skills came from poorer villages in the vicinity of Wusta or even from as far away as the Kurdish districts in the north. In principle, the villagers of Wusta were not averse to manual labor, as are people from Arab states like Saudi Arabia—indeed, they were "do-it-yourselfers" to extraordinary degree—but they preferred the higher returns and prestige of skilled or supervisory positions as long as these jobs were available.

Finally, an important occupational niche traditionally occupied by "outsiders" had also been somewhat modified in recent years. This was the niche belonging to the semisettled nomads. A small group of them had been attached to a leading family in the village who served as middlemen for the sale of their sheep. These bedouin still lived for part of the year in the hills east of the village and for the rest of the year made treks into the mountains to the east to graze their animals. They now sold meat through the local butcher or directly to anyone who wanted to buy an entire animal. While I was living in Wusta, every morning one of these shepherds took his sheep out to the hills beyond the village, stopping on the way at village houses to pick up personally owned animals that he then returned in the evenings.

Most of Wusta's economic successes could not have been achieved by individuals acting alone. Rather, they were a result of the combined efforts of families who invested in the trip of a young man to America, or who agreed to the sale of family land to finance a new venture, or who combined their incomes to construct a large house for the extended family, or who worked together as drivers of a fleet of trucks to build the collective fortunes of all the family members simultaneously. As long as the head of household—in most cases, the father—remained alive to preserve the "corporation," those family members sharing a livelihood usually stayed together. The cement of their relationship was set in the unconditional deference of sons to their father and, in the absence of their father, sometimes to their mother if she commanded their respect. When their father died, the weaker sense of identity among brothers tested the durability of the family corporation. Abu Abdalla and his brothers, for example, and Um Abdalla's brother Nabil and his brother were no longer so strongly bound together as they might have been if their fathers had been alive. The daughters and sisters played little part in these considerations, since they were expected to marry outside and pursue the interests of their husbands' families.

In earlier times, those emigrants who remained permanently abroad also tested the strength of the family's willingness to invest money in those who might not return to serve the communal interest. The two weapons against such desertion were local marriages, preferably between related families, and the formidable bonds forged between parents and their children. In this area, women played an important part in keeping family ties alive.

Looking back at the children's responses to my questions about their futures, it seemed less surprising that they answered as they did. The older boys' interests would logically be bound to their father's as long as he was alive, since he offered them the best opportunities—with chicken farming and construction—to make a reasonable living. Depending on their personal relationships, they might also decide to remain together with their mother if their father died, to run family businesses that remained profitable. Abu Abdalla seemed to be grooming Abdalla and Hanna for such a possibility.

If the boys had been more aggressive or the relationships between parents and children had not been as good, they might have been attracted by the glamour and high profits of the trucking industry, as was the case with deaf Um Yusef's grandson. Or if they showed greater promise in school, they might become eligible for poorly paid but secure jobs with the government or highly paid professional jobs like those of the summer visitors. Only Boulos seemed to possess the capabilities for these options.

The situation of the girls was different from that of the boys. The girls were not limited by thoughts of how they would support themselves or their families. They knew in all likelihood they would marry and be supported by a main income earner, so they wanted to be seen as young women with the potential to attract good husbands. From television and from watching summer visitors like the Doctora, they had become aware that a wife who could provide a second income was becoming increasingly valued in Syria. They also knew it was good for women to have some economic security of their own in case their marriages failed or their husband could not support them. They were aware of the example of the alcoholic Abu Munir's stay-at-home wife who was an object of pity throughout the village, and they saw the other relevant example of the nurse who was forced to support her family after her father's death.

For women, it was respectable to work in professional jobs but not in blue-collar manual jobs like domestic or factory work. Women who engaged in such undesirable types of work indicated either their own desperate financial straits or the inability of the men in their families to support them. The catch-22 of the longer period of education they needed to acquire a professional job was that the more degrees a young woman earned, the more she narrowed the field of men who would consider her an appropriate match. Few men in the village had earned advanced degrees, and men generally did not marry women who were better educated than themselves.

In general, Muna's and Lisa's ambition to work in the professions was not motivated by a desire for self-fulfillment but, rather, was a way to ensure economic security for themselves and their future families through appropriately respectable means.

SIX

Family Concerns

A proposal for an International Year of the Family has . . . prompted appre-
hension and outright opposition, particularly among women's groups who
say the occasion might be used to reverse gains in women's rights. There's a
concern that the new focus on family may turn into a backlash against
women's more independent life style.

— Marvine Howe, "Year of Family Wins Friends and Some Foes"

Conventional wisdom says that life in cities is more exciting than life in small
villages, but after living for a time in Wusta, it seemed just the opposite.
Perhaps villagers live in greater intimacy, and the unfolding of their lives
affects everyone with more force. Or perhaps there is simply more time
to ponder small events. I would hurry back from visits to Damascus eager
to find out what had happened during my absence. Was Abdalla's hand
improving? Had Um Abdalla bought the new clothes for Easter, and had she
paid a phenomenally low price? Which truckers had returned, and what
adventures had they had on the way? Had Abu Abdalla finally found a
source of food for the chickens? Was the tractor fixed in time to bring water
to the sheds? Had Muna passed her latest exams? Was anything else new in
the village?

I would enter my room, throw my things on the bed, and rush over to Um
Abdalla's to find out what had happened. The family would greet me warmly
and politely ask after my news, their faces not yet betraying whether they
had good or bad news to report. I would reply quickly, "Yes, Abu Dawud is
fine and sends his greetings. I received good news from David who is doing
well in school. Nicholas is happy with his school, too, and stayed with his

grandmother over the holidays. Doug will be coming to stay with us for a while, and of course I will bring him to see you. Yes my parents are well; they just wrote to say everything was fine." My news finished, I could begin to satisfy my curiosity about what had happened in the days I had been gone. I would have liked a day-by-day chronology but knew if Abu Abdalla and the children were around, I would get only a brief summary of that news appropriate to convey in front of them and would have to wait for the details until the morning coffee hour came around the next day. Sometimes news I would have been bursting to tell took them days to relate fully. The themes were the same—health, work, school, the price of things; only the details differed.

What about Abdalla, did the doctor finally see him? What did he say? This problem preoccupied Um Abdalla much of the time. The doctor would tell Abu Abdalla to bring Abdalla back to his clinic in Damascus after so many days for a checkup, but when they went on the appointed day, he often was not there. This time during my absence he had operated again on Abdalla's hand where the gunshot wound had left a hole. After this operation, the place on his leg from which the doctor took skin for grafting seemed to be infected, so the day before I got back, his parents had taken him to the clinic again. Although they waited several hours, until nine in the evening, the doctor didn't come. Um Abdalla, tears of frustration filling her eyes, complained bitterly about how inconsiderate the doctors were. "There's a doctor here in the village, but he can't take care of a complicated problem like this so we'll end up going back and forth to Damascus until the doctor decides to attend his clinic."

Um Abdalla had a mental hierarchy regarding the medical competencies of doctors. It started at the negative end with rural practitioners and moved through doctors in larger nearby towns, to Syrian-trained or—in a more positive light, foreign-trained—Syrian doctors practicing in major cities, to finally, at the most positive end, foreign-born doctors practicing in Western countries. She, like other villagers, would select a doctor according to the seriousness of the illness and her ability to see the better practitioners. One way that the summer residents won grudging acceptance from the villagers was by giving them medical advice or referring them by letter to specialists in Damascus. In an extreme urgency, some villagers even had contacts through emigrant relatives to doctors in America where as a last resort they could send X rays or test results.

The problem with Abdalla started when he inadvertently shot himself in the finger with birdshot. The accident left his finger broken and hanging from only a small amount of skin. Um Abdalla bundled him into the car of her cousin and drove to a nearby town down the valley where she found no doctors available in the hospital. Her next stop was the French hospital in Damascus where again she found no one who could operate on the finger, so she moved on to the large government hospital in Damascus. Almost frantic by this time, she finally found someone who could help her. But his reaction was "Is he a girl that the finger needs to be fixed? Better to cut it off!" But Um Abdalla insisted, and so they operated. By now he had had two operations and would have yet another to restore the finger's movement. She was now taking him to a specialist in Salhieh Street (the Harley Street of Damascus, known for its expensive private doctors) where she paid S£30 every visit plus bus and taxi fares. Um Abdalla ended her account of the accident by noting angrily that about five days after the operation, when Abu Abdalla took Abdalla back to the doctor to see how the wound was doing, ". . . the doctor smelled the bandage and reported everything was fine because it hadn't putrefied," and they left without the doctor's even looking at the wound. They were to have returned in five days when the problems started with Abdalla's leg. As an important afterthought, Um Abdalla remarked that the original operation had taken four hours and cost S£1,000, and by now the whole problem had cost a total of S£7,000. It reassured her to think she had done everything possible by using a doctor who was so expensive and who had operated on Abdalla for so long.

The next day, at the coffee break, Um Abdalla casually commented on how her children and Um George's children were born so close in age to one another, the only difference being that Um Abdalla, who was older, had started having her children earlier. "I had one every year for so many years that my body got completely worn out. You could say I was pregnant for ten years," she said with a certain amount of exaggeration. If I had been alert, I might have wondered why she started this topic out of the blue—Um Abdalla was not given to expressing random thoughts.

The following morning, she came for a cup of tea, looking more tired than usual. We talked for a while about the village and about how everyone knew everyone else—a discussion stimulated by my questions asking who was related to whom. "About half the village is related to us," she told me without elaboration, and yet I wondered about the veracity of her statement, since there seemed so little contact between herself and other families. If this was true, the families in Wusta, with few exceptions, kept very much to themselves.

Um Abdalla seemed preoccupied and finally blurted out what was troubling her. She was finally sure that she was pregnant and emphatically wished she weren't. She wondered out loud whether she shouldn't have had an abortion, but because she had discovered her condition so late, it was probably no longer an option. Previously, she said, she had had two abortions which each time cost almost S£1,000, so there was price to consider. After Boulos was born, she had taken birth control pills and that worked for a while, but recently she had had problems and her doctor told her to stop taking them. She was only thirty-two and thought she had enough children but couldn't think of any practical means by which to stop them. Not having sex was an option she would gladly have considered, but she knew Abu Abdalla would not agree. According to her, it was the only major issue she and Abu Abdalla argued about in private. We talked for a while about birth control options, but none was acceptable to her for practical or for what she took to be health reasons. She never suggested religious reasons for not using birth control.

That day, she said Abu Abdalla yelled at her before he went off to work, saying that she shouldn't talk the way she did about not wanting the baby. When she asked him how many children he wanted to have, he refused to say. This made her feel that prevention was her problem, and she saw no easy solution. At my urging, she agreed to ask her doctor about a tubal ligation after this baby was born, but since she had never heard of this method, it seemed unlikely that she would follow up when the time came.

Um Abdalla said she didn't plan to tell the other children yet about the new baby because "it's too long a time for them to have to think about it; they will get too excited." "Women's work is never done," she added wearily.

Lisa can't help out because she needs to study all the time, and it's important not to disturb her this year because of the major exams she has at the end of the school year. And I am completely exhausted from all the guests that came during the Christmas holidays. There I was, running back and forth all day bringing tea and coffee, fruit and sweets. Then the whole family came for the main meal—Um George and her family and my brothers (but not her mother). I stayed up until three in the morning cooking. We killed the goat, and I roasted his innards and made all kinds of other dishes. On top of that, I had to prepare for the holidays by buying clothes for all the children, about S£1,000 for each one.

She continued, enumerating all the work she had done and complaining about how difficult everything was, and finally burst into tears. I found it hard to believe that Um George and the girls had not helped with the holiday preparations—it would have been uncharacteristic for them not to do so. This was a different Um Abdalla from the one who normally accepted her lot so stoically.

I suggested that since she was pregnant, she might not need to wash her floors every day and could lower her standards of perfection in housework. I knew my suggestions fell on deaf ears and that she only wanted someone outside the problem to listen sympathetically. She had no intention of changing what she was accustomed to doing. I mentioned encouragingly that when the baby came, exams would almost be over, and then both of the girls would be able to do the housework. That idea seemed the first to brighten her outlook.

We changed the subject after she said regretfully that it was wrong of her to tempt fate by saying that she didn't want the baby. "God forbid that anyone would think I wished the child ill." Indeed, later when serious problems affected one of the children, she must have thought back to her feelings during this pregnancy and blamed herself for his problems. In the end, however, the despair she felt at starting all over again with a new baby did not seem to diminish her joy when her new little daughter finally arrived, nor did it diminish her conscientiousness in keeping the same standards of cleanliness for the household that she had kept before the birth. The other children, as well, were not greatly enthusiastic at first about the idea of a new sibling, but their enthusiasm also rallied and their new little sister eventually won their hearts.

As was characteristic, Abu Abdalla showed little outward emotion about the child's impending birth, but I knew from Um Abdalla that he was pleased. ("He doesn't have to do the work," she added.) His view was "the more children the better."

Early in the winter, little Lisa came down with a bad cold. Abu Adil detached the cab of his truck and, leaving the trailer behind, went off alone to see the doctor in Damascus. After hearing a recital of Lisa's symptoms, the doctor decided she needed a course of antibiotics for what he decided was tonsillitis. Abu Adil stopped in a pharmacy on his way home and bought the medicines and needles that were required. The next afternoon George was sent to let the nurse, Miriam, know that she was needed to give the antibiotic shots the doctor prescribed. She came immediately and continued to come each day until Lisa had completed the five-shot series. During the winter, Miriam repeated this process several times as one after another of the younger children came down with colds and Um George gave each the same dose prescribed by the Damascene doctor for Lisa. It saved trips to Damascus and besides, what was good for one was probably good for the others. There was no difficulty in obtaining these medicines from the druggist without a prescription.

A nurse like Miriam was a convenience to the village. After secondary school, she had received enough basic training in nursing so she could take care of bedridden patients and administer shots, which were the most common treatment for ailments, along with vitamin tonics and cough syrups. Her father had died when she was young, and the family was therefore dependent on the small amounts she earned. Since her mother was distantly related to Um Abdalla and Um George, they felt obligated to use her services whenever possible.

Miriam was probably in her late twenties, but she was not married. People talked about how beautiful and intelligent her sister was, implying that Miriam was not so well endowed with those qualities, which was true. Miriam's work made it possible for her sister to attend Damascus University where she worked on a degree that they hoped would give her a stable professional position and ensure the family greater economic security. Even though all these topics were discussed in front of her, Miriam showed no resentment that her sister had more praiseworthy qualities than she did or that she, Miriam, had sacrificed her own future prospects to provide for her mother and sister. I asked what would happen if the beautiful sister decided to marry—or whether her commitment to the mother and sister who had supported her all these years might prevent that happening. Um Abdalla and Um George agreed that it would not be right to ask a husband to support his wife's family or for them to move in with the couple. Perhaps the sister might work for a time if her husband allowed it and give her own earnings to them. The mother and Miriam created a liability for her, they felt, but perhaps her beauty would infatuate a man enough so that he would overlook these disadvantages.

In addition to the medicines prescribed by doctors, Um George had her own treatments for sick children in winter. She rubbed their chests with something like Vicks that had a strong menthol smell, and she put some holy oil she got from the Mafraq church on their navels. Then she made sure their stomachs were wrapped in several layers of woolen cloth and pinned tightly. When the days became cooler, she started this procedure as one of their automatic bedtime routines.

At the morning coffee hour one day, she wondered out loud why people caught colds so often in winter—she knew the word *microbe* but was puzzled as to where they came from and to why they so often caused problems in winter. I suggested that the overheated air from the stove in the sitting room might be drying the children's nasal passages and allowing the microbes to gain entrance more easily. She was reluctant to accept this idea because she was sure cold air was more harmful than hot air with respect to infections and went over to turn the stove up another notch. It made me wonder whether my explanation was as much folk wisdom as hers. We often challenged each other's explanations in this way, without convincing the other.

Um George was more interested in herbal remedies than Um Abdalla was. She had bottles of ingredients that she used for different ailments. Some she prepared herself during fall preservation campaigns, and some she bought from a specialist in Damascus. "Dried carnation petal tea is good for colds," she explained, "and rose petals are for the stomach." I wanted to hear more, but she was distracted by Ilyas's cries for food. Um George was a doer and not particularly interested in telling me why and what she did.

While Um George went off to take care of Ilyas, Um Abdalla took up the theme of microbes to illustrate that childhood illnesses could be very serious. She told me about the mayor from a village near Homs who had a child with, as she described it, Down's syndrome. According to her, the girl contracted the condition three months after birth when she developed a high fever. From my "scientific" perspective, I was imagining the mayor's not wanting to admit "bad genes" and falling back on the fever theory as a way to save the family image. Or perhaps, alternatively, they hadn't noticed the problem until the child was three months old. It was difficult to discuss medical cause and effect with Um Abdalla and Um George, who always believed uncritically what they were told by other villagers. Confused by the fact that I was supposed to be a doctor, they often asked me questions about health but invariably rejected any explanations and recommendations I proposed if they had not already heard them themselves.

Without being aware of what she was doing, Um Abdalla was returning again and again to stories about birth problems and handicapped children. I knew she was still feeling guilty about not wanting another child. Now when we talked about the baby, she would always preface her comments with "I only care that the baby is normal." At some point, she had made up her mind to accept the idea and was determined to make no further negative comments that might affect the outcome.

One day I returned from Damascus to find that Um George's husband had been away a full twenty-one or twenty-four days, depending on who was doing the counting. I personally accepted Um George's lower estimate of twenty-one days, for she would have been the one to exaggerate the number. His absence was on everybody's mind, but no one wanted to say anything in front of Um George for fear it would worry her. I tactlessly brought up the topic one day when we were all sitting together, thinking she might want someone to commiserate with her. Almost immediately I wished I hadn't. There was silence, and then Um Abdalla changed the subject. Um George's anxiety when Abu Adil was delayed was heightened by the experience of losing her first husband in a trucking accident.

A week earlier, one of the truckers had returned, saying Abu Adil would be late, but—perhaps not wanting to be the bearer of bad news—he refused to give a reason. Knowing that the reason could not have been life threatening, we were more curious than anxious this time to know what had caused the delay. According to the trucker who brought the news, Abu Adil should be back any day now, so we spent our afternoons with Um George to make the time pass more quickly. Several truckers from the same traveling group also were delayed. If they all had picked up extra work in the Gulf, the delay could mean good news, but if that had been the case, why had the trucker been unwilling to say anything about it?

When Abu Adil finally returned two days later, we learned what had happened. He had accidentally driven his truck under a low bridge in Saudi Arabia, and part of the roof had been torn off. He had to stay behind for fifteen days for questioning by the police, during which time most of the other truckers in the group he traveled with found jobs so they could stay and keep him company. After he returned to Wusta, his truck stayed in the shop for repairs for several weeks, and soon he was behind by at least two, if not three, trips. He and Um George became concerned about the payments for the truck and temporarily halted construction on the additions to their house, which in any case were proceeding so slowly as to be almost unnoticeable because of Abu Adil's long absences.

Trucking carried high personal and economic risk. It was so common for problems to occur that relatives remained in a state of anxiety until their men returned safely from journeys. Truckers from the village periodically had accidents along the highways that ended in injuries and sometimes death, damage to goods and trucks, and, in some cases, the incarceration of drivers for minor or not so minor infractions of the law. As days lengthened beyond the expected twelve days of a normal run, families began to think of little else. Sometimes the news was good—a vehicle had picked up a short-term haul between countries of the Gulf, but more often than not, the problem was a breakdown or costly delays at a border.

The financial risks in trucking also increased during the late 1970s and early 1980s. First, competition was increasing. According to Syrian government statistics, the numbers of truckers on the road tripled between 1971 and 1982 from roughly 11,000 to 32,000,[1] a somewhat smaller increase than in the previous decade but nonetheless significant. The government also was tightening its controls, and border guards created lucrative new ways to extort money out of the truckers. All these problems reduced the truckers' profits and led them to question whether the arduous work was worth it. The most vulnerable families were, of course, those most heavily invested in trucking as a livelihood. Others with more diversified sources of income were better off, but many of them—for example, those in the chicken business—also were susceptible to the same tightening web of government restriction.

The mass production of poultry and eggs, like the trucking industry, had had its main impetus in the late 1960s and throughout the 1970s. Between 1971 and 1982, according to Syrian official statistics, the production of eggs rose fivefold, from 300 million to more than 1.6 billion, and chickens three-fold, from 5 million to more than 15 million. Over the same period, however, the neglect of the agricultural sector meant that the needed quantities of feed could not be provided locally and producers became dependent on feed imported by the Syrian government. By the early 1980s, the Syrian government was beginning to experience serious foreign currency shortages and so imposed strict controls on imports of all kinds. One of the immediate consequences was the shortage of chicken feed that Abu Abdalla mentioned—first only in some kinds of grains but later in the overall quantity available.[2] Abu Abdalla cut back the number of chickens he raised and described to me how some producers were raising fewer chickens in winter when the cost of heating the sheds reduced the net profits and then increased production in warmer seasons with the hoarded allotments of feed carried over from the winter period.

The feed crisis continued until 1984 when it was brought to a head by a severe drought[3] that reduced the locally grown barley and grazing crops. Both sheep and poultry producers were competing for the limited imported feed, and as an indicator, sheep production dropped from approximately 12 million to 8 million head. In 1984, the government finally decided to liberalize import restrictions, by allowing private firms registered with the Chamber of Commerce to import such feed ingredients as vitamins, minerals, and feed supplements. By that time, the Syrian poultry industry needed approximately 400,000 metric tons of corn (of which only 25,000 was produced locally) and 80,000 metric tons of soybean meal (which is not produced locally) annually.

During the time I was in Wusta, in 1981 and 1982, before the liberalization measures, the profits from chicken production seesawed up and down, depending on the availability of government feed or, alternatively, feed that could be bought on the thriving local black market. Black market feed was, of course, considerably more expensive and reduced profits proportionately, since the prices of eggs and chickens were strictly controlled by the government. The government also issued strong controls over the third and final alternative, the limited home production of grains for feed. All farmers were required to sell homegrown grains to the government at predetermined costs, which the government then sold at a higher controlled price to the consumer. On the way to market, not surprisingly, many of these grains were "lost." Government grain was distributed on a rationed basis to mills, livestock producers, and poultry farmers, although none of these groups was able to obtain as much as it needed. In Wusta as elsewhere, farmers began to feed their chickens less suitable feeds like flour, bread, and barley and to cut back production.

Were the villagers' fears about their livelihoods warranted? In certain measure, they were, for even though they were living well, the growing competition and instability in the economy were affecting the size of their disposable income. In an analysis of the Syrian economy, one observer notes that although there was major growth in all economic sectors during the 1970s, including an increase in real GDP of more than 150 percent, the economy began to stagnate during the 1980s, until by the end of the decade, the real GDP was about the same as in 1980, and per capita income declined about 20 percent.[4]

Other problems indirectly related to foreign currency shortages were con-
tributing to the malaise in the trucking business. One problem was that as
earners of foreign exchange, truckers were vulnerable to attempts by the
government to raise its share of earnings, and another problem was that the
villagers operated in a very narrow niche of the trucking trade in Syria[5]—
transporting produce from Lebanon to the Gulf and Saudi Arabia—so any
disruptions in these areas immediately affected their earnings. Eventually,
the government imposed a large monthly tax on all trucks. Trucks were not
allowed across the border until they could show that this tax had been paid.
As far as the truckers were concerned, this was just one more in a number
of substantial bribes paid to have their papers processed on the borders.

Similarly, the Syrian government started enforcing a law that required
truckers carrying freight in bond to travel in a convoy escorted by a customs
official from one border point to another, ostensibly for their own safety but
also to ensure that goods demanding a high price would not find their way
into the Syrian black market. It might take two or three days to cross Syria
instead of the customary one day because of formalities in assembling con-
voys and presenting the proper documentation.

The truckers had even bigger troubles during the intermittent hostilities
between the countries in the area. During these times, for instance, they
could not go into Lebanon to pick up produce for the Gulf countries, or they
were restricted in other ways. There was a particularly long hiatus during the
Israeli invasion of Lebanon in 1982. If the Syrian government's laws had been
more flexible, there would have been ample opportunity to substitute
Syrian for Lebanese produce in the Gulf markets and obtain the foreign currency the country needed so badly. But government regulations inflexibly
prevented local crops from exiting the borders, ostensibly to avoid shortages
and possible unrest at home. As a result of controlled prices, which made it
hardly worth the effort of the big fruit and vegetable producers to sell their
produce, crops were left to rot in the orchards, and fields were left fallow.
Thus the government's efforts proved counterproductive. Poor-quality
fruits and vegetables reached the market at government-controlled prices,
and better-quality produce was sold under the counter at black market
prices. These were particularly difficult times for the truckers, who were
squeezed from both ends, with few goods available and payments on their
trucks still coming due. Later, when the hostilities ceased and the truckers
were able to reach warehouses in Chtura, Lebanon, they also found, for a

time, that the war had disrupted farming to such an extent that there was no longer an abundance of cheap produce.

The repercussions of the war continued for the truckers for some time after its active phase was over. For example, in 1983 several Arab countries banned the sale of Lebanese goods so as to prevent Israeli goods from entering their markets through Israeli-occupied southern Lebanon. And in April 1984, there were reports of 1,300 to 1,500 trucks carrying Lebanese products awaiting clearance at the Saudi border. Eventually, a process was devised by which Lebanon's Board of Foreign Economic Relations could issue certificates of origin for Lebanese products.

Curiously, during the Gulf War almost a decade later, the truckers were reported to have done very well. Restrictions were relaxed on the export of Syrian produce, which enabled the truckers to earn higher profits, and prohibitions by the Gulf States and Saudi Arabia on Jordanian trucking because of Jordan's stance during the war meant that the Syrians were able to buy secondhand trucks cheaply and could stay for long periods in Saudi Arabia and the Gulf, transporting goods for the war effort.

In addition to these problems, many truckers were precariously involved in questionable activities to extract the maximum profit from their investments. Most, for example, registered their trucks in Kuwait to avoid local taxes and the Syrian requirement that a certain portion of trucking hours be given over to poorly paid (estimated at 25 to 75 percent below cost) hauling for the Syrian government.

Three other regulations were especially troublesome to the truckers. One concerned regulations regarding compulsory military service. Young Syrian males could not get visas or passports to leave the country until they had finished their military service of three years. Army service started at about age eighteen, and young men were therefore not able to drive trucks across borders until they were twenty-one or so, thereby delaying the time when they could begin to gather the large sums they needed to marry. Wealthy families like that of Abu Ilyas paid high fines so that their sons could avoid military service, but this option was not open to most families.

A second regulation simply made the driving itself more difficult. The truckers considered it easier and safer if two drivers could go and spell each other on the trip to Saudi Arabia and the Gulf nations, but these countries, fearful of illegal immigration, did not permit more than one driver per truck across their borders.

The third and most serious regulation was the Syrian government's refusal to allow the truckers to bring back goods from the Gulf, where tax-free consumer products could be bought cheaply. Because of this regulation, the trucks returned empty, thus raising the cost of transport and cutting their potential profit.

During this time in 1981 when external controls over both their livelihoods intensified, Abu Abdalla and Abu Adil would return home with anxiety written on their faces. Several times a week, Abu Abdalla scoured the markets from Wusta to Damascus looking for grain for the chickens, and Abu Adil returned grimly from each journey with news of more and more restrictions. He complained that every trip added another regulation to complicate the truckers' lives. Both men worried that they might have to find other ways of earning money if conditions became any worse. Despite all these problems, trucking still held a strong appeal for young men attracted by the money and the romance of travel. It was a macho kind of work that let them prove they were the tough "go-getting" men the villagers admired.

I was in the village a while before I realized the full extent of Abu Abdalla's income-earning activities. He had started out in the *baladiyya* office several years earlier, with responsibility for one aspect of the work, but by the time I came to Wusta, he had responsibility for three aspects. He was charged with billing and collecting water users' fees and taxes; he registered land transfer documents; and he granted building permits and inspected construction work to ensure that the proper standards were met. His position as the highest government representative in the village was of considerable importance, since he possessed so much discretionary power over matters of land and construction. At times, it was said, he stuck to the letter of the law when he wanted to annoy someone or when he thought there might be something extra in the transaction for himself. At other times, he would interpret the regulations flexibly when he found it useful to his own interests. It was not in the interest of anyone in the village to antagonize Abu Abdalla. Though *baladiyya* work might seem routine, no one considered it so, and Abu Abdalla was given credit for both successful and unsuccessful applications.

Before and during the time I stayed in Wusta, increasing numbers of Damascenes were buying land in and around the village to construct summer homes. The village was seen as advantageous because of its pleasant summer weather and its land that as yet was not too exorbitant in price—from S£50 to S£200 per square meter, depending on the location. Abu Abdalla estimated that about a quarter of the village land had already been sold. He was in the enviable position of being able to negotiate some of these land transactions between villagers and outsiders and, through his acquaintance with the outsiders, to contract workers to build houses on the land. It was natural that he should also act as overseer for the work. He rarely let such an opportunity go by to enhance his income. But because he kept this kind of information to himself, I could only guess at the number of projects by the frequency of visitors who came to discuss construction with him. Most of the out-of-towners treated him with the careful consideration given to one who controls the success of projects. They joked in a flattering way that he was the most important person in the village. "If you want to get something done, you go to Abu Abdalla," they would say. On the surface, he seemed relaxed, but in reality, he was under considerable pressure from the numerous projects he supervised. Soon after I left the village, his health suffered from these tensions, or so the doctor told him, saying he should cut back these stressful activities.

Besides the projects related to his official capacities and the chicken farming, Abu Abdalla also had at least one other income source of which I was aware: part ownership in a truck that took goods to Saudi Arabia. This project was also problematic because of an untrustworthy driver who claimed higher expenses than seemed warranted to Abu Abdalla. Abu Abdalla liked activities he could "hold in his own hands," like supervising construction, in which he could strike the bargain himself and the buyer could not be sure which were actual costs and which were "agent's" fees and was afraid to ask too closely out of fear of antagonizing Abu Abdalla. But in obtaining feed for his chickens and in dealing with the driver of the shared truck, he was forced to accept the same treatment he meted out to others.

Although Um Abdalla contributed just as much to the household as Abu Abdalla, there was one important difference in their activities. The expectation that she would successfully accomplish her assigned activities was never really in doubt as long as she was in good health and able to meet her own high standards of perfection. The reason was that her activities were domestic in nature and protected from external interference by Abu Abdalla. Abu Abdalla, by contrast, constantly dealt with problems of external interference that he could do little about. Every day brought new problems—finding feed for the chickens, seeing that he got a fair price for his eggs, keeping the tractor going, keeping the construction on schedule, sending out water bills on time, and dealing with truck drivers who were inflating their costs. As a result, much of his time was taken up with worrisome problems that carried important consequences for the family.

On one lazy evening, we were relaxing after the children had finished their homework. Abu Abdalla wondered whether I knew that the part of the house in which I lived was what he had built for himself and Um Abdalla when they were married. I had heard this story before but listened politely anyway, hoping to hear, as I often did when stories were repeated, more details to add to those I had heard already. My part of the house consisted of a room, kitchen, bath, and one other bedroom; it was the first time I knew there had been an additional bedroom. The house was situated on Abu Abdalla's father's land next door to his parents' house. As long as his parents were alive, the two families formed what was basically an extended family, sharing most of the work and expenses. "You know, Um Dawud, the old broken down house on the hill just in back of our house? That's where they lived." It was an exceedingly modest home, a reminder of how quickly the economic situation in Wusta had changed.

Um Abdalla talked of those times as the most difficult of her life, because of the demands placed on her by her mother-in-law. "I was working all the time, which I didn't mind, because as a new wife I wanted to do the best I could for my mother-in-law. But she was never satisfied with anything I did." In the early days of their marriage, Abu Abdalla tried to make ends meet by farming. During the season when the crops needed most attention, he slept in a hut next to the fields. He also spoke of that time as very discouraging, when no matter how hard he worked, the crops did not thrive because of the lack of rain. For several years, he tried to make farming work but eventually decided there must be better ways to earn a living. It was then that he was able to get the job in the *baladiyya* office, one of four employees there, and soon after looked into starting a poultry business. It took two years to construct the chicken houses on a choice piece of family land overlooking the valley. Abu Abdalla's rendition of the story was full of singular events and the details of building, whereas Um Abdalla's was of problems she faced with her parents-in-law.

One morning when I had brought her some hot chocolate and we were sitting alone in the sun on the back porch, Um Abdalla gave me an expanded version of the early days—one she hadn't wanted to tell when Abu Abdalla was present.

I was married when I was about fifteen years old, and believe me, I didn't know anything at all. I was just like Muna is now. My mother-in-law was always complaining about everything I did, but we were taught to respect our elders, and I never answered back. She made me feel miserable, and my father-in-law was the same. At first they expected help from Abu Abdalla in farming their land but never gave him a say in what was produced or a share in the profits, so in frustration he went out and rented land. The arrangement he made was that the owner would contribute the land and water from his well and that Abu Abdalla would do all the work. They would split the profits evenly between them. Abu Abdalla planted cucumbers, because it was a fast-growing vegetable and could make a pretty good profit if everything went right. At harvest time, we all went out to bring in the crop. One of the villagers with a truck sold the cucumbers in town and asked a commission of S£10 for each two boxes of produce. Things were relatively cheap in those days, and you didn't need much to live on. Even so, we didn't do very well because there just wasn't enough water to produce a really good crop, and by the time we paid the owner and the trucker, there was little left over.

After a few years of farming like this, he realized it just wasn't working out. That was when he got the government job. He was lucky to get it because he had only gone to elementary school—to the sixth grade, like Hanna now—and then left and began to work. In those days, not everyone went to school the way they do now, and so there were not so many candidates for the job which, like all government jobs, was steady but did not pay much.

Finally, he got up enough courage to ask his father for the share of the land he would receive as inheritance after his father's death, and because his father was old and couldn't farm it himself any more, he relented and gave it to him. There are now three brothers who share the inheritance after the fourth, Um George's first husband, died. Abu Abdalla took his share of the land and built the chicken sheds.

I then asked Abu Abdalla if anyone in Wusta farmed land for a living any more.

It depends on water—many nowadays leave the land idle because of the lack of water. Look, you know yourself that the village water is often turned off, and on those days we don't even have enough for the house. There just isn't sufficient rainfall any more. It might get better, but even if it did, young people no longer have the stamina or motivation to farm. It's too easy to make better money in other work. Nowadays, people come from the village up the road and rent our land. They sow wheat on the hillside without irrigation— just from rain, so it doesn't grow very well. Three months later, they come back and harvest it. They do the same with land that has figs and grapes. It requires only two plowings a year and some pruning, then harvesting. They use tractors and cover a lot of land so they make money. But to answer your question, I guess no one from here earns all his money from farming any more.

Some truckers came to discuss with Abu Adil the timing for their next trip to Saudi Arabia. When they had finished their business and everyone was relaxing over tea, the visitors began talking about the prices of winter staples. Um George brought out the green olives that she and Um Abdalla had bought and pointed out that they had paid S£6 a kilo for them. Everyone chimed in with the price of olives at such and such a store or from such and such a farmer. They all complained of how much prices were increasing but agreed that even though they could give examples of where prices were cheaper, Um George and Um Abdalla had probably paid a reasonable price, given the quality of the olives they had bought. And as someone pointed out, in another month, olives would cost S£12 a kilo when the black ones came on the market. I asked whether the best olive oil was made from black or green olives, and surprisingly, no one knew but that turned the discussion to the numerous kinds of olive oil that could be bought, their relative prices, and where the best varieties could be found. They all agreed that the best olive oil came from Telfita, but there as anywhere, you had to watch out for merchants who diluted the good oil with cheaper oil to increase their profits.

As I spent more time in Wusta, I came to see these endless discussions about prices as consumer seminars in which villagers learned how much they should pay for various items. In 1981, according to non-Syrian sources, the inflation rate in Syria ranged between 15 and 30 percent, with food having the highest rate at about 28 percent and meat even higher at 39 percent. Because prices fluctuated constantly and merchants tried to charge as much as they could get, people had to keep informed about the going rate of commodities so as to avoid being overcharged.

The villagers' greatest delight was striking a bargain cheaper than anyone else's. After Um Abdalla's trips to Damascus, she would burst in the door with her packages, ready to show us what she had bought and tell us how much she had paid for each item so we would know what an astute bargainer she had been. But I would agree too quickly that she had done a superb job in beating down the price to a mere fraction of what it should have been, and her elation would fade when she remembered that I didn't know much about the matter and therefore was not a good judge of her talents. A few minutes later, she would dash off to her sister, who was a true connoisseur and would understand better the miracles she had wrought. Um George would say, "But did you get this particular kind [a quality item], or was it only this other kind [an inferior product]?" And Um Abdalla could reply that of course, it was the quality item, which should have cost "such and such" normally, but she had gotten it for a much lower "such and such." Then, and only then, would the practical Um George grudgingly give her seal of approval, and Um Abdalla could relax, knowing that she had indeed obtained outstanding bargains.

When I tried to participate in this contest by showing off my shopping exploits, they always said I had spent double what the item was worth. After a time, I lowered the price I reported to about half what I had actually paid just to prove myself worthy of entering the discussion. Eventually, Um Abdalla and Um George felt so sorry for me spending so much money that they ordered items from Saudi Arabia for me. They would say, "We can have Abu Adil bring such and such for you" and would accept no refusals. Soon I was receiving smuggled ghee and powdered milk in quantities my husband and I could never possibly consume.

The preoccupation with costs reflected another characteristic of the villagers, a deep-seated distrust of outsiders' motives. They assumed that any outsider with whom they were not intimate would seize the first possible opportunity to cheat them. The object of the outsider's "greed," everyone seemed to understand, was not personal gain but, rather, a natural inclination to accumulate as many resources as possible for his or her own family. Seen in that light, the overcharging of sellers was both normal and unselfish. But for the same reasons, buyers had to be on the alert against having their own resources depleted. It could work in one of two ways. Buyers could be "cheated" if they let themselves remain strangers to these outsiders, or they could appeal for "fairness" by reminding the seller of a real or a potential relationship of blood, friendship, residence in the same village, religion, or any other meaningful connection. Discovering a relationship and knowing what a fair price should be were the ways in which buyers kept costs reasonable. Looking back on the discussion between Um Abdalla and Um George and the olive salesman on the first day of my visit, I recognized some of these strategies at work.

Lisa and Muna joined us at Um George's, interrupting the discussion about prices, and I asked Lisa whether she had finished her homework. "Most of it," she sighed. "They give us so much work." She had her physics book open in her lap to continue memorizing the lesson in odd moments. "We have to watch the teacher do experiments in class and remember what she did as well as learn every word in the book by heart."

"How many students are there in your class?"

"It varies from about forty to seventy, depending on the subject—these numbers are just about right—I don't have any especially big classes."

The election results were coming in on the television—long lists of names that nobody in the room was particularly interested in hearing, except when the results for the local area were announced. Even then, the adults seemed only mildly interested in seeing whether they recognized the names, not whether one individual or another had won. When I asked Abu Abdalla why he wasn't interested in politics, he replied that if it didn't affect his business, he didn't care. He didn't know the name of his own member of parliament or the name of the well-known and generally feared minister of interior. All he knew was that the regional member of parliament came from a large town down the valley. Yet as was required of all citizens, he had gone and cast his vote that morning, though for whom was a mystery.

Between results, the Lebanese singer Farouz sang, and a troupe of three women and a man danced and sang traditional selections. Lisa became interested in the women entertainers. "That's the kind of dress I like—an 'Arab' one," she said, pointing out a loose flowing red dress of fine organdy with bodice and sleeves embroidered in gold. It was hard to believe that these were the words of the same Lisa who wore only blue jeans after school and quarreled with her mother over wearing a dress to church at Easter. We talked about the evening serials on television. "I like the Egyptian ones a lot better than the Syrian ones. The stories are better and people seem more real—people you can become attached to. There's a good one on now, but I haven't seen it because of schoolwork."

"How do you know it's good?"

"Because the girls in school tell me about the episodes every day."

The guests, meanwhile, were becoming disgruntled with the long lists of election winners. Etiquette required that they should have left by now, but they stayed, hoping to see the serial that was expected to start any minute. We continued to wait, though it was well past the usual time for the program. Um George came and went bringing nuts, grapes, and coffee. The little diesel stove poured out heat until we were bathed in sweat in our woolen clothing. We had been sitting in one house and then the other since about four-thirty, and now it was well past ten. Um George's four little children had drifted off to sleep, and she had gently changed them into their night clothes and placed all four in the bed in the corner of the room.

It also was past Lisa's bedtime, and the serial was clearly not going to come on. By neglecting to announce the schedule change, Syrian officials had kept viewers tuned in to election results all evening. Was it intentional or just careless programming? We could only guess. The truckers and Abu and Um Abdalla started to leave. Lisa and I slipped away down the mud path to our house, bending to avoid the low limbs of the fig trees. It was a bright cloudless sky with a half moon casting shadows on the ground. The cold air was a wonderful relief from the sweltering sauna of Um George's parlor.

Their preoccupation with money made me curious about the family's income. Although they were open about how much they spent, they never discussed how much they earned. If earnings were known, they believed, the government might tax them; friends might ask for loans and it would be difficult to refuse them; and others might be jealous of them, something they wanted to avoid. The best way I could approximate their earnings was to look at their expenses, since they never seemed to put aside extra money except temporarily to pay for special projects. Trying to add up the expenses was also not easy because they stockpiled items and invested in one-time capital investments like buildings, feed grinders, and tractors that were difficult to add to the equation.

Perhaps it was enough to know that some of their expenditures were very large. For example, the cost of heating fuel alone was considerable. Every can, or *tanaka*, of fuel cost S£20 (almost $5), they told me, and they feared the price would go up to S£30 the following year. There were three heating stoves in the house, one in the bathroom which was turned on only once a week when water was heated for baths, one in the television room where we sat in the evenings, and one in the girls' room where we sat during the day. The heating stoves were filled two times a day or 120 times a month for the two most commonly used ones. A *tanaka* was enough to fill the stoves four times, so thirty *tanakas* were needed to heat the house each month in winter. Thus, heating the house alone cost £30 x 20 = S£600 ($150) per month. To generate electricity for the chicken farm and to fuel the tractor took about 210 *tanakas* more per month, or S£4,200 ($1,050). This cost remained the same every month of the year unless an unusual cold snap required additional fuel to heat the chicken houses. This translated into a total cost in the winter months for the house and chicken sheds of about $1,200 per month for fuel alone.

Um George spent less, since she was trying to save money for the family's new constructions. She used only one stove for her main room so got by on fifteen *tanakas* a month, or half as much as Um Abdalla used.

Um Abdalla's shopping excursions into Damascus invariably ate up considerable sums also. An outfit that she bought for Lisa to wear at a wedding consisted of a S£400 coat from Hong Kong that Um Abdalla bargained down to S£300, gray cord pants from Italy for S£125, and a blouse for S£60. Um Abdalla explained with some satisfaction, "Every time I go to Damascus, I buy something for the girls. I like them to wear nice clothes."To Um Abdalla, ready-made was more prestigious, presumably because it was more expensive, and therefore when the event was something where the girls would be seen in the village, she bought them ready-made clothes. Um Abdalla bought clothing about twice a year for the children at a cost of at least S£1,000 for each child each time. For herself, she thriftily bought material and made her own dresses.

Other costs included meat for S£50 (more than $12) per kilo, bread and vegetables which were insignificant, and well digging which, according to Abu Abdalla, cost about S£125 per square meter. Most of the town's wells were from 100 to 130 meters deep, depending on whether or not the land was on a hill. The big reservoir that stood on the hill above the town belonged to the *baladiyya* and was the source for the water piped into homes. People paid for the metered amount that they used from this source. Rents also were surprisingly steep for the village, but they were, of course, income for those lucky enough to have rental properties. An unfurnished three-bedroom apartment rented for S£10,000 to S£12,000 ($3,000) for the year, meaning basically the summer, but there were few available at the time. Most homes were used by their owners, and most summer visitors owned their houses.

Abu Abdalla was grumbling one day because the tractor was not working properly. "It must be the boys playing with it, or maybe it's because my *silfi* [in-law] used it the other day." He went off to the mechanic to see what could be done about it and came back with the gloomy news that it would cost S£5,000 to fix its "heart"—which I took to mean was something fundamentally wrong with it. He then went off to the office, and a man came to the door asking Um Abdalla for S£3,000 but Um Abdalla refused, referring him to her husband. She came back shaking her head at the expenses piling up.

Another day, the plasterer came to look at the interior of the rooms that Um Abdalla wanted finished. There were two finishers, one from the village, the master finisher—Antoine, son of old Abu Antoine, and the other, his apprentice—a Kurd from the Qamishli area. They agreed on S£75 a square meter of wall, which in the end would take twenty-five days of work for two men to complete at an overall cost to Abu Abdalla of S£6,000 ($1,500). The work required (it was not clear why) four layers of plaster over the cement foundation and finally a layer of paint. The plasterers would work from eight to four each day, and Um Abdalla would prepare lunch for them so they wouldn't need to take time off to go home. Abu Abdalla, who had to pay this astonishing sum for two rooms, remarked, "Finishing doesn't pay much, but at least it's better than going out trucking."

Um Abdalla rarely spoke of religion, nor did she go to church herself except at Christmas and Easter. She liked the children to go, however, and most church days she woke them in time for the eight o'clock service. They were so accustomed to obeying her that unless there was pressing schoolwork to do, they rarely objected. But if they objected, she didn't force them to go. The girls went more regularly than the boys. I sensed, sitting through the service one day, that their presence provided a good chance to be seen publicly under appropriately pious conditions. Even though not many young men came to the services, their mothers were there in force looking over the attractive, well-mannered young women that their sons might consider marrying.

Despite her sporadic churchgoing, there was no doubt that Um Abdalla, like all the villagers, had a steadfast faith in God. This was a given in the village that was beyond discussion. When the children were ill or she heard the story of someone else's crisis, she exclaimed with conviction, "May God help them." What happened and was no longer redeemable, she believed, was a result of God's will, to be borne stoically. Because religion was an accepted fact of life, she never questioned whether she should accept certain beliefs or wondered why she belonged to a particular denomination. These issues were too abstract to be of interest to her. Once I took a relativist position in a discussion, saying that my beliefs were probably a result of the fact that I was born into a certain family at a certain time and place. She looked at me strangely as if amazed by my lack of conviction and answered in a way that let me know she felt, in this case, that it was my misfortune to have been born in the *wrong* place and time. These were discussions that she ended as soon as it was polite to do so.

Um Abdalla carried out what she considered to be her religious duties minimally, however, and hoped this was enough to keep her in good standing with her neighbors and with God. I felt that in her mind there was a higher morality connected with doing her household duties than with going to church; otherwise I am sure she would have attended church more often. I have already mentioned the remorse she felt about rejecting the idea of pregnancy, fearing that God might punish her with some harm to her other children for her failing to accept his will.

Um Abdalla scoffed at the idea of *jinns* or other malicious spirits—ideas that were accepted widely in Egyptian society—and she said she really didn't believe in the existence of "the evil eye." Nevertheless, a number of her actions contradicted this stated belief. For example, she was careful not to speak too flatteringly about her children or the children and possessions of other people, for fear of seeming envious or attracting the envy of others—a more acceptable way of describing the evil eye. She felt that negative speculation about the future made it likely that those negative events would occur, and she believed firmly that to speak badly about people might cause them direct bodily harm. She was careful to avoid these behaviors.

When the topic of different religions was raised, usually stimulated by my presence or a villager's vague curiosity about my faith, people expressed the strong belief that it was not proper to argue over religion, especially those religions sharing the ideologies of monotheism. In practice, they seemed more concerned with distinctions among denominations than with differences in beliefs, and although they publicly professed tolerance of Islam, they obviously thought that Christianity was preferable to non-Christian religions and that their own brand of Christianity was preferable to other Christian denominations.

It was when they arrived at the differences between the Greek Orthodox and Greek Catholics in their own village that they finally had something to say about the superiority of one set of beliefs and practices over another. They would point out that the rituals of their group's faith were more rigorous than those of others, that more of the prominent villagers belonged to one faith than the other, that one denomination had more adherents, that the priest was better, or that Catholics gave their people a paper to marry non-Christians and Orthodox did not. Each was convinced of the greater worth of his or her own denomination but was careful to express these thoughts only in the presence of coreligionists and not in the presence of people from other denominations. Not knowing where I fit in made them reluctant to talk about religion with me except in response to specific questions and then only in a general way. They were well aware of the explosiveness of religious issues and had learned to be careful.

Relations between Muslims and Christians was a topic they especially tried to avoid—they were practiced in not saying anything to an outsider that might be construed as critical of Muslims. Because the village was so overwhelmingly Christian, there were few opportunities for direct contact with Muslims. In fact, Wusta was so much a Christian enclave that the villagers operated much of the time as though they constituted a homogeneous universe of Christians. This was not to say that they ignored Islam or were not sensitive to its possible encroachments. Occasionally, they used stereotypes[6] that reflected their truer feelings: "We Christians say the Muslims will eventually die out—'What is born by the sword will die by the sword.'" "'Christians spend and Muslims save.' You know the Muslim caretaker at the summer house by the chicken shed? He earns S£2,500 a month, has a free place to stay, and uses only one hundred pounds for food during the month. He saves all the rest; *they* are very thrifty." Since spending and generosity were admired, these remarks could be taken as derogatory from the perspective of the person making them.

"Wusta is surrounded by Muslims—half of the next big town, all of the large town down the valley, the next village to us, this village, and that [they name a number of villages]. Islam has lots of children!" There was nothing explicitly negative in this comment, but there was the implied criticism that Muslims breed faster than Christians and that there might be disadvantages to Christians if they were overwhelmed by the Muslims' greater numbers.

Although the people of Wusta liked to think of themselves as a wholly Christian village, the changing economic scene had subtly modified this fact almost without their realizing it. When I asked one man about the religious affiliation of the people in the village, he responded that everyone was Christian, of either the Catholic or Orthodox faith. In the sense that the permanent residents were primarily Christian, he was right. But like the others, he ignored the one prominent Muslim family of several households that had lived in Wusta for some time. In addition to these permanent Muslim residents whom villagers saw infrequently, most of the outside workers attracted by the new opportunities in the village—farmers, chicken house attendants, sheepherders, and unskilled construction workers—were Muslim. Their presence was considered so temporary—even when their relationship with the village had lasted as long as the bedouin's—that it was overlooked entirely in defining the village religious identity. The same was true for the Muslim summer visitors, who were seen as so transient that they did not count in the villagers' sense of who belonged there.

Sometimes in Wusta it was difficult to distinguish feelings about religion from feelings about social class. With the exception of the single extended Muslim family that had lived in the village for some time and the sprinkling of summer visitors, most of the Muslims who came to Wusta were menial laborers. Villagers saw themselves as their employers and therefore superior because of their higher social status and standard of living. Um Abdalla, who was generally a kind woman, assumed a patronizing attitude toward Um Muhammad, the wife of the bedouin who took care of the chicken house, but it was difficult to know whether she reacted more strongly from a sense of class or religious difference—probably both to some degree.

The villagers were becoming wary of the increasing number of Muslims coming as summer visitors. These visitors were not as easily dismissed as the menial workers were, as they were well-to-do and held influential positions in professional or government circles. One was a high party official who, when he came to live in Wusta, arranged to have the dirt road outside our house asphalted up to his own front gate. The lesson was not lost on the villagers, who knew quite well that the summer visitors could ultimately win any arguments that arose between them. It was in the villagers' best interest, therefore, to avoid problems by cultivating a tone of cordiality and deference toward the visitors.

The Wusta villagers would have liked to preserve their identity as a Christian village for the reasons I mentioned earlier, but in exposing themselves to new forms of economic livelihood, to national and international markets, to outside workers and to summer visitors, they had opened the village to the penetration of strangers and to forces alien to their own social image. Whether these changes would reduce the villagers' sense of insularity or intensify it remains to be seen. Almost certainly, the villagers will find it harder to ignore the presence of Muslims or to see themselves as an exclusively Christian universe.

Church services in Wusta translated some of the village's important concerns into ritual symbols. As the village's representative of God, the priest was awe inspiring in his magnificent robes of pale blue and silver. During the sermon, he offered prayers for the bodies and souls of truck drivers on the road. The congregation sat around the nave in physical replication of their social roles: the younger children sat protectively in the front pews, with the small contingent of men behind them in the place of prominence and the large supporting section of women in the back. Contrasting with Islam in general, in which women tend to maintain a more private role, public Christianity was kept alive in Wusta by the active participation of women. I never saw either Abu Abdalla or Abu Adil go to church, but the women usually went on special occasions.

Men and women also reflected a different relationship with the church when, after genuflecting in the center aisle on entering the church, the men walked directly to their seats while the women, with more personal interests in mind, stopped to light candles in front of pictures of the saints to honor them or ask special blessings for someone they cared about. The older women wore scarves to show their respect, whereas the younger ones put them on for communion only; the men wore hats. The priest walked at the head of a procession of altar boys, circulating holy symbols—crosses, Bibles, incense, and candles. At communion time, the children formed a double row in the center aisle for their parents to walk through on the way to the railing, and when the adults were finished, a nun pulled the children into order to take their own communion. The pictures of saints looked down on us as we stood and sat, stood and sat, and the priest droned on.

We spent one morning early in January thoroughly cleaning the house so that everything would be spotless when the priest came to bless the house and its inhabitants for the New Year. All day we trailed after the children, straightening their books, lining up the shoes, or replacing a piece of clothing in the cupboard, all so we would be prepared. The best parlor stood ready with the stove stoked and pouring out a glowing heat. Although we waited in nervous expectation all day, the priest didn't come. "We Catholics are the most numerous in the village, so it takes him several days to get to each house. The other priest [Orthodox] goes around too, but there aren't so many of them and it doesn't take as long," said Um Abdalla, proudly rationalizing the delay.

On the second day, after we had spent the morning cleaning again, the priest finally came at three in the afternoon, just when we had given up hope and were beginning to relax about the recurring disorder. Um Abdalla and the children rushed to the door to greet him and kiss his cross before he went to sprinkle holy water over each room in turn. "Any time after the sixth of January we can expect him to come," Um Abdalla had told me. And, as an afterthought so I wouldn't be embarrassed, "It's traditional for us to give him money—S£25 is about the expected amount because he gets a good salary, but we usually give him S£50." I had my money ready when my turn came to have my tidy room blessed, but I couldn't bring myself to kiss his cross.

Starting late in February, people began a period of fasting for forty days. Both Catholic and Orthodox observed this period, but with variations. According to Um George, "Some don't eat or drink from twelve midnight until twelve noon. Others don't eat from after sunset until the next morning." In either case, it was much less demanding than the Muslims' fast at Ramadan. She said it was only for adults, and most fasted only irregularly. Um Abdalla was exempt from fasting this time because she was pregnant, and Um George managed only about one day out of two.

For a long time, Um Abdalla and Um George had been talking about taking me to see a shrine some distance from the edge of the village, so one day when my husband was visiting with our car, it seemed like a perfect opportunity. Um George, Um Abdalla, and the older Lisa put on their best clothes and bundled the littler children into warm jackets, and soon all of them, including the older boys, were piled into the car. We stopped first at the convent where the nuns kept the keys for the shrine. With the keys in hand, we took the rutted road out to its conclusion, holding our breaths each time the loaded car scraped the road.

The shrine stood alone at the edge of a magnificent precipice, far away from any human habitation. From its terrace, we looked out over the valley as if from the window of an airplane. Um Abdalla pointed out the villages by name, this one Muslim and that one Christian. Even though in distance they were not much farther than Wusta from this site, it would have required a long drive to circumvent the steep cliffs that separated them from the shrine. Um George explained that the shrine had been built on the spot where a saint had escaped his persecutors by hiding in a cave. They were amazed that an educated person like myself, a presumed Christian, didn't know the exact reference in the Bible. The shrine was built within and around the historic cave where the saint took refuge and which most of the time was not used except on the saint's feast day and other special occasions such as baptisms. Other times, families might go to make a request of the saint—to grant a cure, to start a pregnancy, to protect a child, or to give thanks for a request already granted.

The spot and the cave were naturally beautiful in themselves, but when the biblical imagery was added, it was easy to see why the villagers considered it a sacred place. Everywhere, bits of cloth and balls of human hair were stuffed into holes in the rocks or on the altar to connect their owners in a concrete and lasting way to the supernatural powers that resided there.

As they entered, Um George and Um Abdalla and the older children traced crosses on themselves with holy oil from the altar to transfer the blessings of the site. Um George dipped her finger in the oil and anointed the smaller children as they dashed by to explore the cave. We wandered around looking at the saints' pictures and the altar and visitors' offerings, and then Lisa and Um Abdalla and Um George crossed themselves again and genuflected, and we all walked quietly outside again, except, of course, the smaller children who ran circles around us. In a sunny spot in front of the shrine, we took pictures of everyone, in groups and singly, before the precipice and against the face of the cave. Then we climbed back into the car and renavigated the precarious road back to Wusta, first to the nuns and finally home. The women put away their good dresses and put back on their normal house gear. We all referred to the trip later as the "day we went to the shrine."

Several times villagers remarked: "We have a better standard of living in the countryside than do the people in towns with their crowded apartments and more expensive foods, and that's why our children want to stay here and bring up *their* children in the village." It was the first time in the Middle East that I heard rural people claiming a village was a better place to live than a city. Was it because they were Christians and felt safer in an enclave with their own kind away from other, possibly hostile, groups? Or was it a simple declaration of fact—that life was indeed better in the village? Looking around me, I could see they lacked few of the modern conveniences that rural people covet—washing machines, blenders, televisions, irons, gas burners, gas water heaters, motorbikes, and tractors—and their homes were spacious, with indoor plumbing, schools nearby, and every kind of good and service they could possibly want only an hour away in Damascus. More important, an abundance of food was at their fingertips. Indeed, life could objectively be said to be at least as good, if not better, in the country-side.

At Um George's, she and Abu Adil began building on the extra room again in late fall. Most of it was finished by Abu Adil in the short periods he was home. The progress depended on how much time he had available and when there was some extra money. Even when the rooms were virtually complete in the middle of winter, Um George did not use them in order to save on heating fuel, but as soon as the weather turned warmer, she moved a large bed into one room and began putting the children to sleep there away from the confusion of the family sitting room.

Over morning coffee, we were talking again about the baby. Um Abdalla had finally told the other children that she was pregnant, and according to her, they were not happy at all. The day before she had gone into Damascus to buy some basic baby clothing, which came to about S£200. "Why don't you make the things yourself?" asked the thrifty Um George. "I don't have the time, nor are the things as good when they're made at home," answered Um Abdalla. She explained to me, "We always passed the clothes along from child to child, but the clothes Boulos wore are long gone, and Um George's children need all she has." I felt that Um Abdalla enjoyed her excursions to the city to buy clothes and seized on this practical reason for why she now had to go more often. It surprised me to see her preparing in advance for the baby, remembering how strongly Egyptians felt about waiting until the baby came before buying necessities. They believed that harm would come to the baby if preparations were made in advance.

We were sitting watching the last of the homework exercises, and Abu Abdalla was telling me more about his work. This was a subject of most compelling interest to him once he got started, but he always began hesitantly, conditioned as he was to think women were not interested in such matters. He was not used to sharing this information in detail with anyone, including Um Abdalla, his brother, or the boys. To Um Abdalla, he would offer a laconic "Well, the tractor is broken today, and I have to get someone to look at it," not saying how it broke or how seriously or whether it was reparable or any of the details that seemed important, considering the essential nature of the machine.

This time he wanted to continue his explanation of the egg-laying business. Layers, he noted, produce eggs for a year and a half to two years before they are sold for meat. "Generally speaking, the climate here is good for raising chickens. In other countries, they illuminate chicken houses 24 hours a day to make them produce faster, but here in Syria we prefer a longer production because chickens that produce faster need more feed."

Abu Abdalla had brought feed the previous day from Damascus using a cousin's truck, waiting to get it when the cousin wasn't using the truck. For services of this kind, he either could pay his cousin a lower rate and do some service for him or could pay him the full amount outright and keep the arrangement formal. He preferred the first option, which saved him money and helped develop a friendly relation that might have other advantages. This arrangement, however, became frustrating when he suddenly found a supply of feed but had to wait to haul it until the truck was available.

Abu Abdalla was proud of the special grinder he had recently installed for preparing the feed. The various grains were poured in the proper proportions into this grinder, and the milled feed came out on a mechanized track that carried it around the huge poultry house. One time he demonstrated the operation to me with a twinkle in his eye. "Um Dawud, stand right there and listen carefully while I turn it on." I did as I was told, and the moment the motor came on, a long sigh rose up from the six thousand chickens catching their collective breaths in anticipation of the food coming down the track. It was indeed impressive!

Abu Abdalla continued his explanation. The chickens needed a tanker of water each day, but the boys kept the reservoir full in case the town water was insufficient or the tractor broke down. Abu Abdalla installed heaters in the chicken houses for when it became cold in winter, but usually the heat generated by so many chickens in a restricted space was enough to warm them. The bedouin caretaker, Abu Muhammad, was supposed to make sure the window openings along the sides of the houses were closed when the temperature fell, but Abu Abdalla didn't trust him to remember and usually went himself to make sure it was done properly.

Abu Abdalla said he produced 5,400 eggs a day from the 6,000 or so chickens. One afternoon up at the chicken house, I counted a day's production as six stacks of seventeen boxes each, with thirty eggs to a box, or 3,060 eggs in all, fewer than he claimed but perhaps the full production had not been collected that day. "The producers around here sell their eggs to agents in Damascus, sending them down every four or so days, depending on how many there are."

Abu Abdalla routinely examined the chickens to find any that might be sick. "You can tell by whether their combs are red or not—if they are red, they are well." The worry was that an illness might wipe out his total investment in one round of chickens. About ten chickens a week produced enormous eggs, and in the process of laying them, at least one died. He was careful about seeing that the chickens were given immunizations and regular dosages of vitamins. Listening to Abu Abdalla, I was impressed by the extent of the knowledge he had acquired.

Um Abdalla interrupted to tell me that she always took some chickens from each batch to keep in the backyard so that there were fresh eggs and, every now and then, fresh meat for the family. Chicken, more than other meats, was considered a delicacy, and the taste of her free-ranging chickens was better than that of the chickens growing up in the restricted area of the shed. Along with the chickens, she kept a goat that was continually bothering the little children. She would threaten, "I've got to kill the goat this week—he's always after Adil and little Ilyas, trying to knock them over. The rooster is the same; I try to keep him locked up, but he's always getting out." Then she added, in one of the few implied criticisms of Um George she made in front of me, "I can't be watching Um George's children all the time to be sure they don't get hurt." I, too, found myself rescuing them once or twice from the rooster and the goat.

Abu Abdalla came late from the chickens, covered with dust from grinding the latest batch of feed he had been able to find in Damascus. Recently, none of the chicken farmers could find feed, and many were cutting back their flocks. He looked tired and worried, and when I expressed sympathy, he replied that he was worried about the prospects for chicken farming. The girls quickly jumped up from their studies to bring him a cup of tea, but the dust caught in his throat, and he sputtered and coughed until it cleared. He looked forlorn slumped in the corner of the room, wrapped in his discouraging thoughts.

To follow up on our discussion of chickens, Abu Abdalla brought me some brochures from the experimental farm down the road. He explained that he followed the feeding schedule for chickens recommended by a Dutch consultant who had helped set up the farm in 1972. His problem was that he could no longer find the variety of grains he recommended. His solution was to balance the ingredients overall—one time corn, another time barley, and so forth, and so far he didn't see that it had had an adverse effect on the chickens.

A little later, a man in a small Suzuki truck hailed us while we were sun ning ourselves on the back porch. Um Abdalla greeted him and shouted out that Abu Abdalla was down at the office. He went off in that direction and soon drove by again with Abu Abdalla in the direction of the chicken houses to collect the boxes of eggs.

Um George and Um Abdalla were in my room having coffee. It was bitterly cold, and the snow was heaped in drifts around the walls of the house. As usual my "misplaced" stove was not doing its job, causing us to huddle as close to it as possible. Already that morning I had burned a large scorch mark on my shawl trying to get close to the little warmth it provided. It was a kindness of the women to accept my inferior hospitality when they could be better warmed and have better tea next door. Abu Adil had been gone for ten days on another trip to Saudi Arabia. He still needed to make up for the problems with his truck that, in the end, had kept him home a month and a half. One problem was that his was a refrigerated truck and so there wasn't such a premium on his work in the winter. Regular trucks competed for the same business, and his installment payments were higher.

Um George sighed, "If only we had the money to open the store now." Then fantasizing, she went on, "The first thing we would do is buy a small truck to haul things from Damascus because of course, we wouldn't be able to bring enough by bus to stock a store. Abu Adil would get a driver for the big truck and stay home. Trucking keeps him away too much and leaves me here with something always going wrong."

I started thinking how useful a small truck would be for both brothers. Abu Abdalla could use it for hauling his feed from Damascus or bringing pro visions for the family or as backup for the ailing tractor. Abu Adil could bring construction materials for the new rooms. And certainly both could earn money or credit in exchanges with other villagers. Because it would relieve Abu Abdalla from asking others for favors, perhaps he might share the costs with his brother.

I kept these thoughts to myself, aware now as I had not been before, that the women didn't like to talk in detail about monetary arrangements that might commit themselves or their husbands in the future. The subject of sharing a truck was delicate and not easily spoken of in advance of the fact. Besides, they preferred spontaneous to fixed arrangements. Each new spontaneous arrangement generated a warmth that reinforced their relationships better than did any fixed arrangement. If Abu Adil offered the use of the truck to Abu Abdalla, he would never know for sure what kind of favor he might collect in return and therein lay the interest. My American desire to make "fair arrangements" found these ambiguous arrangements unsettling. I would feel uneasy about whether the lender felt fairly compensated. On their side, they felt uncomfortable with fixed arrangements, which took away from the very "stuff" of relationships, the concrete reminders that they existed.

SEVEN

The Outer Circle

The more closely the members of a family are attached to one another, the more often do they tend to cut themselves off from others, and the more difficult it is for them to enter into the wider circle of life.

—Sigmund Freud, *Civilization and Its Discontents*

One blustery day, Um Abdalla decided that it was time to introduce me to a favorite neighbor living not far away. The neighbor had heard about me and had sent word through her daughter, who was a classmate of Lisa's, to say we had delayed too long in making an introductory visit. After the noonday dishes were cleaned up and we had changed into our visiting clothes, we set out on the short walk to her house. Since it was my first visit to them, no amount of urging could keep us out of the formal parlor. The parlor was about the same temperature as the weather outside, and we shivered when our legs came in contact with the plastic covers of the plush chairs our hostess pushed forward for us. She lit the stove and left the room to put on "nicer" clothes.

We had ample opportunity, while we waited for her, to survey our surroundings. The centerpiece of the furnishings was a red velvet love seat with flowers cut into the wood of the curved back and legs. Little gilt tables with imitation marble tops were arranged where guests could reach them easily. They already held the china dishes that the hostess would fill with nuts after an appropriate time had passed. A coffee table in front of the love seat held a tissue box with matching red plush holder and next to it, somewhat incongruously, a statue of a flamenco dancer twirling her red skirts provocatively. All the surfaces were red velvet, "marble," gilt, or carved wood rosettes. Doilies graced the furniture, and unmindful of the cold, a bouquet of plastic flowers stuck stiffly out of a Japanese vase on a corner table.

I shivered uncontrollably in my coat and wrapped my scarf tightly around my neck. Our snatches of conversation echoed against the hard surfaces of the tile floors as gusts of cold air from under the poorly fitting door penetrated the folds of our clothes. The rest of the family wisely remained on their rugs and cushions in a warmer part of the house. A formal parlor seemed thoroughly out of place in a village where muddy roads and hardy occupations demanded more functional interiors. Judging from the older houses, it was a recent fashion.

Fortunately, for the comfort of our toes, we had left our shoes on at the insistence of our hostess instead of taking them off at the door as was normal in rooms with large rugs on the floor, but in doing so we left a line of muddy tracks across the expanse of spotlessly clean tiles. I lapsed into resentful silence at being made to suffer for someone's sense of propriety. Surely, as a guest, I should have some say in arrangements that affected my comfort. But I was still learning the etiquette of visiting and not yet sure of what I might be permitted to object to. By the time our hostess returned in her better dress, the stove had began to do its work and the cold was mitigating. We got on with the business of consuming juice, tea, nuts, sweets, and coffee and exchanging both families' news.

The next time we visited this household, remembering the previous visit, we begged our hostess to think of me as one of the family. Apparently she decided she had satisfied the niceties on the first visit and, with relief on her face, led us into the warm and inviting family room where the *soba* stove sizzled in peaceful competition with the cheerful conversations already under way. This time we left our shoes at the edge of the carpet and stood waiting for the hostess to seat us on the cushions around the wall. By established custom, one place was usually taken by the patriarch of the house, and we didn't want to usurp his proprietorial rights. Although he might offer this seat to a male visitor, it was unlikely he would yield it to a woman. Women were more flexible and usually moved quickly from a customary place to offer it to a guest, even including a female guest.

The happy advantage of being allowed into the everyday sitting room was that we sat together with the rest of the family. Everyone lounged comfortably on the floor in work clothes, the men wearing their at-home pajamas and the women in house dresses. Unlike Egyptians, who felt compelled to stand and shake hands with guests entering a room, the Wusta villagers greeted people with a "marhaba" (hello) from the floor. Only the host or hostess stood up to find places for the guests near the stove, to plump pillows for their backs, and, in the case of women, to bring large scarves to cover their legs modestly.

Despite the informal atmosphere, we were still obliged to sit carefully with our feet tucked under us. For most Syrians, this foot etiquette was all-important. As long as men were present, we women would sit uncomfortably with our legs under us until, if we were lucky, the men left the room. Then we were released in a number of ways: from the formal foot etiquette, from the male-focused and -directed conversations, and from the stiff formality the women usually maintained with men. Our hostess would say, "Why don't you stretch out your legs and make yourself comfortable," and we would feel immense relief as blood flowed freely again through our limbs.

If a man returned, we all would tuck our legs back under us unless the hostess had given us blankets or other coverings to hide our legs and feet. Both respect and modesty were involved in covering the legs, for even those who wore pants were given a blanket to ensure that the soles of their feet were not impolitely facing anyone. When sitting in chairs, we were expected to follow similar rules. We should not cross our legs at the knee, as that would indicate an overly casual informality, but we could cross them demurely at the ankle or keep our feet planted on the ground. In the beginning, because I was not sure of all the gradations of respect, I kept both feet planted on the floor to avoid mistakes.

I was acutely aware of how easy it was to blunder in these matters, from an embarrassing moment in Egypt when I was attending a church service and a total stranger leaned over to tell me angrily that I should not cross my legs in church. Without knowing it, I had been showing disrespect for the sanctity of the church. After that, I watched carefully for the subtleties of "foot etiquette" in the Arab world.

In social gatherings, the Wusta women were less concerned with the distinctions of age, class, and social status that guided men's relations. Distinctions had to be far more pronounced for women to acknowledge them. True, young girls deferred politely to older women, but there was more informality in that deference than there would have been between younger and older men. Depending on the kind of person she was, an older woman might even serve a younger woman of the household in a sympathetic, nurturing way rather than insist on being served herself. Such an act was recognized as kindness rather than a breach of the rule that younger women should serve older women. But in men, such behavior would be seen in most cases as a humbling of the older man if the younger one was not a guest. Guests were an exception to the general respect rules governing gender, age, and class.

Within the family, women always showed deference to men even when the men were approximately the same age or younger. In regard to food, women always served men regardless of their relative ages, the exception being that men might be asked to perform these tasks when no women were present. Boys were expected to show respect to their mothers but were given more latitude than girls in the way that they expressed their respect. The aggressiveness prized in Syrian men gave the boys in some households the freedom to abuse, verbally and even physically, female relatives, though not in those families who considered manners important. In Um Abdalla's and Um George's families, this would not have been considered acceptable.

One afternoon, we decided to visit Um Samir, the maternal aunt of Um Abdalla and Um George. When we knocked on the heavy door, one of her sons appeared. "She's not home?" confirmed Um Abdalla, "Then she must be sitting with Um Munir." "Yes, Auntie, she is over at her house," he answered politely, all the while staring at me. We went next door and, as predicted, found her with her friend Um Munir, the wife of our constant visitor, Abu Munir. After we had exchanged greetings and were settled in Um Munir's sitting room, I remarked on the name Abdalla, meaning "slave of Allah," which I had thought to be a Muslim name, based on those people with the same name I had known in Egypt. "No," they said quickly, "it can be either Muslim or Christian, but if you take the name Abid alone, without the Alla, it always is Muslim." And they proceeded to list all the names they could think of that were either Christian or Muslim.

Our conversation moved to the religious groups in the community and the differences among them. The village was primarily Catholic, but there were also some Greek Orthodox, and after I pressed them a while, they talked about the family of Muslims. "Whom do they marry?" I asked. "Oh, from someplace outside the village." I learned from other sources that indeed the younger generation of Muslims had married outside the village and that many had already left the area for good. They noted, with an expression of disapproval at the audacity of the action, that the Muslim family had told the government they were fifteen families rather than fifteen individuals in order to meet the minimum requirement for the government to subsidize a mosque in the village. The women thought the mosque a waste of money, since "it was never used." But it certainly appeared to be used when my husband and I looked in the window one day and saw some books piled on a shelf and a broom resting next to a recently swept-up pile of dust. Since men were more likely than women to go to Muslim religious services, there could not have been many people from a fifteen-member extended family attending the mosque.

The discussion was becoming perfunctory—the topic did not interest my companions very much, and I was reluctant to be regarded as an apologist for the small group of Muslims in the community. At that moment, Um George came to join us, giving everyone a convenient excuse to change the subject. She had finished cleaning up after the midday meal and had left the children with her husband, who was on a longer stay at home.

Um Samir started telling me about her seven girls and three boys. She explained where each was living and whether they were studying or married. Three of the girls were married, and one was engaged. Um Munir then related the details of her seven boys. As she was talking, a young woman, Um Amir, one of Um Samir's daughters, joined us with her infant son, and not long after, her husband—the young man who had answered the door at Um Samir's—also joined us. They were dressed in their best, she in a nylon dress, stockings, and heels and he in neatly ironed slacks, shirt, and jacket. It appeared that they took this to be a special visit. The young man was Um Amir's cousin (her father's brother's son), the son of Abu and Um Munir. Their marriage had cemented a number of relationships, including the friendship between the neighbors, Um Samir and Um Munir.

After a while, I asked Um Samir what her husband did. "What else? Everyone here in the village is a trucker because of the money," she replied. Abu Samir started trucking thirty-five years ago, according to her account, but if she were correct, it would have made him the first trucker in the village, contradicting other stories that placed trucking as having a more recent origin.

The young Um Amir took out a cigarette and began smoking. The easygoing conversation changed, and the older women looked displeased. Um Samir said to us, as if in apology for her daughter's behavior, that in the old days it was improper for women to smoke but that nowadays young women didn't seem to care. The older women were uneasy that we might interpret her smoking as a disrespect to us. If she had smoked when older men were around, it would have been more serious, but women were expected to be more accommodating. Smoking in front of Um Samir and Um Munir was one thing, however, and smoking in front of guests was another, verging on rudeness. Um Abdalla reassured them that we didn't take offense, but I, unable to keep quiet, remarked that smoking might be damaging her health, a thought that had not crossed their minds. They smiled politely but didn't take my comment seriously, since as far as they were concerned, such matters were in the hands of God and were better not even mentioned.

Baby Amir started crying, and his mother tried to stop him, but nothing she did had any effect: she tried to feed him, she walked around with him, and she bounced him violently up and down. The women offered suggestions, and Um Samir took him and crooned some verses to him, but still he cried. Finally, in exasperation, Um Amir handed him to his father, "Here, he listens only to you." Abu Amir, so young himself that he seemed no more than a boy, took his son in his arms and left the house. We could see them walking up and down outside the house. In an effort to explain why she had turned the baby over to his father, Um Amir remarked that he had to wait anyway for the bus to Damascus, since he was the driver for the next shift. When the bus finally came, he handed the sleeping baby to Um Amir and climbed into the driver's seat.

The conversation shifted from one topic to another, first prices and then their irritation with a neighbor who threw garbage in a vacant lot where it blew around the area. Um Samir and Um Munir complained that they were continually picking papers and plastic out of their front yards. I listened with interest to this conversation because I had been unsure what to do with my own trash. Up until then what didn't go to the chickens and goats, I had been carrying back to Damascus. I asked what the neighbor should have done with her trash, and they answered that the food scraps went to the animals and the rest should have been burned. All that should be left were cans, which eventually rusted and decomposed on the heap of ashes. Every home had its corner for burning rubbish. The next day I went with Um Abdalla to look at ours and thereafter burned my garbage there.

The women wanted to know why I didn't eat more of the food they were offering. Didn't I like their food? Um Abdalla, now used to my ways, answered for me, "Americans are afraid of getting fat, because their men don't like fat women." They all laughed and decided that with their plump figures they wouldn't get far in America. Next they wanted to know whether boys and girls in America were allowed to marry whomever they pleased. When I answered yes, they all agreed that this was no way to form a marriage, stressing how disrupting to family life it would be if children married anyone they pleased. They said it might be acceptable if a boy saw a girl he liked from a distance and asked his parents if they approved of his marrying her. Then if the girl was acceptable, the parents could make the arrangements in the proper way so it would look as though they had selected her themselves. At least in this way, both sets of parents would have a chance to see whether the two were a suitable match. They definitely opposed free choice and were confident that theirs was the only way to produce happy marriages.

The women explained that young people who fell in love weren't in a position to make rational decisions. They were not capable of looking at all the factors that needed to be considered. Only parents knew what was good for children, and since theirs was a selfless interest, the children were best served by accepting their choices. "No wonder you have such sexual laxity in your country and so much divorce. With all those 'love marriages,' what would you expect?" I was glad they didn't know the full extent of Americans' "sexual laxity," such as unmarried couples living together and no one paying much attention. It was impossible to explain the practice to them in a way that did not look outrageous.

"What characteristics do you consider when you select someone to marry your child?" I asked, in order to change the subject slightly.

> Well, they differ for males and females, but basically they are that the two should come from similar backgrounds—one not much richer or more powerful or of higher status than the other, or the higher person will assume "airs" with the other. If there has to be a difference in their backgrounds, then it is not considered as bad if the woman marries "up." But if a man marries up, he will always be at the mercy of his more powerful wife. Also, the family should have a good reputation—no scandals—and get along—you don't want any bad blood appearing in the children or any relatives that might embarrass you and make it difficult for your children's children to marry. You want to feel proud that you are connected to the family of your child's spouse. Of course, you want to know also that the spouse has manners and a good personality so the two will be compatible.
>
> We like to see our children marrying close relatives for all these reasons: they are like us, they have the same interests as we do, we accept the fact that

they are well brought up, and we know our children will be secure with them. When they are relatives, we sometimes are willing to accept things we might not accept in others. Another advantage of marriage to a relative is that if misunderstandings arise between the spouses, the families can quietly get together and resolve them in a way that won't happen if the children marry outside the family. Relative marriage is especially good for girls, since they can always go for help to their parents-in-law, who are also their relatives. We like these marriages because it is our experience that children who marry relatives are more likely to stay in the village and build homes and rear their children among friends and relatives. They are always happier when they live close to home.

"What would be the differences in the kinds of spouses you would choose for your sons or daughters?" I asked.

For the boys, we would want quiet, respectful girls with sweet personalities who dress well and who are willing to work hard around the house. Our sons, of course, also want them to be beautiful. Beautiful means that they have fair complexions, thick hair, and that they be neither too thin nor too fat. Education now is also important because a mother who can't help her children with homework handicaps them. But generally speaking, a girl should not be better educated than her husband, or she might hold that over him. This is becoming a problem for some families, since the boys leave school at the end of the secondary level to go into the army and begin trucking. They usually can't marry until their late twenties when they have saved enough money to support a family. Unless they marry someone much younger than themselves—which, by the way, used to be considered the best type of marriage in our generation but is considered less so today—then they marry girls who are also older than what used to be considered good. While the girls wait for the boys to make enough money, they sometimes continue on to university, which creates another kind of problem. The longer they go to school, the less likely it is that they will marry—they have to consider that fact. How can a man with a secondary school degree marry a woman with a university degree? He would always feel inferior.

At the same time, some girls now say they want to work, and although we mothers mostly accept the idea that this is a fact of modern life, many of the men don't yet agree. In good families, where money is not a problem, it would only be respectable for girls to work if they took professional jobs. People believe, however, that extended education is good in general because even if they don't work, it teaches girls to be more rational and less emotional. Because of this, people accept the idea that educated girls will move freely in society without automatically assuming they are immoral.

"How about the girls, how would you choose their husbands?"

In the first place, we don't choose husbands for them, but if you mean how would we decide which of those asking for her hand we would give our agreement to, then I can tell you. In a girl's case, we want her to go to a secure and kindly environment. Secure means where she is taken care of financially, and kindly means where neither her husband nor her husband's family treat her badly either physically or verbally. We want him to treat her with respect and show good manners, and we watch him carefully when he comes to call to see how he behaves. You can usually look at the family someone comes from and know how the children will turn out. We have a proverb about that: "Turn the pot upside down, and the daughter becomes the mother." Although this applies to daughters, it's also true for sons.

"What about his appearance?"

That's not so important with boys. If they show initiative in earning money and if their families are respectable, they can be dark skinned or even ugly. Of course, it makes it nicer if he's handsome.

We discussed these topics until they exhausted their fund of information and examples. The topic captured their attention. They probably never had occasion to talk about these details in such a conscious way, because everyone intuitively knew the characteristics of a good spouse and looked for them when deciding who would make a suitable match. It took time and many clarifications from each of them before I was able to come up with the preceding version. They assumed that everyone knew as much about the subject as they did.

All the while I was straining to hear their answers, as the roar of trucks circling the house on the main road of the village threatened to drown out critical parts of the conversation. As was customary in the afternoon in Wusta, the young men were out practicing driving in their detached cabs. Um Munir's old stone house, already in a state of serious deterioration, shook with the vibrations. The window glass behind me was broken, and the wind whistled down my neck, but since I was sitting in the place of honor on Um Munir's best couch, I couldn't move to a more comfortable spot without offending her sense of hospitality. I leaned forward to warm my hands over the electric heater. "Are you all right?" Um Munir asked anxiously. Out of concern, she pulled the curtain over the broken pane, but that only made the room darker and more gloomy. I said I was fine and hoped that an involuntary shiver would not make an obvious liar of me.

Having forgotten her duties as a hostess while we discussed these interesting topics, Um Munir suddenly remembered and jumped up to bring more food—nuts, coffee, raw apple slices, and, finally, cookies. Feeling remorse about the cold, she began to complain about her husband's love of *araq* and told stories about how he threw things around the house when he became angry. The broken window was a result of one of these outbursts.

We stayed for the customary two hours. Um Munir said how pleased she was that we had come to see her, even though she had not been the original object of our visit. On our way out, Um Samir reminded us that we had not yet visited her in her home, and therefore we still owed her a visit. She waved from the door but remained behind to talk over the visit with her friend.

On our way home, I grew anxious about the children who had been left so long with their father. Would he have watched them carefully to prevent them from falling against the hot stove or fed them when they were hungry? But my companions chattered on cheerfully about the visit, hurrying less out of anxiety for the children than out of realization that we had been away for some time. As we turned a corner, a cold wind sweeping unimpeded from across the valley caught at our clothes with a force that penetrated to our bones, and I felt grateful for the long skirt whipping around my ankles. Um Abdalla, leaning into the wind, looked blue from the cold, with her short skirt and bare legs. Fashion seemed incongruous here, where in all other respects, people tended toward an almost boring practicality.

When we arrived home, the children, none the worse for wear, were scrambling over their cheerful father who, though glad to see the women, had survived the afternoon without any ill effects.

The following week, we were able to honor our promise to visit Um Samir. Her house, one of the largest and most substantial of the newer houses belonging to villagers, still had the debris of construction surrounding it. I remembered that Um Samir had said her husband had been one of the first men involved in trucking in the village, and indeed, the house was convincing evidence of the prosperity that trucking could bring. Um Samir was distantly related to Um Abdalla, and a girlhood friendship had made their relationship closer. In addition, one of Um Samir's daughters was a classmate of Lisa's. Most of the family was there, Um and Abu Samir, the four unmarried daughters, and two of their sons. The oldest son was "away," which I took to mean was off on a trip, as was so often the case with truckers, but unbeknownst to me, I had stumbled on a sensitive subject. We managed to talk our way into the family room where the males of the household also were congregated. In this family, the females outshone and outtalked the males. The older girls stood out as particularly sociable and attractive.

We spent the first hour of the visit listening to the plans of one of the daughters, who was engaged. Indeed, the original purpose of our visit the week before had been to see her trousseau and other items she was gathering for the wedding. Although she was only high school age, she had stopped attending school when she became engaged several months before and now spent all her time preparing for the marriage. Already it seemed a long time since she had become engaged, and it would be even longer before she would marry. It had been her husband-to-be's decision that she should stay home from school, probably to prevent any meetings with other men that might jeopardize their relationship or her reputation now that they were committed to each other.

Before the couple could marry, the husband-to-be had to earn enough money to build a house and provide the bride's dress, her jewelry, and the house furnishings. During their engagement, she told me, laughing, they would hardly see each other, since custom required that he bring her expensive gifts each time he visited, and each expensive gift only further delayed the time when they could marry. Her family—aunts, uncles, grandparents, and so on—also would contribute clothes and jewelry, and these were what she was eager to show us. The whole family was totally immersed in deciding what clothes she should have and how they should be fashioned and decorated.

A few days after this visit, Um Abdalla and I were summoned to Um George's to help entertain a guest. This time the guest was the daughter of Um Samir, Um Amir, whom we had seen so recently with her baby at Um Munir's. Both Um Amir's and Um George's husbands were away at that moment, and since we had just seen Um Amir a few days before, during our visit at Um Munir's, Um George must have said something like "Um Amir, we haven't seen you in a long while, why don't you come see us soon?" to which Um Amir probably answered, "Well, my husband will be away next

week, and so I will be free. Will you be home then?" and Um George would
certainly have agreed enthusiastically to the visit. The fact that they had seen
each other recently and exchanged all their current news did not prevent
another visit soon after the first. What was more important was that Um
George have a chance to provide hospitality to Um Amir in her own home.

Um Amir was trying to establish herself as a married woman who went
visiting and made her own independent relationships in the village. She
explained to us that in the short period she had been married, she had been
fully occupied with her obligations. At first, her time was spent learning
how to cope with all the household chores and how to be a good wife to her
husband. Um George and Um Abdalla clucked sympathetically, for they
knew that during the first year of marriage, a bride is supposed to be fully
engrossed in caring for her husband. This period became something of a
weaning period for a young woman as she became part of her husband's family and learned to live away from her own family. Um Amir was fortunate in
this respect because her mother lived next door and was best friends with
her mother-in-law. Under these conditions, it would be difficult for her to
stay away too long from her mother. Within the first year of their marriage,
as was ideal, Um Amir found that she was pregnant, and when the new baby
arrived, motherhood took up the better part of the second year of their marriage. All of this explanation was to let Um Abdalla and Um George know
why she had not called on them sooner.

Um Abdalla and Um George had given gifts, made visits, and attended the
festivities of Um Amir's marriage and the birth of her child, out of indebt-
edness to the couple's parents and not because they had a special relationship
with Um Amir, who was considerably younger than they were. Now it was
time for Um Amir to establish her own social relationships with people like
Um Abdalla and Um George, who were predisposed to neighborly relations
because of their connections to her family. Before she was married, it would
have been inappropriate for Um Amir to go visiting independently or even
for her to accompany her mother more than occasionally on visits to friends,
for the same reasons that Lisa did not go with us, for fear that people might
say the family was advertising their daughter for marriage. Now on two
counts, as wife and mother, custom allowed—demanded, in fact—that Um
Amir establish a social identity of her own, for herself and for the future
opportunities her connections would provide for her child.

Um Amir was explaining that her husband was usually away during this
time in the afternoon on the late shift driving the bus. Before this job, Abu

Amir used to work in the local *ballot* (tile) factory. The women talked about some problems Um Amir was having with her teeth and how she had gone several times to her cousin, the son of her mother's brother, who was a dentist in Damascus. They all complained about the difficulty of going all the way to Damascus for medical and dental care. Um Amir said her cousin would have liked to open a clinic in Wusta but was afraid there wouldn't be enough business to justify opening an office there.

They turned to a discussion of Amir's birth. They obviously had not seen one another for a long time before we met at Um Munir's, and I could see they were enjoying having a "good talk" unconstrained by the presence of the older women. I asked where the women from the village had their babies, and they replied that they usually went to hospitals in Damascus, but a few still had them at home. Um Abdalla said she had had her first two children at home but after that had gone to the hospital, "because it was too difficult having a baby with the other children around." There was also a woman doctor in the neighboring town who could come in an emergency.

Next they talked about the new priest, who had only recently returned to the village from many years away. Since he had left as a very young man, he was returning almost as a stranger. They were very much impressed by his learning and degrees, although they could not recall what kind of degrees he had received. They also had heard that he had spent some time abroad with some sort of international work. The gulf in education and experience that separated him from most others in the village and the fact that he had lived longer away from the village than in it did not detract from his standing as "a person who came from the village." The women were very proud of the fact that a son of the village could have such illustrious credentials.

The following evening, the deaf Um Yusef came on another of her periodic visits to Um George's. I was beginning to discover all the interconnections between the people I was seeing. Um Yusef had heard that we had been to visit her son's house a few days before and wanted news of what was going on there. Suddenly I put the pieces together: the missing son at Um Samir's and Um Yusef's argument with her son, Yusef or Abu Samir, about something that affected her grandson Samir. I had everything but the final piece of information, the subject of their quarrel. Um Abdalla, at all times unwilling to gossip about people, had been reticent about telling this story.

Although Um Yusef had difficulty understanding us, we could listen while she told us stories. This time for my benefit, and forgetting that she had already told me several of these details already, she told me triumphantly that she was seventy-nine years old, as if it were a great accomplishment to have lived so long. She was married at fourteen and had had sixteen children all together, of whom nine were still alive: five girls and four boys. One of these sons was Abu Samir. She then began talking about the problem that no one had wanted to mention. Samir had pleaded for a long time with his father to let him leave high school and begin trucking, but even though his father was a trucker himself, he had been adamant that his son finish secondary school. But Samir was impatient to earn money and felt that more schooling was only wasting his time when he was so sure that he wanted to go into trucking. When his father would not relent, Samir simply left school and went to live with his grandmother, Um Yusef, in the house she had shared with her husband before he died. Um Yusef, who had been living with Abu Samir's family much of the time, was banned from their home for defending the boy. Now she missed the contact with her other grandchildren and wanted to hear how they were. In sign language, we replied that they all were well. "Did they say anything about Samir?" she asked. We said no, and she sadly shrugged her shoulders.

Um George interrupted at this point to say, "Parents tell their children not to go into trucking because the work is too hard and too dangerous. The money is what attracts young men, so you can understand why they want to do it. We expect them to take initiative in earning money, and if they do, they have little choice but to go into trucking. There is no easy alternative."

One beautiful afternoon with a hint of spring in the air, we decided to visit Um Muhammad, the wife of the bedouin caretaker of Abu Abdalla's chickens. The air still had a touch of crispness, but the sun warmed our backs, and the earth by the side of the road was bursting with new growth. Um Muhammad lived about a mile up the road, and the three of us—Um Abdalla, Um George, and I—trekked up the hill to the chicken houses. Even though they were on their feet all day, Um Abdalla and Um George quickly tired when faced with even a short walk and soon complained that they should have waited to ride on the tractor. They felt none of the compensation I felt in the healthiness of walking or the pleasure of seeing such a beautiful landscape. They were willing to take this long walk only to get out of their homes for a while and to show me something new. Um Abdalla had told me she liked to visit Um Muhammad from time to time, but from the way

she complained about the walk, I was sure she must normally come by tractor if at all.

"She's a good woman with a difficult life," Um Abdalla said sympathetically
of Um Muhammad, and she brought along gifts of tea and sugar for her. In a
hospitably bedouin way, Abu and Um Muhammad greeted us heartily. Um
Muhammad rushed to set the kettle on the stove, and before long we each had
a strong sugary cup of tea in front of us. Their house was modest, consisting
of one room furnished with thin mats on the floor, a wooden cupboard for
their few belongings, and the stove. A goat skin filled with ghee hung from a
hook on the wall. Abu Abdalla had furnished the room for them, in addition
to giving them a salary of S£1,500 ($375) per month, a sum he considered
exorbitant. They also could eat broken eggs and a defective chicken now and
then, and so, as Abu Abdalla put it, "They live practically free."

Abu Muhammad was a slender toothless man with adequate manners,
though not the aristocratic graces of nobler lineages of bedouin I had met in
Saudi Arabia. Accepting a job as a manual laborer already signified that he
was not from the discriminating tribes who looked on manual labor as
demeaning. Apparently, chicken farming had become one of the common
ways for people of Abu Muhammad's semisettled tribe to supplement their
livelihood of sheepherding. Through their networks, Abu Abdalla was always
able to replace his caretakers when they decided they had had enough of
chicken farming. Abu Muhammad talked to us for a few minutes and then,
because we all were women whom his wife could entertain without him, left
to help Hanna, who had come with the water tanker.

Um Muhammad shouted to her daughter, Laila, and son, Muhammad, to
spread the greasy quilts lying around the room in a more orderly way so that
we could sit on them. The children were already moving quickly to pick articles off the floor and make a place for us. They automatically knew what was
required when a guest arrived, but her shouts emphasized the urgency of
giving us an especially hospitable welcome. Um Muhammad's attention
focused on me even when she was talking to Um Abdalla and Um George,
and she chortled gleefully every now and then as if pleased with this delightful apparition that had appeared on her doorstep. I was just as interested in
her, for she was quite unlike the other women of the village. She wore a
strange but practical collection of clothes—a number of skirts topped by a
light ankle-length cotton one in a subdued calico print, a khaki waist-length
army jacket, and a black wool scarf wrapped tightly across her forehead and

neck so that it looked like a kind of ski helmet. From the ingrained dirt in the folds of the cloth, it was unlikely that she had taken off this outfit for most of the winter. Tattoos covered her chin in a delicate goatee.

She knew well how to defer to her husband's boss's wife and at first spoke only in response to our questions about her family and her origins in the area northeast of Homs. She said she missed the sociability of being with her own people but then ingratiatingly said nice things about the treatment she had received from Um Abdalla.

I was wondering whether her children went to school and, if so, how they managed to walk the long distance to the center of the village every day. She answered my questions about the children's education without much enthusiasm. She herself was in favor of educating both the boy and the girl but was not fully convinced that education would have any practical benefit for the family, especially for the girl. She didn't want to venture a guess as to how long the children would go to school; "It's up to God," she said.

The boy was a so-so student who was having trouble in mathematics. When I asked, he brought out his English book, looking pleased to be able to show me what he could do. We made several tries at communicating in that language, but soon it became clear that, as with Lisa's schoolwork, he could only recite paragraphs from memory and not communicate orally. In a singsong voice, he recited pages of the book, but when I asked questions using the same words, he only looked bewildered. If I read questions from the book exactly as they were written, he could respond in parrot fashion with prepared answers, but if I deviated by even a word from the book, he became confused and offered something at random. "What is your name," I asked hopefully. "My name is Muhammad," he said grinning from ear to ear. "How old are you?" I continued. "Fine, thank you." he returned, and we foundered on from there.

This exchange left me feeling sad that so much time was wasted in the memorization that the school substituted for learning. Perhaps Muhammad would never need to speak English, but if he was going to spend so much time studying it, he might as well do a better job of learning it. It was much like the feeling I experienced later in Pakistan when, looking in the English notebook of a little shepherd boy who had just had the same kind of garbled conversation with me, I saw these words written:

> Apostrophes are used when liaising persons with objects except in [I think it was twenty-six] cases.

The twenty-six or so cases were listed. The little boy could repeat this grammatical principle with all its exceptions but could not answer the most basic questions in the language. Could there be a more ineffective way to teach a point of grammar?

Abu Muhammad showed more interest than his wife did in the boy's doing well in school, even though he himself had had no education and knew little more than that education might make it possible for the boy to become a doctor and earn a great deal of money. Always, it was the hope of every Syrian parent that their children would become doctors.

Neither parent was much concerned about educating the girl. It cost money for uniforms and books, and she would only go off eventually and marry into another family. They could not see that it would do her any good, and besides, it might hurt her chances to marry. She sat there following every word of our conversation, quiet and shy and quite willing—expecting, in fact—to let her brother receive the major share of the attention. I asked to look at her schoolbooks, and she took them out for me to see. When she read, it was with expression, as though she not only understood but actually enjoyed what she was reading. Um Abdalla praised her, telling me that she was at the top of her class. It was a long walk to the primary school, and I could imagine that if she didn't like the experience, her parents would have been happy to keep her at home to help with the chickens.

I asked the children what they did after school, and both said they spent most of their time working in the hen houses. By my question, the boy Muhammad was reminded of the work he should be doing and went off to help his father. I watched his awkward gangly stride that must have put the egg boxes in peril. How sad for the family to rest its hopes on this boy when next to him his efficient, hardworking sister with many more talents was ignored. After reading to us, she kept her book open, as if it was too compelling an object to put down, and, taking out her notebook and pencil, began doing her homework. She must snatch moments like these to complete assignments when she was not needed by her parents. Her scarf and wool helmet–covered head and longish dresses made her already a miniature of her mother. In noticing her dress, so unlike the jeans of the village children, I realized the usefulness of the unattractive military school uniforms in obscuring the differences among children. At least in this case, one little girl would not seem so different from the other children.

Um Muhammad soon opened up and began talking in a lively and animated fashion, no longer mindful of the reticence she should show in front of such important guests. I hadn't experienced this kind of lively conversation since visiting with villagers in Egypt. She told stories in the same manner they did, with one episode following another in an endless stream with no clear conclusion to the tale. The pleasure was in hearing the colorful details and the neat turn of phrases. She kept an eye on her guests to see how they were reacting and, depending on our attentiveness, interspersed wild stories with more sedate ones, all supposedly based on true events with magical or supernatural interventions at the right or the wrong moment. Her guests were well entertained; even my usually serious companions couldn't help laughing at her "nonsense."

We were transported to a "tribal" world for the duration of a few hours, and the time passed more quickly than we thought. Suddenly we realized the sun was setting and we should be getting back to the house. We said our good-byes quickly, with Um Muhammad urging us to come again soon, and started down the hill. Soon Hanna overtook us with the tractor and offered us a lift. The women looked to me to see if I would accept, and when I did, they gratefully climbed up, too. We bumped along the rutted road clinging to one another and laughing as we were jostled almost to the point of falling off. The sun set behind the western hills in a last burst of reds, purples, and fuchsias. Up ahead, Lisa had remembered to turn on the outside light to guide the tractor to its place underneath the grape arbor.

Many afternoons we would see Um Yusef's grandson, Samir, driving a truck around and around the village in preparation for taking his test for his license. We could count the minutes almost exactly when he would come whooshing around the corner. He looked capable and efficient up there in the cab at the wheel, a born driver if there ever was one. His father owned the truck he was driving, Abu Adil told me, so it appeared they had reconciled their differences over the school issue. No one had remarked on this turn of events, and when I asked about it, they shrugged as if to say, "Well of course, what did you expect? It is in the nature of families to reconcile their differences."

Samir was only seventeen and so would have to wait until he became eighteen before he could get out on the road. Then, according to then existing laws, he would be able to go to Lebanon without any trouble over his army status, since Syria and Lebanon treated each other's citizens as if they were one contiguous country. Samir would need only his identity card to cross the border. However, if he wanted to make the round trip to Saudi Arabia, he would have to get an exemption from the army. One way to do it at that time was to pay the S£25,000 fee and remain abroad for five years. Many of the young men did it and came back with earnings that more than compensated for the fee. No one seemed sure what Samir planned to do about resolving these problems, as they were his business and not our concern.

A few months later, Samir discovered that he could not avoid being drafted into the army by paying a fee and going to work abroad, because the government had closed another loophole.

Once I was later than expected getting back to the village from a stay of several days in Damascus, but I had stopped for a few minutes after a visit to Homs to let them know when I would arrive. Everyone was concerned about the problems in Hama, a town quite far north of Wusta where a confrontation between the government and the rebellious townspeople had left thousands dead. Because the government-controlled newscasts gave little information about the problem, the villagers were relying on rumors and the conspiracy theories that were rampant during any period of unrest. Um Abdalla and Abu Abdalla said they had heard that troops were killing "children in the streets." Being Christian, they were ready to place the blame on the Muslims who "instigated" the confrontation, rather than on a heavy-handed response by the government. "Islam is the criminal of Hama," declared one of our Christian visitors, implying that the destruction and death in that town were the fault of the Muslims but forgetting that it was also mostly Muslims who died under the guns of the government's counterattack. They wanted to know if I had seen anything on the road coming from Homs, which was near Hama, but I had not, except for trucks loaded with plain boxes in the shape of coffins moving toward Damascus.

A few weeks later, after the road was reopened, I was returning on a bus from Aleppo and passed directly through the city of Hama. It was appalling to see the beautiful old city almost totally destroyed and in its place a flat plain where bulldozers were swiftly removing all evidence of the confrontation. It was then that I understood how deceptively expansive the space in old cities seems, with their endless winding alleys and intricate constructions. The field to which this old city had been reduced was perhaps a tenth of the space I would have imagined from seeing the city intact.

Um Abdalla's mother, Um Nabil, came by one day for a short visit to complain to Um Abdalla about her son Nabil. It seemed that he wanted to buy a new truck for S£800,000. She felt it would be a mistake to invest so much when they had just finished building their expensive house. It would mean tightening their belts for two more years to find the S£25,000 he would need each month in payments. "And where will he scrape together the down payment?" she asked Um Abdalla, with irritation. She was unwilling to confront her son directly but could vent her anger on her daughter. Um Abdalla sighed, not ready to take on the troubles of another household and feeling resentful that her mother came to her only when she had something to complain about while reserving all her affection for this favored son. This was the son who told me he was too sophisticated for village life—who hated trucking and everything about living in the village. Now it seemed that the magnetism of money was drawing him ever deeper into the trucking business he claimed to despise.

A few days later, we visited Nabil, who was just back from Dubai. He was trying to decide about the new truck. Somewhat flippantly he asked if I couldn't arrange for him to go to America where he could earn lots of money and wouldn't have to work so hard. He reiterated conversations I had heard before about how boring the village was and how he would rather be drinking and spending money instead of sitting around where there was nothing to do. He talked with admiration about the profligate life, images of which I presumed he had observed in the Gulf. He seemed to think the indulgences of the Gulf States were "modern" and something I would appreciate.

His mother explained again how he had spent most of the fall and early winter sitting around the house because he was fed up with trucking. In an effort to discourage him from buying a new truck, she used the same negative arguments with him about trucking that he himself had used before. He replied that he wanted to buy the truck so he could earn money more quickly and then decide what to do with his future.

He talked proudly about his children—now there were three. "Time for the fourth," he said. There was the boy that his mother doted on and two daughters, the youngest just one year old. Um Nabil ignored the two girls and tagged along after the boy wherever he went. The boy's young mother seemed passively indifferent to her mother-in-law's usurpation of her son. Perhaps she was relieved to care for two rather than three children.

Nonetheless, Nabil changed from playboy to kindly father when he was with the children, whom he clearly adored. He played gently with them on the floor, wrapping his head cloth around them until they fell in a tangled heap in the middle of the rug, and he roared a belly-shaking laugh at their antics. "I know your son's name is Kamal, but what are the names of your daughters?" I asked. He replied that they hadn't yet decided on names for the girls, even though one daughter was already more than a year old. We all suggested ideas, but there was something wrong with each name. No one seemed in a great hurry to name them, so I let the matter drop. Somehow, the casual attitude toward the names was typical of the disarray in this family and its overwhelming focus on males.

There was news that the elderly Abu Antoine was not well. As soon as the dishes were cleared away, we went to visit him. Abu Antoine and Um Antoine were the parents of the man who was refinishing Um Abdalla's walls. They had lived next door to Um Abdalla while she was growing up, and so she felt a special affection for them—"Almost the same as relatives," she said. She used the same term *neighbor* with them that she used with me, and I was happy to hear the term used with people for whom she felt such deep affection.

Abu Antoine was in bed with an injured arm. He looked exceedingly frail when he struggled to raise himself to greet us. The bed was near a window that provided the only light in the dark, damp room. The couple's poverty was apparent in their humble home with its low ceilings and cave-like interior. Abu Antoine's and Um Antoine's clothes, the bedding, and the furnishing all showed signs of wear and neglect, the last perhaps the oversight of their advancing age. I imagined this house—so similar to that of Abu Abdalla's parents—to be an example of the homes the villagers inhabited before their fortunes improved.

Abu Antoine became more animated during our visit. Soon he was reminiscing about the old days. He had always been a farmer, caught at too elderly an age when times changed to contemplate another way of life. His mainstay has been the cultivation of figs and grapes. He was proud of his three sons, who had been old enough to cash in on the economic boom: one drove a truck, another worked as a tile layer, and the third worked as a painter-plasterer, finishing the inside of newly constructed houses. All earned a good living.

Abu Antoine observed,

> In the early days when I was farming, we earned enough money to take care of all our needs. But now young people need so much more than we did, a

big house, washing machines, fancy furnishings. They aren't content to live simply—each one wants to be a millionaire. That's why they abandoned farming, because they see how other young men earn more money with comparatively less effort. No matter what they say about trucking, the work is still not as hard as farming. Farming was good enough for us because we didn't expect to have very much, but trucking and construction offer much higher wages so are attractive for the young men who want all those material things. To persuade someone to work in the fields, you now have to pay them S£70 a day—a fortune in our day! That and the other rising costs of farming add up, so you can't make a profit anymore. Not many people in the village want to do the hard work of farming anyway, so they rent the land and let others do the work.

In Abu Antoine's case, the grapes and figs were already planted, and he only plowed them now and then, pruned them, and finally harvested them. Abu Antoine and Um Abdalla continued to talk about how the construction industry was booming these days. "Yes," agreed Abu Antoine, thinking of his son Antoine, "just now, there is plenty to do right here in the village. Men can work full time here. The only problem is timing. Jobs tend to come one on top of another when the workers are busy, and then there is a lull for a time when they have nothing to do." His son took jobs in neighboring towns or even in Damascus when there was no work in Wusta, but he preferred to work in the village where he knew people and was close to home.

Um Antoine took advantage of a lull in the conversation to launch into stories about her daughter-in-law, all of which were negative. We listened to her politely, and Um Abdalla offered some suggestions about how to mend their relationship. Um Antoine rejected each suggestion for one reason or another. On the way home, Um Abdalla commented dispiritedly that she liked the old man very much but felt annoyed with the behavior of the old woman. "She says negative things about her daughter-in-law to everyone, and they repeat them to everyone else. Every day, Abu Munir comes by the house with a new story about the daughter-in-law. She should keep those family things to herself."

The signs of spring finally appeared in earnest. Each house of the village was wreathed in the blossoms of their surrounding fruit trees. Two men were out plowing a small orchard when I went out to take my walk one day. One led a mule and the other was steering a wooden plow. An odor of trampled flowers and overturned mounds of dirt accompanied the rich wet smell of new growth floating across the fields. The day before, about two hundred sheep had gone by my door attended by three men, an older one with a donkey carrying supplies and leading the flock, another a middle-aged man with a stick rounding up the stragglers, and a young boy skipping along at his side. Abu Abdalla reported that they were bedouin who wintered in a nearby village and were now starting out to their summer pastures.

Abu Abdalla would soon be digging up the ground between the two houses under the new fruit trees that he and Abu Adil had planted the previous spring. The trees were still small enough to let the sun through to the vegetables they would plant in rows underneath.

Visitors

Let your money be insulted but not yourself.
The one who is alive is always approached for something.
The person who knocks at the door will get a response.
Having faith in men is like having faith that water will remain in a sieve.
Kiss the hand over which you have no power, and call on God to break it.

— Syrian proverbs

Friday was Abu Abdalla's day off from the office. With the extra time he had on those days, he would turn his attention to his side businesses. The house was relatively quiet on Friday, with the younger children in the Wusta primary school still attending classes, even though this was the normal school holiday in most Syrian schools. The government allowed villages with mainly Christian populations to take Sunday holidays instead. The older children in the school across the valley in Mafraq took Friday holidays because of the many Muslims attending school there.

People started coming to see Abu Abdalla early on Friday morning. The first man who came wanted to borrow the tractor. Abu Abdalla would be reluctant to say yes because he needed it every day, and since it was old, he was afraid something might happen to it if it was used for rough work. So he refused, but with many apologies. But some people were difficult to refuse, like his brother-in-law who had borrowed it before, but the man who wanted it that day he only saw infrequently and so it was easier.

Next came some Damascenes, a man, his wife, and her younger sister. They wanted Abu Abdalla to find them someone to build a grillwork fence. Their neighbor with one of the most ostentatious summer houses had one, and they wanted to have something equally impressive. The atmosphere changed abruptly when they entered the room in their fashionable dress, polished shoes, and patronizing airs. The wife took the only chair in the room without being asked, a breach of etiquette in the village, where men were usually made comfortable first and women fit into whatever space was left. Um Abdalla ran to bring more chairs for the husband and his wife's younger sister. We immediately felt at a disadvantage looking up at them from our places on the floor. Abu Abdalla, perhaps purposely, went to sit on the day bed so that he was almost at eye level with them. The visitors then crossed their legs, with their feet swinging casually in our direction, and the man began asking in an ingratiating way about Abu Abdalla's news as if he were an old friend. The words were standard, but he said them in a way that revealed his lack of interest.

Um Abdalla's and my attention was riveted on the more aggressive of the two women, the man's wife. She interrupted the conversation to ask Um Abdalla to open the door because it was too hot in the room. She accompanied her request with a loosening of scarves and a fanning motion of her gloves. Um Abdalla rushed to comply, and I imagined the practical Abu Abdalla thinking of the money floating out the door on the current of expensively won hot air. A few minutes later, it was too cold for her, so the door had to be shut and Um Abdalla had to turn up the stove.

The woman explained to me in French, over Um Abdalla's head, that they only stayed overnight in their house in summer, because during the rest of the year the weather was too cold for her. I replied in Arabic, my French too rusty to trust. Her next sentence was drowned in the roar of a truck passing the house. As if on cue, she remarked that they had located their house as far off the road as possible so they wouldn't be disturbed by the annoying noise of the "awful *camions*" driving around the village night and day. She sniffed with distaste at the thought of the trucks, adding that they had come to the village for quiet and had found instead that the village was as noisy as the city.

No, they didn't have time to take coffee with us because they had several important appointments back in Damascus and couldn't stay long. Um Abdalla ran to get them some tangerines, which she carefully peeled and sectioned and placed on plates in front of each person. The wife picked up two or three sections and spent a long time pulling off the remaining strings before daintily breaking them in two and putting them in her mouth. Um Abdalla and I were mesmerized by this display of rudeness but intimidated, too.

I looked at the three of us, for the first time seeing how she must be per-
ceiving us. What had seemed ordinary now seemed dirty: Abu Abdalla had
kept his muddy boots on for their benefit, not to be outdone, since it was
considered more sophisticated to keep your shoes on and not to leave them
at the door as the villagers were accustomed to doing. His pants were spattered with mud from his early morning trip to the hen houses. Um Abdalla,
looking very stout but not yet recognizably pregnant, had on her work dress
with men's socks stuffed unmodishly into high-heeled house slippers. I tried
to pick the lint off my long skirt and tucked my legs with my son's striped
soccer socks under me. I was the only one who hadn't kept on my shoes, and
now it was too late to retrieve them. We all looked decidedly scruffy, a fact
that had not been apparent before. We sat woodenly, not sure how to arrange
ourselves, looking somehow, well, like dumb peasants. I was shocked at how
quickly their expectations transformed us into a reality that was different
from the images we usually had of ourselves.

Um Abdalla ran back and forth serving them—they wanted water and
then Um Abdalla thought the wife might need a separate plate for her tan-
gerine strings, and so forth. We were used to women carrying on conversations with women during village visits, especially if the men were engrossed
in business conversations. But except for their complaints, the two women
were not the least interested in talking with us. Their attention was focused
on making Abu Abdalla understand what they wanted. They left most of the
talking to the man of the family but interrupted when they thought he was
not explaining the details well enough.

At one point after their business had been proposed and Abu Abdalla was
digesting the details, the man turned to me and expressed his surprise at
finding both an American who spoke Arabic and one who would want to live
in the village. From his tone of voice, I felt he didn't regard Americans very
highly, probably ranking them in terms of taste and culture somewhere near
the bottom of a list of foreigners headed by the French. I threw in my lot
with Um Abdalla and helped her peel some more tangerines, even though
they had hardly touched the first.

Eventually they came to an agreement with Abu Abdalla, and as if talking
to a child, the wife repeated, "Now remember you promised you would do
this . . . and this . . . and this," and she reiterated each technical point about
the fence that showed she had been listening carefully. With an annoyed sigh,
Abu Abdalla replied that she needn't worry, he could remember the details,
and her husband, fearing a collapse in the negotiations if his wife badgered

Abu Abdalla further, launched into polite requests that Um Abdalla and Abu Abdalla come to visit them, feigning a familiarity that he hoped would ease the situation. With a few parting words, he whisked the two women away before they could do any more damage.

When they were gone, Um Abdalla and I burst into laughter, with no need to explain how we felt about the visit. Abu Abdalla looked more serious, still smarting from the insulting way he had been treated but not so upset that he would refuse a new piece of work. I was beginning to understand why the family did not associate more than necessary with some of its neighbors.

I was invited to spend one Friday with a summer resident very different from the unpleasant visitors who had come to see Abu Abdalla. The Doctora and her husband had been some of the first to build in Wusta, coming there for the simple reason that they were looking for what they took to be a less complicated life in rural areas. She took me on a tour to show me their house, which was a blend of modern and traditional details. "My mother convinced me I should build an old fireplace like the one they cooked in when she was a girl." She pointed out a huge fireplace in a corner of the dining room. Her mother had her own large apartment on the second floor and spent the summer with them in the village as well as the rest of the year in their apartment in Damascus.

"At the time, we decided to build our house of stone like the villagers', but it was difficult to find good workers. We had to go all the way to Lebanon to find stonecutters. In those days, Syrians were not so used to living away from their homes to work on construction projects. Now people in the village bring them easily from Hama." The Doctora had her medical clinic in Damascus, and her husband had his own travel business. They were well off but not enormously so. Theirs was a romantic view of village life not very common among urban Damascenes, who, if they built summer homes, usually did so because it was fashionable at the time or because they wanted what they thought would be the peace and fresh air of country living.

As my hostess led me around her house, I was reminded of rustic pictures in *House Beautiful* magazines and, sure enough, on an end table in the living room was a well-thumbed stack of past issues. My hosts had built a veranda with vistas out over the valley on one side of the house and, on the other, a veranda shaded with grape arbors for the summer. In summer they rolled up the rugs and sat on cushions on the floor to feel more relaxed, little knowing that the villagers they thought they were emulating did just the opposite: sat on the floor in winter nestled in cushions and rugs, so the cold air wouldn't send drafts up their legs, and on couches in the summer, so the air could circulate better underneath them.

From the ceiling of the veranda hung flowering plants, an idea definitely imported from the magazine pictures. Herbs and spices were also drying in bunches on the walls of the living room and kitchen—basil and a native saffron that they grew themselves and considered essential to coloring their rice dishes. Um Abdalla dried wheat on her courtyard floor and left most of the plants she grew in the garden until she was ready to use them or preserve them for the winter. I couldn't imagine her using them as decorations by hanging them on her wall, and as far as I knew, although she used spices for taste, she never used them to color food.

The city couple had four children, three sons and a daughter. Only the younger ones still came to Wusta on Fridays, probably because their parents made them come. The older children used the time for studying and preferred to see their city friends when they had extra time. We often saw the youngest boy and girl playing outside on Fridays while their parents entertained friends. The boy would stalk the bushes in a camouflage uniform playing freedom fighter. The girl, in blue jeans and army jacket, rode her bicycle around the tiled courtyard and paths of the garden or joined her brother in an imaginary battle that had them hopping over stone walls and blasting the opposition on "distant" peaks.

Um Abdalla's children would stand in a silent line observing the self-confident city children while the city children, knowing they were being watched, would ignore their audience. Um Abdalla's children looked as though they would like to join in but for the fact that, unused to this type of fantasizing play, they were uncertain how to go about it. They were accustomed to playing the flat-footed roles of serious adults and not these children's glamorous commandos. Besides, they knew only the unromantic side of military life from the experiences of their young uncle, who could hardly wait to get out of the army and get on with his life. The observers exchanged unsmiling glances, looking for one or the other to make a move. They knew something superior to their experiences was going on, but they didn't know what to do about it; not one of them had ever ridden a bicycle or worn a camouflage uniform. They were learning the lesson of what it was to be "rural," as opposed to a finer category of "urban."

The summer residents showed me their garden, which with a good deal of effort they had planned themselves. A man from the village had done most of the heavy work and looked after it while they were away from Wusta. They talked easily about the future, with none of the anxiety the villagers felt about the possible bad luck such talk could bring. Some day, they said, there would be an orchard where the little trees now stood, producing a wide variety of fruit on their approximately one-acre plot. At the moment, however, they were having problems with their well, which for some reason was producing only a small trickle of water not sufficient for the needs of their garden. The same was true in the well down the street, and they were worried that it might mean the beginning of a serious water shortage or, at the very least, require an expensive redrilling of their well. In the old days in Wusta, the husband explained, people had shallow wells from which they brought up water by hand. Naturally, they didn't use very much water this way, only enough for the house and a few nearby gardens. The fields then were watered entirely by rain. Now most of the people had electric pumps, and many had connections to the village system, so water could be obtained more easily, and people used larger quantities than previously. He felt this was partly why water was becoming scarcer. He reiterated the discussions I had listened to before, about the problems of the decreasing quantities of water that had contributed so much to changing the agricultural character of the village. His argument was couched in environmental terms: technology in the shape of pumps and deeply drilled wells was ruining what was once fertile agricultural land and a simple peasant way of life. Abu Abdalla talked about it differently, as a matter of nature, that is, the smaller rainfalls and the government's not paying the cost of drilling deeper wells.

Vegetables of all kinds were planted among the still immature fruit trees of the man's garden, and in front of the house, flowers bloomed in attractive profusion, another contrast with the villagers' gardens, in which only practical "flowers" like basil or thyme grew. Suddenly, we noticed men on a hill in back of the house looking at a plot of land. Our host expressed his fear that the inevitable was about to happen and that by the next summer there would be a new summer house occupying a vantage point over his property, robbing him of the privacy that he had so carefully cultivated by buying at the edge of the village and constructing high walls around his land.

These Damascenes came to Wusta on most Fridays during the times of the year when they were not living there full time, unless snow made it difficult to come. Central heating supplemented the fire they built in the big fireplace in the living room. "Soon after we arrive," they said, "we always stop in to see Abu Abdalla. He is the unofficial mayor of the town, and we can count on him to give us the news of what's going on." They seemed to have cordial relations with the villagers and took an interest in what was happening there, even though their ideas about rural life were so different from those of the local people that it was difficult for them to be more than friendly neighbors.

On Friday "weekends" when the weather was warm, guests would come out from Damascus to sit on the vine-draped veranda of the Doctora and her husband, and we would hear their laughter floating across the vacant lot that separated our house from theirs. The guests sat in folding chairs and ate a feast of several kinds of meats, side dishes, mounds of rice, fried potatoes, and so on, most of it cooked in the couple's Damascus kitchen and brought with them early that morning to the village. The friends relaxed in easy chairs until late in the afternoon and then, after drinking Turkish coffee, departed down the road again for Damascus. Their host and hostess would follow an hour or two later after cleaning up the dishes and packing up the remaining food. I admired the energy of these two, who with their busy schedules during the week also seemed to complicate unnecessarily their one day of rest. The husband was a kind and gentle man who helped his wife a great deal around the house, bringing coffee for the guests and even doing a considerable amount of the daily cooking and washing up himself, a fact that amused Abu Abdalla a great deal when he heard about it. They were nice people, even Abu Abdalla and Um Abdalla spoke highly of them, and I enjoyed being with them very much. It seemed sad sometimes that they pursued their dream of country living with such passion that they missed the peace and tranquillity they seemed to seek.

They were certainly much nicer than the summer people who had come about the grillwork fence or another couple who came by Abu Abdalla's one day to check on some work he was having done for them. They were very like the others, and I marveled at how inventive bad manners could be. This second couple stood waiting for chairs to be brought to them, rather than sitting with us on the cushioned and carpeted floor. When Um Abdalla went to call Abu Abdalla and they were left a few minutes alone with me, they asked pointedly if I didn't find these conditions much more primitive than I was accustomed to. Their attitude of intimacy with me suggested that as upper-class Damascenes, they were the only ones capable of understanding an American's deprivations in such a setting. I replied that on the contrary, I found life in the village qualitatively better than the pseudo-European lifestyles in Damascus—perhaps stated a trifle too defensively on my side but sufficient to make them change the subject. I left the room quickly to help Um Abdalla prepare the coffee. It was hard liking this kind of summer person, and I began to think that our neighbors next door were the only exceptions to the rule.

The priest sent word that he wanted us to visit. His sister and her husband had just returned from America and wanted to meet the American living in the village. I suggested that we wait until my husband came the next day so we would have a man along to make talking with the priest a little easier, and Um Abdalla agreed that it was probably a good idea. Abu Abdalla never went visiting with us, so there was no question of his going along. We sent one of the boys to schedule our visit for late the following afternoon. It was my idea to set an approximate time convenient for us, against Um Abdalla's feeling that the priest was so important that he should decide the time. But she wavered when she realized that my husband perhaps was important enough that we could fix the time without offending the priest. She made me write the note, however, just so the priest wouldn't think she was the one being presumptuous. If I made a mistake it wouldn't matter, since I wasn't expected to know local customs.

On the following day, we dressed in our best and set out on foot to the other side of the village. Um Abdalla had outdone herself; she was wearing a coat I had never seen before and had made up her face into a garish carica-ture of the fresh rosy one that was natural to her. She struggled along the road in her newly shined high-heeled pumps, rapidly turning gray from the mud. I managed a knee-length skirt for a change, and my husband fortu-nately still had on his clothes from the office. We felt a little ridiculous step-ping carefully along the muddy road, trying to avoid puddles and watching the inevitable disappearance of the shine we had so carefully cultivated on our shoes. I thought back to Egypt and remembered how urban bureaucrats wore Western suits and ties when they went to the countryside, to let the vil-lage people know how important they were.

The priest's brother-in-law, Boulos, had spent most of his life working in the United States. He was old enough, however, when he left Wusta to have nostalgic memories of his childhood there. The whole time he was in America, he dreamed of retiring and returning to the village as a wealthy and important man. He had been one of the first ones in his family to start the exodus to America, and he never lost a feeling of connection with home. He had left because a Lebanese friend told Boulos's father and his brother that they could earn a great deal of money in America, and so in the early decades of the century the two men went. When Boulos's turn came, they arranged for him to go also. He worked in the police department and then as a private security guard in Los Angeles, on Wilshire Boulevard. During one of his visits back to the village on holiday, he married a neighbor woman. Boulos learned to speak fluent English during his stay in America, though with a strong colloquial accent that marked him as working-class American. His wife had spent nearly as much time in the United States as he had, but although she understood much of what was said in English from the soap opera serials she listened to each day, she never learned to say more than a few words herself. She shared his dreams of retirement and return to the village so that she could be reunited with her friends and family.

Now, after fifty years in the States, they were back in Wusta, and Boulos, probably as a result of depression, was sick in bed. The priest was gallantly trying to cheer him up by bringing the Americans he had heard were in the village to see him. Boulos gave us the litany of his complaints in his heavily accented and, to us, somewhat absurdly idiomatic English. He had been disappointed to find out how "primitive" the village was and how little there was to do here. He spoke longingly of his favorite television shows in America and the house where he had lived with all the conveniences of central heating, air conditioning, and labor-saving devices. He had sold everything in anticipation of his return to the village. In the end, he said sadly, "I just didn't realize I had become so Americanized while I was there. Now here I am, a stranger in my own country." We tried our best to cheer him up, but there was little we or anyone could do, and his illness bespoke his own realization that this was true.

His wife was a different story. She beamed with delight when she spoke of being back with her relatives and friends, where all day long she could speak Arabic. If she was anxious at all, it was at the thought that Boulos might want to return to the United States.

One night in early January 1982, Abu Abdalla listened to the newscast twice with more than his usual interest, hoping to find even a glimmer of an explanation of what was going on. He and Abu Munir, who was sober for a change, discussed their concern about the possibility of hostilities breaking out in the deepening crisis with Israel. The previous night, the adults sat talking about the likely effects if anything should happen. A major concern was whether war preparations might tie up foreign currency reserves in weapon purchases and thus reduce the importation of animal feeds even further. Hostilities might also interrupt trucking from Lebanon to the Arabian Peninsula or halt imports of construction materials. The two men worried that villagers might be drafted into the army. Almost anything that happened would directly affect their lives.

Usually they dismissed television news as a waste of time and listened to newscasts with only half an ear. Indeed, Syrian newscasts mostly pictured dignitaries going here or there and meeting this or that personality or showed formal ceremonies at commemorative anniversaries of such and such. Names and places were mentioned, but rarely anything of substance. People met and we occasionally speculated on why they were meeting, but we never learned what they discussed, except as carefully screened bulletins after the completion of meetings. Urban Syrians became adept at reading between the lines to find out who was in or out of favor by who met whom and, by means of other nuanced bulletins, how foreign affairs with various nations were progressing, but the villagers were too remote from political personalities to understand the subtleties of national politics. Their lack of information in times of tension made them anxiously seek out people coming from the city who could tell them the latest, usually worst-scenario, rumors. That night they quietly awaited the news, but the same pictures of dignitaries appeared without a hint that a crisis was brewing.

After the second newscast, Abu Abdalla brought out a letter he had received from his father's brother in Argentina. The uncle had left Wusta when he was about Muna's age (twelve) and had come back to visit only once, bringing his wife. Um Abdalla and Abu Abdalla remembered the visit well. The uncle spoke Arabic poorly and his wife not at all. Despite his difficulty with the language, the uncle talked continuously about all the wonderful things available in Argentina and, by his invidious comparisons, made Um and Abu Abdalla happy when he left. Now in the letter the uncle was offering Abu Abdalla a ticket for a twenty-day visit to Argentina, presumably to see for himself all the luxuries that abounded there. Abu Abdalla was asking the others, with contempt in his voice, why he would want to go to Argentina. The others urged him to go just to see what it was like, but he remained adamant. Tapping the letter for effect, he retorted that even the way they offered the trip was insulting—"twenty days, as if after the time was up, they would throw me out." He made a few humorous remarks and then dropped the subject, but we all could feel his deep humiliation.

It was Friday again, and several people came to see Abu Abdalla. This time, most were workers on constructions he was supervising. There was a great deal of talk about how much certain components of the construction would cost and about obtaining building permits. After a while, Um Abdalla and I excused ourselves and, leaving Lisa in charge of refreshments, went to sit with Um George. Abu Adil had been gone this time for nineteen days, and Um George was becoming concerned again. Nothing was said, but going to sit with her on Friday when Abu Abdalla was home and Um Abdalla should have been caring for his guests showed the extent of our sympathy for her situation.

One day, the largest trucker in town, Abu Ilyas, invited for lunch the family of a Damascene doctor who now owned some of Abu Ilyas's land. As a friend of the Damascenes, I was invited to go along. Abu Ilyas explained that the doctor had saved his eldest son's life when he had tetanus as a small child, and so he, Abu Ilyas, repaid his debt of gratitude by giving the doctor a choice piece of his land for a reasonable price. The son, Ilyas, drove one of the family trucks, and Abu Ilyas farmed the doctor's land for him.

When we arrived, the elderly Um Ahmad, the mother of Abu Ilyas, was in the kitchen surrounded by her daughters-in-law and her married daughter, who had come from her house on the other side of town to help prepare the meal. Um Ahmad was a kindly old woman who insisted that after the meal we come to have tea with her in her own part of the house. The family's old stone house stood impressively high on its foundations, with a commanding view over the village and out down the valley. Um Ahmad needed only to step out of her kitchen to a railed balcony that ran the length of the second floor to see a breathtaking view. She told us that she had no other wish than to die in this house where she had lived for so many years. This remark was an obvious comment on the large and expensive house that Abu Ilyas was building higher on the hill behind him, with an apartment for each of the sons and their families. There would certainly be a place for Um Ahmad if she cared to move there, but she sniffed when the idea was suggested and stated that she never intended to leave her own home.[1] Abu Ilyas laughed at his mother's intransigence but added that it would be her choice when the time came.

The doctor politely asked Um Ahmad about the health of her sons, and she answered briefly about each in turn. When she came to Samir, she pleaded with the doctor to do his best to help them solve their problems with him. The doctor knew about the problem, and although he had tried to intervene, he had been unable to help. Still, he listened sympathetically. Abu Ilyas added, to show their helplessness that now his brother had been in prison without trial for four years. The family felt they had exhausted every avenue open to them, and there was nothing left to do but to continue to pursue contacts with high officials who might be able to exert enough influence to obtain his release. So far, these high-level contacts had not achieved any results, and they were not certain why.[2] They wanted the doctor to give them names and lend his support by influencing these important people to make an effort on Samir's behalf. The doctor suggested some names, but Abu Ilyas had tried most of them. The doctor said he would talk to some people he knew but felt that it must be a very difficult case if nothing had worked even with the intervention of such important people.

I wondered whether the doctor felt any reluctance at having his name connected with a prisoner whom no one was able to help. There must be some danger in such a connection, especially since it was not clear why Samir had been arrested. Perhaps the doctor would make his inquiries appear to be a matter of obligation—"The family of the people who sold me my land have asked me to make inquiries on behalf of their family member in jail"—in order to distance himself from the problem and show that he was connected by a commercial rather than a personal relationship to the prisoner.

Abu Ilyas had three brothers and a sister. The sister was married to a villager and lived nearby. She had a four-year-old granddaughter, the daughter of her son, whom she brought with her to "help" in the kitchen. One of Abu Ilyas's brothers had worked for the Ministry of the Interior (the dreaded Internal Security) but was now retired and wealthy (even he, it seemed, could not obtain the release of his brother). The second brother was the one in jail. They returned again to the story, this time providing more information. According to the authorities, when they searched Samir's house on a tip, they found pro-Iraqi, anti-Syrian pamphlets. Samir insisted that he had casually picked up the antigovernment flyers on the street in Damascus. There had been no trial, and no one knew when he would be released. At first, the family didn't know where he was being held but finally discovered he was in a prison in Mezze on the outskirts of Damascus. The family was told unofficially that the authorities weren't letting him out because they wanted to exchange him for Syrian prisoners in Iraqi jails.

It was curious that one brother could be so closely involved in government affairs and the other accused of running operations against its interests. It was explained with a shrug that "work is work"; that is, it allows one to live but doesn't capture one's "loyalty." Government work, in particular, required little commitment, except by higher officials who had a stake in maintaining themselves in power. Syria's domination first by foreigners and then by narrow interest groups reinforced a mind-set in the general public that resisted political authority. Ordinary citizens felt no compulsion to follow government rules if they conflicted with their own interests and if the risk of getting caught was not too great. This attitude was widespread in the countryside, so much so that people were not in the least reluctant to discuss their "illegal" activities. Neither side trusted the other, and their antagonism was kept under control only because the villagers knew they could not win against the massive forces at the government's disposal. In Wusta, people knew enough to level complaints at the rules and not the authorities.

The third brother, a trucker who drove back and forth to Saudi Arabia, sometimes spent six months or so inside that country hauling goods from town to town. According to Abu Ilyas, he would come back with as much as S£600,000 (more than $150,000) profit per visit. One time, on a trip to Yemen, he was caught smuggling guns, was sent to jail for several months, and had his truck impounded—another side of being boldly entrepreneurial, as the villagers saw this activity. Abu Ilyas had to go to Yemen to get him released and finally paid someone to take his place in jail. They spirited the brother out of Yemen, and now he also was "retired" and living in Wusta. I asked Abu Ilyas whether the brother hadn't brought his problems on himself by illegally smuggling arms, but he shrugged his shoulders and reiterated the truckers' criticisms of the restrictions placed on their activities. They felt it was a kind of retribution for the officials who extracted so much illegal income at the borders.

All the brothers owned trucks, and all sold pieces of their land to Damascenes when they needed money. Abu Ilyas had sold the least amount of land, the other brothers more. At one point when they needed money quickly, they sold some of their good orchard land for S£20,000, very little indeed in those days of soaring land prices.

Abu Ilyas farmed his land himself and took care of the doctor's orchards, but he maintained that he lost money in the process. He recounted the problems I had heard before about government controls on prices:

> Now they're even controlling the price of fruit. We can never be sure in this

area about fruit because the size of the crop depends on frosts. We often get late frosts at this altitude that kill the blossoms, and then we have problems. We haven't had a good crop of cherries in five years. One thing I'm thinking of doing is putting in apples because they bloom two weeks later, and we might have better luck with them. We used to plant potatoes, but they take a lot out of the soil, and after a few years you can't produce good ones any longer. Because of these problems and the uncertain situation with government controls, no one wants to farm any more.

Abu Ilyas described the usual pattern of trucking in which young men hired themselves out as drivers for two or three years until they earned enough money to buy a truck. Then they hired a driver or kept on working to buy another truck. "Most men who work hard can retire by thirty-five with money in the bank. The young men in this village show initiative unlike the others down the road." "What makes this village different?" I asked. "Maybe because the boys here see other people who have made a success of it; or maybe because we are Christians and that makes us more practical; maybe just because we are more aggressive." His son, who had just joined us, added that the net profit on a single trip to the Gulf could be anywhere from S£10,000 to S£20,000, his tone indicating that it was obvious why young men would want to become truckers if they had an opportunity like that. To make the trip cheaper, he told us, they filled their fuel tanks in Saudi Arabia, where diesel fuel was cheaper, S£7 compared with S£12 per liter in Syria. It cost about S£2,000 to fill the truck's tank for the round trip. Some of them even built large storage tanks on their truck to accommodate the extra quantities of fuel. Once again I was impressed by the sums they spent and the way they took advantage of every opportunity to increase their profits.

We were called into a large room where there was a long table and enough chairs for each of us to sit at the table. It seemed to be a thoughtful arrangement so that we city folk would be comfortable sitting up off the ground. Lunch was an enormous feast that included many dishes in a traditional *mezze*: small *kibbee*, *hummos bi tahina*, *babaganouj*, wilted cabbage salad, *tabuli*, fried potatoes, and other dishes, all served with homemade *araq* brewed, our hosts explained, before the government ban on the production of alcoholic beverages shut down home production in the village. Then they brought out the specialty of the house, a twelve-layered kibbee about ten inches in diameter. They laughed with delight at our surprise to see such an enormous kibbee. Each layer of the ground wheat and meat shell had to be applied and then deep fried, until the end result was the large ball before us.

Despite all the cooking that should have toughened the ball, the finished product was delectably succulent. After we had finished the meal, the doctor's daughter and I went to thank the women who had remained out of sight and were still cleaning up in the kitchen. They were pleased we had found the food so good.

Abu Ilyas took us for an inspection of his new house on the hill. The palatial house had long arcaded balconies on the side overlooking the view. As we stood there, he reminisced:

> One of my first memories was of my father's father's father, who was the one who built our original house more than ninety years ago. That house was destroyed three times since then, one of those times by the French when they came and bombarded the village.[3] Our family included the heads of the village at that time, and so we became the target of every group trying to control the village. But each time they destroyed the house, we built it back again better than before. We never gave in to them.
>
> I am building this house so that every son will have a floor of his own. Here they will have more room than they would if they had a whole house to themselves. They all will move here from the old house as soon as it is finished, all, of course, except Um Ahmad, who says she won't leave the old house. [He laughed and shrugged his shoulders.] One of her sons will have to stay there with her if she persists in that idea, but as you can see, the distance between the houses is nothing at all, so we will be with her every day.
>
> When will the house be done? It's difficult to say. We are building in stone, and that takes time and money. We want everything to be just right.

Behind the new house was a flock of sheep, watched over by a bedouin who rushed to greet Abu Ilyas. Abu Ilyas explained that his father had been the middleman for the sale of sheep in the area, and therefore the family had had a long relationship with this family of bedouin, who were his suppliers. They continued to camp here next to the house, using the water from his well and the downstairs storage rooms as living space during the three coldest months of the winter. In spring, they took their flocks out to the flowering plains of the Ghutta for the rest of the year.

I went with the women of the doctor's family to keep our after-dinner appointment with Um Ahmad in her room, and we had tea with her as promised, even though we were full from the meal we had just eaten. There was a neat practicality in the arrangement of her rooms: no frivolity, no unnecessary items. Off her tiny private kitchen was an indoor bathroom, most certainly an afterthought placed as close to the existing plumbing as possible. A curtain covered the entrance, its thin substance serving the purpose of privacy. She was obviously tired from supervising the making of the large meal we had just enjoyed but was nonetheless a gracious hostess, seeing to the making of tea and ensuring that each of us had sugar or cream as we desired. She asked me whether I was happy living in the village, and when I answered yes, she looked pleased, adding, "We like it too; the air is good; it is quiet; and the children have a good place in which to grow up," echoing the words of Um Abdalla in an earlier conversation with me. We settled back contentedly in her worn chairs and watched the afternoon sun sink behind the hills out her side window. The glow set her doorway ablaze and struck a long red finger of light across the floor. The stillness was complete . . . until a motor revved up on the other side of town.

I suspect I would not have been invited to Abu Ilyas's house that day were it not for the fact that the doctor had invited me personally to come along, a guest's prerogative. I noted the coolness in Abu Abdalla's voice when I told him about the "wonderful time" I had had at Abu Ilyas's house. At first, I took it to be the usual cool reception whenever I spoke in a complementary way about someone in the village not immediately related to the family. It seemed to be a kind of jealousy: "Why is she seeing them? Aren't we enough for her? Maybe she likes them better than us?" In this case, however, it seemed to be something more. I remembered that Abu Abdalla never talked about Abu Ilyas, even though he was one of the leading men in the village. Each time when I asked about him, Abu Abdalla said very little.

From others I learned that a few years back when Abu Ilyas sold some of his land to the doctor, the doctor decided to build a wall around the trees to mark off his property and to prevent people passing by from helping themselves to his fruit. He did not bother to get a building permit from Abu Abdalla, perhaps because he didn't know one was needed for something as simple as a wall. But Abu Abdalla did not let this oversight go unchallenged and took the doctor to court. The doctor, however, was an influential man and eventually got off with only a minor fine. Abu Ilyas was angry that Abu Abdalla raised such a minor issue with his client whom he was trying to please, and for a long time there was bad feeling between the men. Looking back, I remembered that there was also a coolness in Abu Ilyas when the name of Abu Abdalla was brought up. It was a credit to both of them that they didn't speak ill of the other in front of an outsider.

Lisa was studying for her midyear exams; Miriam was curled up by my side;

and Ilyas was making a nuisance of himself pulling his cousins' schoolbooks out of their bags. No one said anything to him until he took a pencil and began his favorite attention-getting trick of decorating the schoolbooks. Muna went over to him and removed the books, putting them back in their cases and placing them too high for him to reach, saying affectionately, "You're a little devil, Ilyas." Boulos returned from the bakery with a pile of hot loaves of bread. He handed all but one to Um Abdalla and began tearing the remaining one into strips that he handed out to each of the children to press against the curved belly of the stove. They gathered around the stove to watch their pieces become crisp enough to peel off and pop into their mouths. Boulos shyly offered me a piece, and I had to agree that it was extremely delicious hot off the stove like that—like popcorn.

A neighbor arrived and regaled us nonstop with stories of happenings in the village. She was not one who came often, nor was she immediately related, nor did she owe us a visit, so we waited patiently to discover the purpose of her unexpected visit. She began with comments about the neighbor's engagement gifts and then told us, as if the topic of the engagement had reminded her, that she and her sister were making their own wedding plans. This was news to Um Abdalla, who concealed her surprise with expressions of congratulations. The visitor explained, mostly for my benefit because I didn't know the people concerned, that she and her sister were becoming engaged to men fifteen and twenty years older than themselves. She mentioned this in a way that showed she thought the difference in age was a serious disadvantage. However, after pausing for effect, she went on to say that they had been willing to accept this situation only because certain other characteristics of the men had been more than satisfactory. She hastened to explain: these men were marrying late not because they were poor candidates for marriage, unacceptable to other families, but, rather, because they had wanted their sisters and brothers to marry before them. Their father had died before the children were grown, and so these two older sons felt responsible for seeing their sisters and younger brothers married before they did so themselves. She particularly emphasized this point to demonstrate what good men they were, men who carried out their obligations even to the detriment of their own interests.

The guest went on to say that her husband-to-be was a driver and therefore earned good money but that all his money had gone for his siblings' marriages, and therefore he had little left to put toward his own marriage.

At present, he had just one room in his mother's house that would belong to them, but he planned to build a separate house when he had saved more money. She added that he was urging her to marry him in the summer before he completed their house, even though this would mean living with his mother for a while in the single room. She was not sure she was willing to agree to this arrangement but was wavering. After all, it had been his sense of responsibility that had put him in this predicament, and perhaps she should accept this inconvenience as long as it was only for a limited time. She explained these points in such calculating terms that it was hard to believe she felt any affection for her fiancé. Rather, we were being given a "news bulletin" justifying her decision to marry a man who had not built a separate house for her so that no one would suggest this was less than a perfect match.

After being with her for just a short time, it became obvious that she did not possess many of the characteristics of the ideal wife that the women had enumerated during our visit to Um Munir's house. Her personality was not very pleasant, and she was plain in appearance—short, with sallow skin and dark circles under her eyes, unremarkable features, frizzy hair pulled back in a clip, not much attention to dress, in her late twenties, and with an unattractive way of squinting her eyes when she spoke that made her words sound conspiratorial. The fact that her older sister also was still available suggested that the family was not one whose daughters were eagerly sought in marriage in Wusta. In truth, they both were probably ecstatic to receive a proposal finally—Um Abdalla's expression of surprise was enough to confirm the startling nature of her news. I could imagine that when it finally came time for the men to marry, they had found all the agreeable women already taken. Few families would have accepted the idea of marrying their daughters to men so much older or to one who offered no more than a room in his mother's house, unless they were desperate to marry them.

Now she came to the second point of the visit. Had we heard that one of the truckers from a nearby town had been attacked and beaten with an iron pipe in Saudi Arabia? The reason behind the attack, she said, was that his name was Ilyas, and therefore the Saudis knew he was a Christian. "Saudis don't like Christians," she announced with conviction. Um Abdalla looked skeptical but didn't say anything. The trucker had been flown back the day before and was in critical condition in a hospital in Damascus. He had six daughters—whom she mentioned to heighten the effect of his calamity—so no income earners in the house if he should die. His truck, she said, was being held in Saudi Arabia by the authorities. After she exhausted this topic, she went on to the prices of things and a special story of where she had found a particularly good bargain a few days before.

This was the kind of person Um Abdalla disapproved of, one who went around taking satisfaction in the misfortunes of others. She sat throughout the conversation concentrating on her sewing and commenting infrequently on what was being said, though she offered her the routine foods and drinks and congratulated her at the right moments on her impending marriage.

Abu Abdalla was recovering from an operation to remove a benign cyst under a gland in his neck. He spent a week in the hospital and afterward had official permission to take thirty days off from his *baladiyya* work to recover. This seemed like a long convalescence for what appeared to be a minor oper-ation. He lay in his pajamas all day on the bed in the television room. The boys had taken over the chores at the chicken house while he was sick, and he questioned them carefully each day about what was happening there. Twenty to thirty people came by each day to see him, most to commiserate with him because of his illness, but some came on business.

When I came back from Damascus and went to express my concerns by sitting with him for a while, I found him talking with the driver of the truck in which he had a quarter interest. Originally this man had been brought to him by the second son of Abu Antoine, Nabil, who was a tile layer. Nabil met the man through his work and brought Abu Abdalla into a deal that included two other people. To justify why he had become involved, Abu Abdalla explained that it was better to make deals with strangers than with relatives. "You can't trust anyone in the world, including relatives, but you can at least strike a harder bargain with strangers." If it had been a relative, he would have had an equally apt phrase expressing the greater trustworthiness of relatives.

As if to contradict his words, Abu Abdalla was having trouble with this driver whom he didn't trust at all. He was certain the man was taking money on the side or cheating him by fixing the books. Abu Abdalla gave him a thor-ough going over about the expenses that should have been written down in the account book. The driver was supposed to have noted every time he took a new job or crossed a border. Next to these entries, he was to write the expenses he incurred and the money he earned. Abu Abdalla was not happy that the man had taken so long to come to make his accounting, and he was even more upset that the driver kept only vague summaries in Syrian rials.

The driver said somewhat ingenuously that he had kept the books in this fashion because he hadn't wanted "to trouble the others with too many details." He thought his summaries were sufficient and hadn't known that he should keep receipts of everything. He looked frightened as he told his side of the story, and his eyes darted back and forth as he tried to explain the paucity of figures. Abu Abdalla told him angrily that from now on he wanted the man's expenses written out in full in the local currency where the driver incurred them and then a note stating the exchange rate whenever money was paid out or taken in. And Abu Abdalla wanted to see all the receipts.

The driver had made four trips to Saudi Arabia over the previous eight months, staying about two months each time to work in the country. He said he had S£150,000 left in net profit after his expenses had been deducted. For each trip, he received S£2,000 for driving. Then he and Abu Abdalla each took a quarter of the profits, and another villager, who owned several trucks, took the remaining half. Abu Abdalla's share was therefore about S£35,500 (about $9,000), a sum he seemed to think was less than he should receive for eight months of trucking.

After a heated argument, the driver agreed to keep the books more carefully in the future, and the conversation shifted to more friendly topics as they sipped a second cup of coffee. Both wanted to leave on a friendly note, the driver to keep his job and Abu Abdalla to try to preserve some goodwill that might translate into better profits next time. Finally, the driver asked Abu Abdalla's permission to leave to return home where his wife was preparing food for his next trip to Saudi Arabia. He was a Sunni Muslim from Deraa in the Hauran area near the border with Jordan, and he mentioned some food that his wife was preparing that was new to me. When I asked what the food was, he described it to Um Abdalla and Abu Abdalla as well, who also were unaccustomed to the food from that area. "Every place has a different name for its food," explained Abu Abdalla, unwilling to admit that he didn't know the dish.

To my surprise, after the driver left, Abu Abdalla seemed pleased with himself. Perhaps he had only been posing as a tough negotiator to keep the man honest, or perhaps he was relieved that he had any accounting at all of his investment after the driver's long absence. I was left wondering how many of Abu Abdalla's other money-earning ventures I had not yet heard about. It was the first time I knew he had investments in trucking.

I told Um Abdalla that when the baby came, she should take thirty days' holiday as Abu Abdalla did. "What," she exclaimed, "a woman would never get thirty days away from housework—she'd be lucky to get one or two days!" And then pensively, "Tell me, neighbor, why is it that women's work has no end?" I had no answer for her, or maybe the discussion was too long to begin at that time.

Abu Adil returned from a twenty-day trip and came immediately to visit his convalescing brother. He complained that trucking was again getting more difficult because of the problems at the border. He now spent more time sitting at the border waiting for permission to cross than actually on the road. He told us the details of his trip, but they differed little from his reports on previous occasions. Abu Abdalla was waiting for him to finish his report to ask whether the driver who had made an accounting with him had been overcharging. He brought out some notes he had made, and the two went down the list of expenses and earnings. Um Abdalla, Um George, and I turned back to a conversation about what we would make for the noonday meal. The men's conversation ended inconclusively. Abu Abdalla hated to admit he had been cheated and began defending the possibility that each figure might be correct, and Abu Adil, wanting to show how clever he was at getting low prices for everything, disputed each expense. In the end, they decided there was no way to know for sure what the figures should have been because the driver had not noted distances, dates, and exchange rates.

The following Friday, Abu Abdalla was still recuperating from his operation. Because it was a holiday, the house was full of well-wishers. Each one entering asked courteously after Abu Abdalla's health and then listened patiently while he described all the details of his operation. Then, before the next visitor caused an interruption, the talk turned to trucks and money. One old farmer sitting next to me told me that his daughter had gone to America with her husband some time ago and had remained there and that he had not seen either of them for years. His son owned a poultry farm on the edge of Wusta. He told me the story I had heard before about how only older people could afford to farm because their expenses were limited and their children who were doing well economically could help them out. The economic boom was a major event during his lifetime, and he, like other older villagers, was proud of the achievements of his children's generation in making the transition to better-paying jobs. He spoke of his children's accomplishments as some kind of miracle he hadn't quite gotten used to.

To illustrate the initiative of the people in the area, he recounted the story of a driver from a neighboring town who thought he would branch out and carry goods to neighboring Iraq, which was closer than Saudi Arabia. It didn't matter to the driver that Iraq and Syria were bitter enemies—he chortled with toothless glee when telling this part. Somehow, the driver managed to cross the Iraqi border, but when the officials realized their mistake, they detained him in Iraq for twelve days, and he lost a lot of money in government red tape before he could get out. The farmer thought the whole story was a great joke and ended with the understatement that it might be too early to branch out in the direction of Iraq. He seemed eager to impress me with the aggressiveness of the young men in Wusta. Without any difficulty at all, I could appreciate this young man's feat in confronting the most sensitive of political obstacles—the Syrian–Iraq border—since a Syrian's deciding to trade with Iraq was not unlike his deciding to trade with Israel.

Antoine came by to pay his respects and to collect the rest of the money owed him for finishing the walls. In the end, it had taken him thirty days, but he kept the price as agreed. He talked wistfully about how much more he could earn from trucking, perhaps as a way of making Abu Abdalla feel he had gotten a bargain with the plastering.

Abu Muhammad also appeared in the middle of the morning, from the chicken houses, bringing the money for the week's eggs. Abu Abdalla questioned him carefully about how the chickens were faring and ran through a list of jobs that Abu Muhammad should be sure to do. The chickens were Abu Abdalla's major concern during his recuperation. One slip like forgetting to give them vitamins or medicines or water might mean the death of many, and he could not afford to lose so much revenue at a time when he had to pay his medical expenses.

A young man came in a small truck that he parked at the side of the house. He talked, too, about the profits of trucking and claimed that all you had to do was work four months a year and rest the remainder of the time. He talked about different models of trucks, especially ones that used less gasoline and thus cut the cost of trips. That led to more discussion of costs. Finally, turning to me, the young man said he had seen on television that farmers in America used helicopters for spraying insecticides on fields. Was that true, he wanted to know, or just propaganda, and if true, would it make a difference in productivity? I said I thought it would make a difference but reminded him that the farms that used such methods were very big, which made it feasible to do the job with planes. Although I tried not to compare

America in ways that made Syria look less favorable, my listeners invariably construed my statements to mean that America was better. Hearing my comments about the large farms, he remarked sadly that it seemed much easier to make a lot of money in America, and did I know any way he could get a visa to go there?

For an irrational moment, I imagined the large settlement that would exist in America if I were able to respond to all the requests for visas directed at me during my years in the Middle East. Syrians were particularly prone to this disease, despite the vitriolic attacks on the United States in their media. Whenever I was sorry I couldn't respond to a personal request, I thought of emigrants' stories about the difficulties of adjusting to life in America—the loneliness, the homesickness, the almost total dependence on other immigrant families when they arrived. What could a trucker like this do—he had few skills other than truck driving and knew no languages but Arabic. I could never explain these disadvantages to him, but in any case, etiquette demanded that I not answer his request negatively. I told him I wished I could help and left it at that, without giving him a definite no. It was so far fetched an idea for him that he dropped it anyway, a desultory attempt when the opportunity presented itself.

I would rather have spoken the truth openly, to say that it was not within my power to provide visas, nor was it likely to be of any help for me to try to intervene. I would have liked to have said that the laws of the United States determined who could and who could not go there and to have directed the person to the appropriate consular office. The Syrian, of course, would have thought that I was lying and that for some personal reason I did not want to bother myself about his case. They all were convinced that important business was always accomplished through personal intervention and that any barrier might be overcome with the right influence exerted in the right places. With a husband in the embassy, I was obviously one who should be able to make the right connections. Hadn't they done favors for me?

Later, when my husband and I went to live in Yemen, a Syrian we knew flew all the way to Yemen from Europe to obtain a visa to the United States from his "friend," my husband. No amount of explaining that the procedure was the same in the country where he was living or that he was not given special consideration would have convinced him that he didn't need the special intervention of his friend. He had to stay in Yemen for more than a week before he received his visa—through routine channels.

One couple who stopped by early in the morning to offer their expressions of concern over Abu Abdalla's operation were the Damascenes who owned a cottage across the street from us. Abu Abdalla had supervised the construction of their house, and it would have been impolite if they had not come when they heard he was sick. They didn't stay long because they were expecting coworkers from their office to come out from Damascus for lunch. Um Abdalla told me that their house was built through the combined financing of the unmarried sister from Damascus, her unmarried brother, and their mother. Um Abdalla found the most interesting fact to be the unmarried status of the sister and brother and expressed sympathy for their mother that her children were not settled in life, nor would she ever have grandchildren from her son—a most pitiable situation. Both sister and brother worked in the same company in Damascus and commuted to work every day from Wusta during the summer months. Another sister who was married and had children was not involved in the house construction but came often to visit them. When they left, they apologized profusely, saying they would have stayed longer were it not for the visitors they were expecting. Guests were always the best excuse for any behavior that didn't quite meet the mark.

NINE

Parents and Children

[Speaking about Arab children,] dependence on peers or on siblings or on an extended family is not ordinarily referred to as "dependency." The "other-oriented" child is said to have a strong affiliative impulse, or strong need for affiliation, rather than to have a great deal of dependence.

— Edwin T. Prothro, *Child Rearing in the Lebanon*

I arrived from Damascus fairly late in the morning on one of my visits to Wusta and saw Um George's little boys, Adil and Ilyas, playing by my back-door. Ilyas had only recently begun to walk well enough to join the preschooler group. The children recognized me but, in their shyness, played peekaboo, hiding behind the corner of the house for a while before running off to announce my presence to their mother. I played along with them, hoping thereby to make my return known without interrupting some vital activity going on at either house. While I was gone, the weather had changed from crisp fall days to a bitter chill, and my room was especially damp and cold from staying unheated for so long. As I entered the room, I heard a scurrying sound and turned just in time to see a mouse disappearing into the kitchen. When I changed the sheets on the bed, I found that mice had made convenient use of the warm blanket by chewing up pieces and arranging them into a comfortable nest. That night, looking for the missing nest, they ran insensitively across my face.

I stoked the stove, and before the room was even partially warm, Um George had come for coffee, and then Um Abdalla and Lisa and eventually Muna. I turned the heater as high as it would go, and we sat close to it, catching up on news. They were concerned that Abdalla was not recovering from his second operation as quickly as he should, and they wanted to know whether the anesthesia may have weakened his body in some way that could have given him an attack of tonsillitis. They noticed that each time he was anesthetized, he seemed to become weak and ended up with some kind of illness. I went with Um Abdalla to see him lying in his bed, and he did appear to have a low fever. I was afraid, however, to suggest more than a doctor and an aspirin in case he was seriously ill.

Um Abdalla suggested that we move over to her part of the house, and we readily agreed. I found that they were no longer using the television room for family sitting, and when I asked Um Abdalla why, she explained that they always shifted to the back room in winter to take advantage of the southern exposure that made the room a more pleasant place to sit. Conversely, the television room on the north side of the house was shaded by a grape arbor that made it cool even during the hottest days of summer.

A stove had been newly installed in the middle of the back room, making it delightfully warm and cozy. At night, this room doubled as the girls' bedroom. On my previous visit, there had been two beds in the room, but to increase the space for sitting, Um Abdalla had removed one. The remaining double bed, in which the girls slept together, occupied one corner of the room. I could imagine the uproar if one of my children had been told his room was to be taken over for general family use or if he had been told he had to sleep in the same bed with a sibling. The girls, however, showed no sign that they found it inconvenient to share their room or their bed or even that they had to wait to go to sleep until the family's evening activities were over. The only way I could explain this behavior was to assume that the girls did not consider these spaces or objects to belong to them personally, as my boys would have. Where people bedded down at night appeared to be of less significance than that the family was comfortable in a room more suited to the conditions of winter.

In Egypt, the rural and urban lower classes always used multipurpose living spaces so that family members ate, entertained, and slept in the same room at different times of the day. Part of changing to a middle-class lifestyle meant reorganizing living space so that there were separate rooms for cooking, sleeping, and receiving guests. This had important resource implications, for it meant that as lower-class populations became educated, they expected to adopt more elaborate middle-class consumption patterns.[1]

In Wusta, the affluence of the last decades made it possible for the villagers to adopt what were also largely middle-class lifestyles. From the evidence of the older houses in Wusta, especially those of ordinary citizens, it was clear that fewer rooms served a greater variety of functions. For example, in Abu Antoine's old house, we found him resting on a bed in the large multipurpose room that made up most of the living space. Um Abdalla's house, by contrast, though still relatively simple, was typical of those of modern, more affluent families, with a separate kitchen, bathroom, bedrooms, and living areas and special furnishings for each. However, even if they had considered it desirable, there were too many children in Um Abdalla's house to move to a level of consumption in which each child had a separate bedroom and living and sleeping areas could be completely separated. From an early age, just as with Um George's children, the children became accustomed to sharing beds with siblings—at first all together and then, as they became older, separated into single-sex beds and bedrooms. By the time they were teens, sleeping together probably felt more comfortable than sleeping alone.

The girls' room became our favorite place to sit all winter, and unless formal visitors came, in which case we shifted to the television room, we spent almost all our days there. Along the wall of the room next to the bed in a place the sun reached as it streamed in the window during the day, Um Abdalla arranged comfortable cushions for sitting. The rest of the space on the wall with the bed and between the backdoor and the cushions was cupboards to hold the children's clothes and schoolbooks. On the remaining wall were a table and benches that stood in the path between the outside door and the door opening into the rest of the house. The table was ostensibly for study, but it was the favorite sitting place of Abu Abdalla when he came in from work. From his height sitting on the bench, he commanded a good view of the homework and anything else going on in the room. As soon as he appeared at the backdoor, Lisa or Muna would run to bring him tea or coffee, and he would sit in a spot nearest the stove to warm himself before taking off his heavy jacket.

That evening of my first day back in the village, Abdalla joined us in the girls' room, pitifully dragging his painful leg from where the skin had been taken for the graft. His mother began to weep quietly when she saw his pathetic appearance. Although he was most certainly not feeling well, he also was using his illness to elicit as much sympathy from his mother as possible. For a week, he had been allowed to stay home from school and relieved of all his chores, but now the sympathy of other family members was beginning to wane. As a reminder, Abdalla ordered Hanna, who had just come in from finishing both their chores, to bring him a cushion and asked his sisters to bring him tea. Everyone complied without hesitation.

Breakfasts on school mornings were uninterestingly the same: cheese, bread, olives, and tea. There were no choices, no efforts to make it appeal to individual children's tastes, no encouragements to eat. Um Abdalla put it on the table, and the children either ate or did not eat it. If they did not eat, however, they would be hungry later in the day; this had happened enough times so that they ate what was put in front of them.

Watching the lack of fuss over food, I remembered, in a layover stop at an airport hotel in London, watching an American couple trying to feed their three-year-old son. All three were standing in front of a cafeteria array of breakfast foods. "Now what would you like for breakfast, Johnny?" asked the mother, pointing at the display of goodies. Johnny took his thumb out of his mouth and reached for the nearest stack of doughnuts. "That isn't good for you. Wouldn't you rather have a nice bowl of cereal and a glass of milk?" and the argument was joined. Johnny ended on the floor, screaming and kicking, with the sticky chocolate doughnut clutched in his fist and his parents wringing their hands over their inability to make him see reason.

Little Johnny was learning the lesson from this experience that he was an important being separate from his parents. He was given choices[2] that would be honored if he forced the issue. If he insisted, he could control the behavior of adults unwilling to force him to do anything he adamantly refused. He also was learning, though he hadn't yet assimilated the notion into his behavior, that rational reasons were expected for choices. Later he could use the same logic to win arguments with his parents. These were important first lessons for the child of a culture that reveres individual rights and independent choice and likes to think that it bases actions on rational premises. The scene in the London hotel was all too familiar; it could easily have been myself and my own small sons.

In Wusta, Um Abdalla's children also learned important lessons in the way that food was presented to them. They learned that they were not fully differentiated individuals, that they were people in relationship to other people who made important decisions for them. They learned that parents knew better what was good for them, and because their actions were carried out in a genuinely loving way, they came to look to their parents to make decisions for them in all important aspects of life. Parents had not only more experience but also the best interests of their children at heart. How could they possibly make decisions detrimental to their welfare?

Wusta's parents made decisions about clothes, marriage partners, jobs, length of schooling, and other more or less significant events in children's lives. This way of thinking saved a lot of turmoil for both children and parents, especially during adolescence when, most of the time, children docilely accepted the choices made for them by their parents. They might express their behavior in adages about the propriety of children's respecting their parents, but the results were the same.

The fact that Syrian parents decided what their children ate for breakfast might seem like a minor detail in all that went on during the day, but it reflected a pervasive pattern in which parents directed the lives of their children in all major respects and the children were expected to obey. It also was consistent with a worldview structuring life around homogeneous, stable family groups whose members honored their obligations to one another.

Food reflected another important aspect of life in Wusta. We always took our main meal together at a time when everyone had assembled, usually as soon as Abu Abdalla arrived home from work. The time varied by as much as an hour from day to day, but no one seemed irritated at having to wait for meals. Rather, everyone assumed we would wait until everyone was there. As in all matters in Wusta, we did things as a group, and it would have felt strange to leave out someone simply because one or more of us was impatient to start. People knew the approximate time for eating and assembled at that time.

Before I adjusted to Wusta's mealtimes, I would find myself becoming increasingly hungry waiting for the meal to start; I was uncomfortable and wanted to get the meal over with so that I could move on to other things I had planned for the day. It seemed inconsiderate of Abu Abdalla to keep us waiting or of Um Abdalla not to have planned the timing of the meal better. When my own family and relatives assembled for the summer holidays and we felt we needed to plan some time together, we always ate our evening meal precisely at six so that each person could plan his or her separate evening activities. No one would need to waste time waiting for the meal to start. We all dropped whatever we were doing to be home by six, knowing that if we did not arrive on time, we would be inconveniencing everyone else waiting for us. We made sacrifices by adjusting our schedules to accommodate others and in turn expected the same consideration for ourselves. This was our behavior in summer when schedules were flexible, and we could schedule a time convenient to us all.

In the winter, on weekdays, we found it impossible to coordinate our schedules well enough to sit down for even a single meal together. The children were hungry before their father came home or had sports or other after-school activities that made scheduling difficult. There was little tolerance for spoiling our separate activities with preplanned events of as little significance as eating.

One day in the family room, the children were studying hard for midterm exams that were starting the following Saturday, and there was a palpable tension in the air. Miriam and little Lisa had come over to Um Abdalla's house for a change of scene while Um George stayed behind to care for the little boys and to "study" with George. This week, there would be little visiting among the adults, as everyone was concentrating on the important work of studying. An Egyptian once told me that everything shut down in Egypt during exam time, when parents concentrated on studying with their children. Government employees took leave; even hospitals were less busy, as elective surgery was postponed and patients who were not too ill went home. In Syria also, an unnatural quiet pervaded the streets and homes during exam time.

The little girls knew they were not supposed to interrupt the students, but they were tiring of the prolonged study periods and began to view the prohibition as a challenge rather than a deterrent. For a while, Miriam tried to get Lisa's attention by pointing at the pages of her textbook and asking for answers to the math problems. Then she made up some nonsense words that were supposed to be Lisa's assignment in French. Lisa and Muna giggled at her antics for a minute or two but then quickly returned to their books. Miriam retired to a corner to think up new ways to distract them. No one intervened to deter her from the annoying provocations, even though the children and their parents took seriously this time before exams and knew she was having a certain success in distracting them.

Exams or no exams, tonight was also bath night. Um Abdalla had fired up the hot water heater in the bathroom and called in each of the children one by one, from youngest to oldest, to take their baths. Each came back in clean pajamas with wet hair, wafting the perfumed smell of soap throughout the room. The cold windowpanes of the room began to drip beads of perspiration with the overflow of humidity. Muna, happy for the opportunity of a legitimate diversion from her studies, dried her shoulder-length hair in front of the stove until, with Um Abdalla's brushing, it became a burnished gold. With the exception of Um Abdalla, who bathed later, Abu Abdalla was the last to disappear and come back in clean flannel pajamas glowing from the warmth of the bath. This ritual was repeated twice a week, Um Abdalla used to claim, on Tuesdays and Thursdays, but I had not noticed it so frequently. Perhaps this was her plan, or perhaps she was trying to impress me with her standards of cleanliness. Like most other activities, baths were orchestrated en group when Um Abdalla decided it was time and only under her strict supervision.

Basic education in Syria is based on six years of primary, three years of intermediate, and three years of secondary school. In rural areas like Wusta, the idea that children should complete a prolonged period of education is fairly new. Between 1960 and 1982, for example, the number of primary schools in Syria more than doubled, from 3,500 to 8,100, and the number of primary pupils increased roughly fourfold, from 424,000 to 1.64 million. The increases in the same period were even more dramatic at the intermediate and secondary level, with the number of schools rising more than threefold, from 460 to 1,440, and the number of students almost tenfold, from 69,500 to more than 600,000. Syrian officials estimated that in 1975, more than 90 percent of the six- to eleven-year-old primary school–age children were enrolled in school.

Abu Abdalla's family exemplified this growing trend. He had completed primary school, and Um Abdalla, intermediate school, but they and most of the parents in Wusta expected their children in the current generation at least to finish the secondary stage. The advent of education in Syrian villages has had an impact on the relations between parents and children. Whereas previously, households were primarily adult focused, with the parents almost exclusively providing the training and direction in household labor as well as the main source of values for their children, now forces beyond the family are taking over much more of this kind of training. The immediate effects are that children are surpassing their parents in certain kinds of knowledge and skills, that they are becoming exposed to important sources outside the family for determining values, and that large parts of daily life are organized around the children's study needs.

In Abu Abdalla's house, the children had not yet reached a level of schooling at which they could challenge the limits of their parents' knowledge, nor had they been allowed to mix freely with their peers, from whom they might pick up contradictory values. The household was, however, investing considerable time in the child-centered pursuit of schoolwork. Consequently, there was some contradiction between the way the parents were brought up and the way circumstances were forcing them to bring up their own children. This created tensions in the household most often between the contradictory demands of schoolwork and household work.

Theoretically, school might be a place where children learned to think for themselves. But instead of teaching independent thinking, the education program in the schools the Wusta children attended reinforced the idea that the children need only memorize the words of certain authoritative sources, such as teachers and textbooks, in order to assimilate the knowledge they contained. In essence, the teachers took over the authoritarian roles of the parents for a time during the day, and the system, by the way it had been set up, prevented the children from developing critical analytical skills that might make them challenge the thinking of their parents. As a socializing institution, perhaps not unexpectedly, everything in the education process reinforced the hierarchical and authoritarian aspects of the relationships the children learned at home.

The American school system, of course, also socializes children to become the kind of people Americans admire—independent, self-sufficient, creatively original. I was not entirely prepared for the horror expressed by an educator from a developing country that I once took to see a good primary school in Cambridge, Massachusetts. During the morning, he saw little in the program that he regarded as positive. Rather, he saw as "undisciplined and chaotic" the children's individualized learning activities, in which they talked to one another about their projects and moved from place to place around the room to collect materials. He saw as a waste of time ("not the important things to learn") the third graders' presentations of their original projects on Egypt—a play, an essay on Nefertiti, a painted picture of the pyramids, and a poem. He thought "irrelevant" the kindergarten's cutting and pasting of Valentine cards. He thought that the students "did not show the proper respect to their teachers" and that the teachers "let their classes get out of control." Even though he had come to learn from the experience of seeing American education in action, he could not put aside his mental picture of what education should be. And indeed, a teacher who let such things happen in his country would be out of control.

We all tend to act according to these cultural assumptions. I, too, find it hard to understand the long hours of memorization in this visiting educator's country, the disciplined and unmoving lines of children, the students' very deferential attitude toward their teachers, and the almost total absence of discussion and questioning. And yet my discipline of anthropology has taught me that something in these behaviors is important to the society for the upbringing of their children.

Since midday, we had been sitting in the sun on the back porch—Um Abdalla, Um George, their mother, Um Nabil, and I. It was one of those lovely winter days when the sky was brilliantly blue and the air was exhilaratingly crisp. The sun streamed down on us in our sheltered nook and made it seem like a far warmer day than it really was. The rays penetrated deep into bones that were chilled from a morning spent in rooms with the stoves turned off to conserve fuel while Um Abdalla cleaned.

We turned on one of their favorite programs on the transistor radio that we usually forgot to turn on at the right time. It was a broadcast of Radio Damascus at 1 o'clock about topics of interest to the family. Often, as on that day, the topic concerned measures that parents should take to bring up children properly. No one seemed bothered by the didactic preachy tone of the commentator's voice. Along with short lectures on a subject, there usually were dramatized vignettes. In the one we were listening to, the father was continually interrupting his son, who should have been studying, and ordering him to run errands, fetch a glass of water, or whatever he needed. Later, the child failed his school exams, and we heard the father complaining that the child wasted his time instead of keeping his attention where it should be, on his studying. The narrator summarized the lesson by saying parents needed to help their children establish good study habits and to provide an environment in which they could study without interruptions. The women who were gathered to listen to the radio agreed that the father in this case had been the cause of the child's poor marks on the exams. "Some parents just don't realize how to help their children with schoolwork," said Um Abdalla reiterating the point of the broadcast.

That same evening, we were sitting together in the winter family room helping the children study. Um Abdalla was folding laundry and listening to each child repeat his or her memorized lessons. Muna was procrastinating as usual and disappearing into the television room where Hanna and Boulos, who had finished their studies, were watching cartoons. Um Abdalla called her back to sit down and continue her studies. A few minutes later, there was a knock at the door, and since Um Abdalla was listening to Abdalla's lesson, she called Muna to open the door for Abu Abdalla and help him with some packages he had brought from Damascus. Next, Muna was asked to turn up the stove and get her father some tea. It was another half hour before Muna was free to go back to her work again, but by that time, everyone was too busy talking to Abu Abdalla about what he had bought in town to notice that Muna never returned to her studies.

Although Um Abdalla understood the radio program at a theoretical level, it did not change her behavior. If she had been introspective enough to examine her actions, she might have excused herself by rationalizing: "Abu Abdalla needs help; I am doing something important that shouldn't be interrupted; Lisa is engrossed in her work and is also a better student than Muna so her studying is more important; Muna isn't working much anyway, so it is better to leave Lisa alone and call on Muna." It was characteristic of Um Abdalla to calculate the best interests of the group and interrupt the one individual she assumed would be least affected by the action.

I shouldn't have found it surprising that Um Abdalla's behavior contradicted the narrow meaning of the radio lesson. Although she believed that parents should do the right thing by their children, doing the right thing in her mind was set in the context of what was, first of all, right for the whole family, not a single child at a given moment. By contrast, my concept of "right" would have focused on the relative needs of individual children. In this case, I would have called on Lisa or one of the boys who had already finished his homework, in order to avoid disturbing a child who needed more time to study. Um Abdalla, however, could not ask a boy to help Abu Abdalla because he wouldn't have known how to make tea. And she could not call on Lisa who, as a "successful student," was protected from interruptions. In the end, from her perspective, there was no other choice but Muna.

Um Abdalla didn't feel compelled to be "fair" to her children, that is, to ask them to share equally in work that needed to be done or to be equally competent in all aspects of life. Her children were, in her mind, specialists: she had a child who was a good student, one who was a good tea maker, one who installed stoves, one who was an errand runner, and so on. She encouraged the children to be good at what they were good at, rather than trying to make them good at everything. As a result, each child occupied an indispensable niche in the family, doing what he or she did best.

This was one of the ways in which education contradicted earlier practice, for it demanded similar effort from every child, not just from the "specialist" in the family.

Parents tend to mold children's behavior according to sets of assumptions
that they have learned themselves and of which they usually are not fully
aware. Hall differentiates between formal and informal cultural learning.
The first occurs when a child makes mistakes and, when corrected, learns
the limits of an accepted principle of behavior. The second occurs when a
child learns clusters of behaviors by imitating a model, like a parent, without being aware that rules govern that behavior. Hall criticizes parents who
try to explain formal behavior too extensively, for this suggests to the child
what is not true, that there are alternatives to the acceptable behavior.[3]

I cannot remember a time when I heard Um Abdalla or Abu Abdalla praise
the children directly for work they had done. Rather, they expected their
children to do jobs well and therefore didn't make a fuss when they did.
Children were supposed to keep busy, as their parents did, during most of
the day. They moved automatically from one task to another until they went
to bed at night. There was no block of time they called leisure and no activities that were purely for pleasure, unless the moments of television the children saw in the evening could be called this. It was hard to imagine what they
might do during their leisure time other than watch TV: they were not read-
ers or painters or hobbyists, and they did not play with children other than
their sisters, brothers, or cousins.

When leisure time does not exist as a recognized entity, people do not
expect it as a reward for completing "work." Life was not arduous in Wusta;
children were not overworked; and their parents were not obsessed with
work. People moved slowly but steadily through the day, doing what needed
to be done, and when they had accomplished enough for a while, they rested
over a cup of tea or sat enjoying the sun before going on to the next task. At
the end of a period of relaxation, Um Abdalla would stand up and Muna and
Lisa would follow, and together they would go do what needed to be done.
Working together was more pleasant than sitting idly apart from others who
were working. By the time the small children were Muna's and Lisa's ages,
the habit was ingrained.

Praise was not relevant as a reward for finishing a joint task. Since the
children were closely supervised by their parents, there was no question
whether the work would be done properly, for they did not leave the job

until their parents were satisfied that it had been done right. On the other hand, the parents talked openly about joint household accomplishments with the children. Abu Abdalla would come in with Abdalla to report with satisfaction to anyone willing to listen: "We managed to plow all the garden plot today," or "We ground all the feed before the sun went down," or "We got in the winter store of fuel today," and the boy knew that he was included in his father's self-congratulatory comments. The parents talked matter-of-factly about each child's strong and weak points. Abu Abdalla would say, "Hanna is good at putting in the winter stoves, so we let him do that," and Um Abdalla would say in front of Muna: "Muna does housework well, but we are afraid she may not finish high school because her grades are so poor." These comments were taken as statements of fact by everyone, and not as critical measures of either the children or their parents' love for them. Parental love in this household was an accepted fact and not something that needed to be demonstrated continuously.

Censure was also milder than I expected in such an "authoritarian environment." Naughty children were almost never rebuked, at least when they were small. Ilyas "wrote" in Lisa's notebook, a scribble that started eating up page after page before anyone noticed. When Lisa finally realized what had happened, she gently took the notebook away from him. Everyone said, "Never mind!" sympathetically to her, and she tore out the damaged pages and taped the remaining ones so that they were still readable. It was not that she didn't care about the spoiled pages; on the contrary, she was obsessed with keeping her notebooks neat. She simply realized that he didn't know any better and felt a parent-like affection that enabled her to excuse his bad behavior. All the older children tended to develop this affectionate feeling toward the younger ones from spending so much time taking care of them. Part of Lisa's irritation with Muna's fidgeting during study time most certainly came from a genuine desire to see her sister do well, again a sense of parent-like responsibility to help her succeed.

The worlds of children and adults were almost seamless in Um Abdalla's and Um George's households. There were no activities exclusively for adults, no parties for adults only, no quiet dinners after the children were in bed, no evenings on the town while a babysitter watched the children. Taking a vacation from the children was unheard of and never even contemplated. Instead, children and adults composed a complete package that could not be disentangled.

For most of the day, the activities of adults and children intersected naturally; the exception was when some had activities to perform, such as going to the office or school, that took them away from home. When the women gathered together while the children were young, they accepted that children would be there and constantly interrupting their conversation. A hostess could leave a guest sitting alone for some time while she took care of her children's needs without being considered rude—it was assumed that her duties toward her children took precedence over even those she owed her guests. In any case, adult conversations were not characterized by long expository monologues that excluded children, and therefore people were not much bothered by legitimate interruptions. People exchanged brief news items, exclaimed over somebody's problems, made a few comments to include children in the conversation, noted changes in the furnishings of the house they were visiting, and so on. The children could enter the conversation at any time, and the adults would stop and listen to them—not as an interruption in their own conversations, which then continued, but as short episodic comments interspersed in their own strings of comments. What was true for eating—that it put adults at a level where children could enter the activity more easily—was also true for adult gatherings where people sat on the floor. Adults were not set off from children, and the flow of children into and out of the adults' attention was less traumatic or obvious. It was difficult under these circumstances to distinguish "a child's time" from "an adult's time" or "a child's space" from "an adult's space," categories that have significance in Western society.

To appreciate the difference between these two lifestyles, I thought back to my own household when relatives gathered for Thanksgiving dinner. Except for the very youngest, the children were expected to disappear outside, into a recreation room, or into a child's bedroom so that "the adults could talk" before dinner. In addition, the adults would often have a drink that was forbidden to the children. If the children wanted to penetrate adult space, they were expected to wait patiently until the discussion, perhaps lengthy, was finished. If they wished to speak, they were supposed to excuse themselves and quickly convey their urgent messages, before disappearing again out of adult range. It is interesting that Americans, who believe themselves to be an egalitarian society that is profoundly youth oriented, draw more distinctions between adults and children in certain contexts than does a society that stresses concern for "respect" distance between older and younger generations.

In Wusta, the main exception to this casual interpenetration of the generations and sexes occurred when Abu Abdalla entertained male acquaintances for serious discussion. At that time, the children could remain in the same room with the visitors only if they sat quietly and did not speak unless spoken to. Since they were seldom interested in the conversations, they usually left the room of their own accord. Unless the matter concerned her, Um Abdalla would also leave the room and return only to serve or replenish the refreshments. A number of times, because I was curious about what the men were saying, I would stay on when only male guests were present. As long as I stayed, Um Abdalla felt she also must remain, in order to give the gathering a semblance of mixed-gender company. It was a kindness to me to avoid my appearing to be a woman who lingered unduly with men. After a time, she would usually say, "Come on, neighbor, let's go where we can relax."

Although the children had easy access to adults, with few formalities interposed between them, they were nevertheless expected to show respect for their parents at all times and obey them without question. The children of Um and Abu Abdalla rarely resisted their parents' requests. One day while we all were sitting watching television, Abdalla, from a spot lolling on the floor, told Muna to get him a glass of water. I did not see what went on before the request, but it was clear from the way they exchanged looks that Abdalla was retaliating for something Muna had done and knew he could force a concession by making this request of her in the presence of their parents. She looked sideways at her mother and then in a whiny voice retorted, "You get your own water!" Um Abdalla turned to her and said calmly, "Get your brother some water, Muna." Muna twisted in her seat for a minute and then said pleadingly, "Umi, let him get his own, please." Um Abdalla repeated her request, and Muna went reluctantly to the kitchen grumbling remarks to her brother as she passed him. "Muna!" said her mother in stern warning. Girls were expected to serve their brothers where food or drink was concerned, and Um Abdalla was not about to let a rebellion by Muna go unnoticed.

One day when Abdalla was assuming his pitiful look during the problems with his infected hand, he didn't openly defy his parents' orders to go to school but, instead, tried to show them in every way possible that they were asking him to do something that was not right in his painful condition. He went slowly off to school dragging his feet, and when he returned home, he went groaning to bed. In sympathy, his mother brought him hot drinks and sat anxiously by his side for several hours. Later, when the family was all together doing homework, he joined them without any evidence of his previous problems. Rebellion against parents was possible only in appropriately concealed form.

Two of the few household battles I witnessed concerned clothes. One day Um Abdalla was planning to go into Damascus to buy clothes for all the children for Easter. Within hearing of the children, she described to Um George what she planned to buy. When she mentioned the dress she intended to buy for Lisa, there was an explosion. "I don't want a dress, I want pants. I can't go to church wearing a dress," said Lisa. Um Abdalla gave in and bought her a new pair of slacks. She probably didn't want to insist on a dress if the current fashion among the girls in the village was slacks. She trusted Lisa to know but seemed genuinely surprised by such a strong reaction.

The other problem involved Muna. One day she finished her homework early, or at least she said she had finished, and went over to the closet to take down a pair of her school uniform slacks. She began quietly to sew the seams of the slacks. No one noticed for a while until she had been at it for perhaps half an hour. Um Abdalla suddenly asked why she was doing so much sewing on the uniform, since Um Abdalla had not noticed any need for repairs when she folded the laundry. Muna looked embarrassed and didn't say anything, but Lisa volunteered, "Oh, she's making them tighter." The boys snickered, and Muna turned a deep red.

Abu Abdalla turned slowly to her and asked for an explanation of what she was doing. She answered somewhat defiantly, "Well, they are too baggy." "Put them on," ordered Abu Abdalla. Muna left the room and came back in a skintight pair of pants. "You remove every stitch from those pants immediately, and I don't want to see you doing anything like that ever again," he said sternly. Um Abdalla sat quietly on the side frowning while Abu Abdalla was dealing with the matter. The other children watched with glee as Muna became more and more uncomfortable.

We visited Um Samir again, sitting in her warm family room. Um Abdalla had been telling me in uncharacteristically negative detail about Um Samir's daughter, whom I had seen only briefly the last time I visited. She was an example, according to Um Abdalla, of what happened when a child was brought up badly. Um Abdalla blamed the parents entirely for this problem, ignoring the fact that the other children in the family fit her model of how well-brought up children should behave. The young daughter in question,

Lina, who was about six years old, was immediately identifiable. Her parents allowed her to do almost anything she wanted, and she wanted everything. She was what U.S. doctors might have called a hyperactive child, with a seemingly inexhaustible store of nervous energy. Our visit turned chaotic almost immediately as Lina continually broke into our conversations to claim the spotlight for herself. An older sister brought a plateful of nuts which Lina immediately snatched away. Trying to coopt her help, the mother, reinforced by the father and elder siblings, beseeched her to offer nuts to the guests to show "hospitality." In a gesture of partial compliance, she grabbed her own fistful of nuts first before offering the rest around with such haste that some slid off the plate and spilled all over the guests and the ground.

Two boys of primary school age were doing their homework in a corner of the room but were, not surprisingly, distracted by our visit and the antics of their sister. Seeing that their attention was wandering, the father went over and thrashed them violently with a stick to make them concentrate on their work. The older son, Samir, who had been absent during our last visit because of the disagreement with his father, was now home like a prodigal son, sleeping on cushions in the far side of the room, undisturbed by either our visit or the commotion caused by Lina.

Two pretty, sweet-mannered teenage girls automatically took over, offering us hospitality without being asked, doing as much as they could to discipline their younger sister. Their manner was much gentler, more affectionate, and less authoritarian than that of either their mother or father, and they seemed embarrassed by the impression that their sister Lina's behavior was making on us. Their admonitions, however, had little effect on the behavior of the "monster child." The mother soon tried to ignore the behavior of her youngest daughter, even finally outshouting her when the din became too great. When she could no longer tolerate the noise, she became irritable and snapped at the girl. In fact, the mother was so consumed with the girl's behavior that she almost completely forgot to offer us the customary hospitality of tucking pillows behind us, asking about our comfort, insisting that we eat her special nuts, feel comfortable, and so forth. All these niceties were left to the teenage daughters, who showed themselves fully capable of handling them alone.

I knew by Um Abdalla's silence that she was seeing the mother's lapses as gross deficiencies, setting a bad example in the household and responsible in some way for how the difficult child behaved. Um Abdalla was fond of Um

Samir but disapproved of these aspects of her behavior that made her a "bad" mother. A woman who ignored the most common of courtesies was unlikely to teach her children proper manners.

The older girls were finally able to distract Lina long enough to give Um Samir a chance to talk. Once she began, she became animated and talked so incessantly that the rest of us could do little more than sit back and listen. Her husband continued to reprimand the sons harshly, paying little attention to the errant daughter, who was "her mother's problem." He also ignored the older daughters as he sat back and allowed them to serve him. After her husband left the room, our hostess remembered her manners long enough to tell us to stretch out our legs and relax and called the girls to bring us blankets to cover them.

On the way home, Um Abdalla remarked that bringing up children required love and patience and that although firmness was sometimes required, it rarely needed the kind of physical punishment this man used on his sons. "Look at the boys—they are like rabbits—frightened of him. In this family, they have problems with the boys because of their harshness and with the girl because of their laxity." Um Abdalla shook her head sadly when she thought of the problems they would have with this unruly girl when she grew up if she didn't learn to submit to control. Girls especially needed to learn self-control if they were to get along in the world, "Who is ever going to marry a girl like that one?" asked Um Abdalla mournfully.

A determined knock came at the front door one day, and Abu Abdalla shouted around to the visitor that he was at the side of the house. I looked out the window where I was working at my table to see Abu Abdalla standing on an overturned box, retying poles of the grape arbor that had come loose. A portly man rounded the corner with a frightened young boy in tow. He greeted Abu Abdalla curtly and immediately stated his business, which was that his son and Hanna had had a fight on the school ground that day and his son had suffered bruises on his face. He roughly pulled the boy around in front of him and pointed to the bruises—an area of swollen red on the side of his face. Abu Abdalla said nothing but climbed down slowly from the box and went over to stand in front of them. "What do you want me to do?" he asked without malice. "I want you to give your boy a good beating and make sure he doesn't do it again," was the answer, and the man launched into the details of the quarrel as told to him by his son. Abu Abdalla listened to this tirade without a word. When it was over, he turned to the boy and said, kindly, "Do you want to be friends with Hanna?" The boy wiped the tears from his eyes and nodded. "Well, go back to school now, and don't be afraid. I don't think you and Hanna need to fight any more. The problem is over." The father continued to demand some form of redress, but Abu Abdalla simply told him to calm down and not to worry, that he would take care of Hanna. Finally, assuming that Abu Abdalla would give Hanna a beating, he shook hands with Abu Abdalla and left.

Later that evening after the homework was done, Abu Abdalla turned to Hanna and asked, "Did you have a problem in school today?" Hanna nodded and started to explain, but Abu Abdalla stopped him, "I don't want to hear about it. I've already heard enough about it from the boy's father." Hanna looked embarrassed. "It's probably not a good idea to do what you did, is it?" "No," Hanna answered. "Tomorrow you go shake hands with that boy," Abu Abdalla advised. Later to Um Abdalla, he said, shaking his head, "I never saw anyone make such a big problem out of a simple difficulty between boys." It was characteristic of Abu Abdalla to make it appear to the boy's father that he had resolved the problem while still letting his children know he supported them in their difficulties with outsiders.

I had just come back from Damascus and was eager to hear how the children's hours of studying had paid off. In the study period that evening, they told me that most of the children had done well on their midyear exams. Abdalla got 240 out of 350; Lisa scored 225; Boulos was first in his class; and Hanna did well too. There was an ominous silence when it came to Muna, and they all turned expectantly toward her waiting for her to report the bad news. I asked her how she had done, and she admitted sheepishly that she had received only 160. "What does that mean?" I asked. "My teacher said that if I work very hard, I still may be able to pass grade 7 this year." Um Abdalla confessed later that they didn't know what they would do with her if she failed. "She's too young to stay home and do housework or run back and forth to the bakery. Maybe I could teach her sewing and let her make clothes for the family." It was a reflection of the times that they didn't immediately think of marriage, although Muna was already almost the same age as Um Abdalla had been when she was married.

It was a two-day school holiday, and the children had more free time than I had seen them have before. The weather was beautiful—an early spring day, not too hot and not too cold. Rain the night before had dampened the dust and released the odors of an earth coming back to life. I could see that the emotions of spring had stirred the older boys—Abdalla, Hanna, Boulos, and George—to gather spontaneously on a plot of land separating the two houses. They were kicking an empty can back and forth when they saw several classmates pass by carrying a soccer ball and heading down the main road to the village. They called out to the boys, and almost immediately a game of soccer was organized in the large empty area where they had been standing.

They were minutes into the game when Um Abdalla appeared and called Boulos—she needed him to do some shopping for her at the village store. Soon after, Abu Abdalla interrupted with a request that Hanna and Abdalla accompany him to the chicken houses, where because of the nice weather, it would be a good time to clean out the sheds for a general changeover of the chickens. The boys reluctantly left the game, dragging their feet but not verbally protesting their father's orders. I resisted the impulse to plead with their father to allow them to continue the game. "They're only boys," I would have said. "It's such a beautiful day, and they need to have some time to themselves to play." If I had, Abu Abdalla would have looked at me with surprise. "What, and leave the work undone? It's more important that the chicken houses are prepared for the next batch of chickens." The game continued on for a while with only George—his father was on a trip and so there was no one to demand his attendance at a job—and the village boys. Soon, from the lack of people to make it fun anymore, the other boys continued on their way toward the village center to find more players.

Later in the morning, when Um Abdalla felt the time was right, she sent the girls off to the kitchen to make the noonday meal while she remained in the "homework" room. The girls came back every now and then to ask her if the meat was thawed enough, where the oil was, how much of a certain spice they should use, how long they should cook the meat, and when they should add the vegetables. Um Abdalla sat with me peeling potatoes and then later, while they cooked, continued some sewing she had been doing before. I could feel that she was tempted to go help them but knew she was purposely restraining herself to give the girls practice in cooking by themselves so they would be prepared to do the work when the new baby came.

It was well into the evening. The boys were talking together and the girls were still at their homework. An old Lone Ranger show was on television, but the only one watching was Boulos. We all had gravitated to the television room when Abu Munir came by. That night he was not as deep in his cups as usual. He and Abu Abdalla were explaining their relationship to me. Their fathers were father's brother's son to each other so they were the same once removed. The reason for telling me all this, besides giving me a vital piece of information that I should know, was so that I would understand why Abu Munir stopped by so often and why Abu Abdalla took him in so graciously. The explanation was, of course, not completely valid, only convenient, since Abu Munir came around more frequently than did other relatives who were more closely related.

They began talking about the past and the time when Abu Abdalla was married. He was fifteen years older than Um Abdalla. "Women wear out quicker than men," Abu Abdalla said in my direction with a twinkle in his eye. As he hoped, I rushed to defend womankind by saying, "Not in my country, they don't! The women live, on average, to be older than men." "Well, in your country the women wear out the men from ordering them around so much," he returned, enjoying the discussion. "Here in Wusta our women take better care of us. There are several old men in the village who are over one hundred."

Um Abdalla sat quietly during this discussion, putting in a word now and then and sending me supportive glances, but continued to concentrate on folding laundry and repairing the seams of the school uniforms. She made each child two such uniforms at the beginning of the school year with material she bought in Damascus, blue for the children at the preparatory level and green for the ones at the elementary level. Though somewhat crudely tailored and given to pulling apart at the seams, the tailored uniforms nevertheless showed considerable sewing skill on Um Abdalla's part.

Abu Abdalla and Abu Munir were talking about why so many of the young men these days did not want to finish school. About half, they estimated, left school before they finished the last year of the secondary level, and some even before that. Abu Abdalla said that in his day, there really hadn't been any choice. By the end of the primary or intermediate school, times were so bad that most of the boys had to work to help their families. They blamed trucking for providing too attractive an incentive for young men now, even though most parents could afford and wanted to keep their sons in school until the end of the secondary level. Abu Abdalla had been one of those who had had to work immediately after elementary school.

There was a lull in the adults' conversation. Tonight the children were concentrating well on their homework, and there had been no interrup-

tions. The adult conversation had passed over the children's heads unre-
marked. Muna was happily doing the homework for her favorite subject,
sewing. She was supposed to cut out a piece of cloth to a certain measure-
ment and sew lines of different lengths and styles across it. Her father, undis-
tracted by his conversation with Abu Munir for a minute, became interested
in what she was doing. After watching for a while, he couldn't resist taking
the measure from her and cutting the right size cloth himself. She accepted
his help reluctantly but without protest. This was one subject for which she
had some aptitude. But Abu Abdalla felt that measuring the cloth correctly
was something he could do better than she. However, when it came to the
stitching, in which he had no interest, he gave it back to her.

A week later, the children were home again on holiday. Um Abdalla was
catching up on housework that was not part of the daily routine; this time
she was ironing a stack of clothes. The girls had just finished several hours of
housework and had come to sit with me near the stove. As usual, the fire had
been turned off at night and was not started up again until the chores were
done. The boys were up at the chicken house, and Abu Abdalla had gone into
Damascus to see if he could find some chicken feed. Um Abdalla was telling
me that the next day we really had to go to visit a friend's daughter who was
getting married. She had heard that the girl had received her *mahbass*. I
thought she was using a word meaning "bread-baking oven" and was surprised that the people of the village, who always bought from the bakery,
would find a bread-baking oven such an important gift. They laughed when
I asked about it and explained that no, I was thinking of another word. They
were talking about the word for *shebka*, using the Egyptian word more familiar to me that they had learned from the television serial, the gift of gold
jewelry that the bride received from her bridegroom.

   Lisa was sitting with us the following day when we were about to leave
for the visit, and in a rush of feeling for her, I asked if she couldn't come with
us as a diversion from her studies. Um Abdalla looked uncomfortable and
replied that it would be better if she stayed home and did her studying. Since
this was a time of day that Um Abdalla was usually not so insistent on the
children's doing homework, I was puzzled by her refusal. Later, when we
were alone, I asked why Lisa never went visiting with us, and she replied,
with some hesitation, that it would not look proper to take a daughter who
was close to marriageable age visiting to a household where there were eligible young men.

During the visit, even though we went especially to see the jewelry and were told it was worth S£60,000, we were unable to see it because it had been delayed in coming from the store. Apparently our visit satisfied the family, however, and Um Abdalla didn't feel she had to return to see the *mahbass* when it finally did come. The important thing was that we knew the price of the gift and had seen some of the dresses that were to make up the bride's trousseau.

One afternoon, Um Abdalla's mother, Um Nabil, came by with her small grandson Kamal. She announced, somewhat untactfully, that the only reason for her visit was that Kamal would not stop crying until she brought him to see his cousins. She regaled us for some time with stories of Kamal's delicate constitution and why it was wise not to disrupt it. She remarked that it was a full-time job for her to make sure he ate enough and didn't get sick; in her mind, the two were connected. She described how she sat with Kamal and encouraged him spoonful by spoonful to eat his meals. Even though she did the best she could, he often rejected most of what she offered. Just to show us what she meant, she interrupted her conversation to take some biscuits out of her purse and push them toward Kamal's mouth. He had been sitting next to her quietly watching the other children, momentarily so overcome by shyness that he was afraid to join them. Automatically, he responded to her overture with a shrug and a whiny rejection, pushing the biscuit away from his face and out of her hand. He then turned his attention back to the other children tumbling around the room.

Um Nabil turned back to us, and Kamal, now partially distracted by her attempts to push food at him, tried to take her hand and pull her with him to play with the children. But she had started another story, raising her voice higher and higher as his screams grew louder. Finally, he drowned out what she was saying, and she stopped abruptly. Mistaking his motivation, she turned and again offered him the biscuit he had rejected earlier. He refused it once more, with a frantic flailing of his arms that knocked the biscuit again from her grasp. During the rest of the visit, we watched with fascination this battle between the two, as the elderly Um Nabil scurried behind him with food and he alternated between rejecting the food and screaming to attract her attention if she turned to do anything else.

By this time, Um George's children had stopped their own play and were also watching the tug-of-war with interest, as though they were at a spectator sport, the two little boys soberly and the girls giggling at one another.

They found it considerably more entertaining than the television program—the Arabic version of *Sesame Street*—turned on in the background.
They had been engaged in a game of somersaults performed off the cushions
in the far corner of the room, but even though their play had been interrupted, none of them showed any interest in doing anything with little
Kamal, whom they regarded as not very much fun.

Finally, Um Nabil decided she had to get Kamal home before he became
"too tired." After they had gone, the room seemed strangely quiet with only
the ten of us left. Um Abdalla, always ready to see the bright side of things
and at this moment particularly disturbed that I had seen such a negative side
of her mother, remarked, "My father was a great man: he was strict but very
kind with all of us. Everyone in the village respected him. Unfortunately, he
died young from a lung disease when he was about sixty. My mother was a
good woman while he was alive and able to control her. Her problem is that
she loves her son and this boy to a point that is not good for either one of
them." Um Abdalla felt keenly the lack of warmth in her relationship with
her mother. Because Um Nabil showed little interest in her other grandchil
dren by Um Abdalla and Um George, they also showed little interest in her.
Indeed, when she visited, she ignored the children, not even bothering to
greet them when she entered the room.

According to Um Abdalla, though Kamal certainly was indulged, his situation was different from that of the girl, Lina, in the house we had visited
earlier. There the problem was more serious, everyone agreed, because people would be less tolerant of a spoiled female than of a spoiled male. The girl,
already difficult by nature, was subjected to inconsistent discipline from the
other members of the household, whereas little Kamal was consistently
overindulged by his grandmother, who had assumed full responsibility for
his care.

Um Abdalla didn't feel very well in her seventh month of pregnancy. She
couldn't sleep, and her hands and feet had begun to swell. For some reason,
during one of our morning coffee breaks, we started talking on the subject
of orphans. Um Abdalla and Um George were saying that there were not
many orphans in the village; in fact, there was only one case they could think
of offhand. This was the case of a family in which the wife died while delivering her sixth child. "Her husband had no one to look after the children,
so he put them in an orphanage in a nearby town. He wanted to marry again
but couldn't find any one from the village who would take care of some-

one else's six children. Eventually he found a woman from some other village who would marry him." Um George added, "You can imagine that she wasn't a woman who was being eagerly sought after in marriage. No one who had other options would leave her village and take on this kind of burden." Immediately after the marriage, the man brought the children home from the orphanage, and soon afterward when his second wife had her own baby, she was taking care of a total of seven children.

I realized that Um George's definition of orphan was different from mine. In her view, children became orphans when because of the circumstances of their parents, they could not be cared for at home. Indeed, according to her, under most circumstances, even when both parents died, children were not orphaned in the general sense as long as close relatives took care of them.

Um Abdalla went on to talk about another woman who died in childbirth from an asthma attack. "This woman had been told it would be bad for her to have babies, but what could she do? You can't get married and not have babies." I felt she was drawing a parallel with her own condition of endless babies. She continued on in a happier vein. "Our climate is good for people with asthma. One man from the village went to Algeria and nearly died from the condition, but when he came back to Wusta, he became well almost immediately." The implication was clear. If the woman who died in childbirth had only been left alone by her husband, she would be alive and well.

Muna burned the dinner last night and again tonight, and Um Abdalla was particularly bothered because she was hoping the girls could assume more of the work in the late months of her pregnancy. Uncharacteristically, she shouted angrily at Muna that she needed to be more careful and pay attention to what she was doing. Muna looked downcast and didn't answer. The next day, when Um Abdalla was out, Abdalla used the Molinex to grind some hard kernels of wheat just to see how the machine worked. Coming in while the experiment was in process, Um Abdalla shouted at him that it was not good for the machine to use it in that way. After such shouting outbursts, their mother walked around with a glowering look on her face while the children looked contrite and hurried to do things they were asked to do or anticipated things that would please her. The children looked genuinely distressed when they upset their parents. Both nights, when their father came home, Um Abdalla reported their misbehavior, and Abu Abdalla added his own words of more measured rebuke while the child in question hung his or her head silently. "Did you do what your mother said you did?" he questioned sternly. "Don't you know that you could break the Molinex?" It would not occur to them to contradict the reprimand outright. However, sometimes they would try to put their behavior in a more favorable light. Muna would say, "Well, I burned the dinner because I was out in the backyard getting fuel for the stoves and the goat had broken his tether. I was trying to tie him up again, and that's why I was late checking on the food." In such a case, Abu Abdalla would continue by saying that she was big enough to do things right.

During the time I was in Wusta, neither parent used corporal punishment that I was aware of, but there was the implied threat that such punishment might be used in cases of extreme misbehavior.

One night Lisa was reeling off the day's social studies in a monotonous chant. The lesson went something in the vein of "America is an imperialist nation bent on the destruction of the Arab homeland." It was the usual fare from her social studies book. I was listening and wondering, as I often did when I heard her memorizing these lessons, how she reconciled in her mind the fact that her parents harbored a guest in their house who came from this "imperialist nation destroying the Arab homeland." Lisa was a sensitive girl, and it seemed that if she were conscious of the content of what she was saying, she would either lower her voice or recite her lesson somewhere else where I couldn't hear what she said.

Suddenly, she broke off in midsentence as though reading my thoughts. I assumed that she realized she was saying something very negative about America in front of me, and I expected apologies or at least confusion about what she would do next. Instead she turned to me and asked very seriously and directly, "Is it true what they say, that America is a much better place to live than Syria? Which place do you like best?" Her question took me off guard, since it so obviously contradicted the sense of the lesson she had been memorizing and showed an inherent skepticism about the materials she was given in school.

Where had she heard that America was better than Syria? From the summer visitors? Apparently so, since these books or, for that matter, her teachers didn't require her to think about the content she was learning; she simply memorized the books mechanically and dutifully recited them the next day in school. There were many times when her far-off gaze or quick rejoinders to snatches of conversations showed how little of her attention was engaged in the memory work.

I returned to her question, which was not easy to answer.

I can't really say that America is better than Syria. They both have their good and bad points. I guess people always feel more comfortable where they grow up, near the people they know. America is a very beautiful country with a lot of variety in its scenery and people—you can find almost any kind of climate or geography you like. You would also probably like the technological parts and maybe the skyscrapers in the big cities. But I think I can tell you at least one thing you wouldn't like very much. Imagine that one of my sons lives in a part of the country I would have to drive almost a week to get to. My father lives about five hours' drive from me, my sister three days away. I don't get a chance to see them very often. Would you want to live where your close relatives lived so far away? I asked, not wanting her to think everything would be perfect there.

"Well no," Lisa answered, getting the point, "I could never live so far away from my parents and sister and brothers or my cousins." And then she added impatiently, "But still you haven't told me which country you like best."

"I like it here in Syria, and I especially like it with you in Wusta, but eventually I want to go back to be with my family in the United States. Do you understand that?"

She nodded and went back to her memory work: "America is an imperialist nation bent on the destruction of the Arab homeland. . . ."

Lisa stopped going to school on the first of May and spent the full month before exams studying at home. Already in April, she said, very few children in her ninth-grade class were attending school, even though it was still in session. Everywhere she went during that time, she had a book in her hand, reciting out loud the passages she was required to memorize for the exam. In the afternoon, her classmate Muna, a daughter of Um Samir, joined her, and the two of them walked back and forth in the lane behind the house. First one girl recited while the other listened and corrected, and then the other took a turn. This was the first time during the year I had seen the two girls meet after school to do things together. They were allowed to meet only at that time because their parents believed it was essential for them to study together to do well on the exam. Um Abdalla was taking great care during these days to be sure the children did not spend much time on chores, but this meant more work for her. There was an air of seriousness and much greater quiet during the evening study sessions. Unlike the midyear exams, there was no second chance with these end-of-the-year exams.

TEN

Toys and Play

[American child rearing] produces achievement-minded, independent, and future-oriented individuals who are largely free of ties that bind them in time and place.

— Florence Kluckholm

After the children were old enough to move around independently, that is, beyond the stage when they depended almost completely on their mother for their needs, they spent most of their time with brothers and sisters. I watched Ilyas go from babyhood to this stage while I was living in Wusta. When I arrived in the village, he was spending most of his day scooting around in a canvas seat on rollers that let him accompany his mother on her cleaning chores but left her hands free for her work. She had a high tolerance for his crying and came to his aid only when he didn't let up in his demands. The situation changed in the afternoon, when he was released from his walker to crawl among the cushions on the floor of the sitting room. There he commanded the bigger and more receptive audience of his brother George, his cousins from next door, Um Abdalla, Abu Abdalla, and often a guest or two. At that time of day when the hard work of housecleaning was over, his mother also was more accessible, and she became the magnet to which he returned between forays out to the others.

The children responded quickly to Ilyas's friendly overtures, seeing him as a delightful plaything to be included as much as possible in anything they did. They showed less resistance to his tears than the adults did, giving in easily to his demands. Um George or Um Abdalla rarely interfered in the children's play, even when it became rough, and consequently, pleas to them were useless in attracting sympathetic attention.

No sooner was Ilyas walking steadily than he was bundled up in the morning like the others and sent out to roam the space between Um George's and Um Abdalla's houses. For several hours the four preschoolers entertained one another, returning to their mother occasionally for a piece of bread, or care for cuts or bruises, or to go to the bathroom. Their shouts drifted cheerfully across a quiet landscape, where at that time of day, the only other movement came from the tethered goat and the chickens. Occasionally, their shouts turned to screams of disagreement, but Um George rarely paid any attention unless a hurt sounded serious. The children worked out their arguments alone or under the refereeship of their brother George or their cousins. The older children, however, could be just as indifferent to minor problems as their parents were, and as a result, children with grievances became accustomed to solving their problems themselves.

Because parents and older children were not around in the morning when the four youngest ones were left to their own devices, they resolved minor squabbles on a "might becomes right" basis, by which the older, stronger children took what they wanted and the younger children accepted their dominance. Parents wasted little time in arbitrating "fairness"—in seeing that each child was given equal treatment or in assessing the rightful share of blame or innocence in a child's argument with another. An implication of this situation—which seems like a contradiction—was that there were few conflicts among the children and that whatever conflicts there were, were over in a very short time. Children had no reason to establish either their "right to something" or their blamelessness in a quarrel, as these were not issues that attracted the attention of their elders, or anyone else for that matter.

It was not that judgments about right and wrong or fairness were not made in this household—just the contrary, there was a strong and uncompromising sense of what was right and wrong. But rather than holding children accountable to absolute standards, parents adjusted their expectations to what they felt were appropriate according to age, sex, and social criteria. If you were the oldest child in a group, you were likely to be held responsible for something that went wrong. If you were younger, your crime was likely to be insubordination to an older sibling or parent. If you were female, you were supposed to fulfill the expectations of appropriate feminine behavior, and if male, appropriate masculine behavior. There was no effort to mix these categories by treating children "equally." Thus, judgments about the rightness or wrongness of children's behavior were based on expectations regarding their age and gender characteristics relative to those of the persons with whom they were interacting at the moment. Within the space of a few hours, a child might be expected to behave in different ways if the cast of characters changed. Miriam, for example, was expected to obey her older cousins in the afternoon when they were together, but as oldest of the preschoolers, her mother held her responsible for any difficulties that the group encountered during their morning wanderings.

In general, not much was expected of children before the age of five or six. Until this age, behavior of almost any kind was tolerated. Adults and older children were quick to indulge the whims of little children as soon as they were expressed. Abu Adil would rev up his big truck and take the little boys for rides even when it was inconvenient, simply because they wanted to go. Um George would pick up one of the small boys who had persisted in harassing the older children during homework and give him a playful slap and then hold him in a long bear hug until he laughed with glee and forgot what he had been after. She did not tell him to stop bothering the students or reprimand him for his behavior. *No* was not a commonly used word in the household. Um Abdalla indulged her small nieces and nephews in the same way when they stopped by her house during the morning, and she rarely complained, despite the extra work they made for her. The children moved freely between the two houses—self-confident and assured of a good reception wherever they went, scattering clothing, pillows, and other household items and disorganizing the careful arrangement of the houses, yet they were never made to feel there was anything wrong with what they did.

One day I watched a father in the village playing ball with his four-year-old son. The game involved kicking the ball gently to the boy who then had to make a "goal" between two stones placed behind the father. This game went on for some time, and each time the ball went to the son, he made the goal without much resistance, even though on each attempt the father feigned difficulty in holding him off. The father didn't challenge the child or prevent him from making the goal; he simply let him win time after time. I had seen American fathers in similar situations "challenge" their sons by making a few goals themselves or occasionally wresting the ball from their children. Whereas the Syrian father built his son's confidence by ensuring that he was not frustrated by a lack of skill, the American father challenged his son to improve his skills. Both fathers undoubtedly acted out of conviction that what they were doing encouraged their children's development at this stage in their lives. Perhaps it was my imagination, but many Arab children—boys in particular—seemed to possess a confidence that is not so evident in American children of the same age.

An Egyptian once told me, when I remarked on this "indulgence" of small children, that it was necessary to develop a child's personality at this age, or the child might either become timid or develop personality disorders. It was, she said, much better to indulge than to discipline young children, since discipline suppressed what was natural in them and might even change traits that gave them their unique personalities.

The kinds of indulgences that parents chose to provide, of course, molded the children according to deep-seated assumptions. Abu Adil, for example, was much more likely to "indulge" the little boys in their desire to ride around in his truck than he was to do the same for the little girls, and Um George was more likely to "indulge" the little girls in their desire to shape a cookie than she was to do the same for the little boys. Generally speaking, however, there didn't appear to be rigid prescriptions applied to the children at this age, and Ilyas might also be given a chance to form cookies if he insisted. The indulgence was more a "giving in" to the child in what he or she wanted to do. Parents in no way construed the indulgence as an excuse to "teach" children to cook or learn other adult skills. I could see myself in the same situation turning the indulgence into a learning experience so that my boys would become familiar with the tasks of adulthood.

It was the kind of rainy morning with low clouds hanging over the valley that made it pleasant to stay indoors next to the stove. The small cousins had come over to see us and were momentarily absorbed in a box of Legos their father had brought back from the Gulf the day before. They scattered the pieces widely while searching out the pieces that interested them. It took them some time before they could make the pieces stick together, and none of the adults thought it important to show them how to do it properly. Eventually, as they became proficient with the little blocks, they put together more and more pieces until they formed a kind of building structure. The older children looked longingly at the Legos but wanted to get their homework out of the way so they would be free for their holiday the next day. Every now and then, Muna, who was sitting on the cushions closest to the little children, stopped her work for a minute and suggested an innovation in their construction before turning back to her work.

None of the adults showed any interest in the blocks, although it was probably the first time they or the older children had seen such a toy. It was likely that Abu Adil had seen the Legos in a store in Dubai and, attracted to the pictures on the box and wanting to bring something back to his family, had purchased it. The bigger boys on their bench, who were also concentrating conscientiously on their schoolwork, seemed oblivious to the construction and the noise of the younger children. As soon as they finished, however, they joined in a game of trying to use up every piece in the kit to make a gigantic construction. The next day in their spare time, the children again worked together, building a single new construction. Thereafter, the kit disappeared and was not seen again. Their mother had become tired of picking up the tiny pieces and had removed it to a high shelf.

Toys and their use in children's play reflect significant aspects of growing up in different societies. I thought of the houses of my American friends who, when their children were small, had walls of shelves to contain the numerous toys considered a necessary part of a household with children. Most were "manipulatives" that usually came as parts of puzzles, construction sets, or alphabet letters or numbers and were supposed to be assembled creatively or in some specified pattern that provided a learning experience to give a child a head start in skill development. Neatly packaged in the store, such toys promised much more than they delivered, and as usually happened, they ended up as a heap of plastic bits on the playroom floor.

During my children's early years, our household managed to avoid the mountains of plastic, not so much from intent as from the fact that in Saudi Arabia where we were living in the late 1960s and early 1970s, children's toys of any kind were difficult to find. Once a year, we ordered from the United States a single "big" toy for each of the boys, and the rest of the year they made do with the "natural" toys in our vicinity, riding the donkey cart bringing water to neighborhood gardens, helping the man next door build his house, turning a packing crate into a cabin, working with the gardener to construct a flower bed, building sand castles, playing in swimming pools. By the time we returned to the United States for a home stay of several years, I was ready to make it up to my children for the years without American toys. What a surprise to find them uninterested in the "manipulatives" I produced. To them, they were merely toy replicas of the real objects that had been at their disposal in Saudi Arabia.

Looking back on these experiences from the vantage point of Wusta, I was beginning to see how toys reflect the way a society perceives its children. Some, like ours, think that children need many years of fantasy practice with toys as props to learn the various roles of adult life. Activities such as sports and play groups create arenas in which children practice relationships of teamwork, competitiveness, cooperation, leadership, and the like before being entrusted with the same real-life adult relationships. Other societies, like Wusta, see children as miniature adults who are eased into adult roles by working side by side with adults to learn the skills they need for everyday life. From an early age, the Wusta children practice adult behaviors and responsibilities in relation to children who are younger than themselves. Like learning to chop the parsley under the watchful eye of the adult, they first learn to do the peripheral jobs well before being entrusted with more critical responsibilities.

Is there significance in these separate approaches to preparing children for adult responsibilities? Is the American approach of "playing roles" a way in which our society procrastinates, by keeping children busy until they complete the lengthy educations they need to become successful adults? In Wusta, is it for practical reasons that children are hurried into meaningful responsibilities so soon?

Toys accomplish other missions for a society, I was told by a Dutch friend who raised her children beside mine in Saudi Arabia. She explained that her compatriots believe a child's aesthetic sense is developed by the quality of the toys they have around them—their purity of color, the simplicity of their basic lines, and their overall artistic quality. It was always a pleasure to visit her home and see her children's playthings. For the most part, they did not break into little bits, and each was intended to have many purposes, so that little children could make up their own minds about how they should be used.

I hardly had time to set down my bundles on my return from the Christmas holidays in Damascus before Muna and Um George appeared simultaneously at my door. Abu Abdalla and Um Abdalla had gone to pay their condolences to a family in which the old father had just died. My room was still cold, so we went over to the warmth of Um George's kitchen where the fragrance of molasses hung in the air. Um George had just finished making *dips* pudding for the New Year. While the kettle was heating, she took me to see their Christmas decorations in the newly constructed best parlor. There, in a corner, stood a plastic Christmas tree decorated with tinsel and colored balls, exactly like the one Um Abdalla had in her best parlor—the sisters had bought two at a special bargain price. The tree's location in the cold, not yet regularly used, best parlor suggested that its primary purpose was to bedazzle guests who came to call during the holiday season and was not a main part of the family's festivities.

Um George caught me up on events. Abu Adil had been delayed again during his most recent trip to the peninsula, but this time it was for a happier reason. He had found extra work to make up for the income lost during the disastrous trip when his truck was damaged. He had been away twenty-five days but had promised Um George he would compensate for his long absence by staying longer at home until after the holidays were over.

This time, along with the complicated embroidery I usually worked on, I brought a simple piece of cross-stitch work from Damascus for Miriam to do. She was a serious little girl who seemed unusually good with her hands. When I had offered to let her do a stitch or two on my embroidery, she had been pleased, but the stitches of my embroidery were so tiny that she had difficulty finding the right holes to stick the needle through. Nevertheless, she did her best, as much, it seemed, to please me as from any pleasure she got out of the work itself.

For some reason, I had become a love object to Miriam, which made her embarrassed when the other children called attention to it. On my way over to Um George's this morning, I saw her playing with her sister, Lisa. The two were almost identical in size, although Lisa was younger by a year. But there the likeness stopped. Miriam had dark hair and honey-colored skin, and Lisa was an ash brunette with pale skin. Their personalities differed, too. Miriam was quiet and intense like her father, a born presence whom the younger children readily deferred to. Lisa was more sociable and preferred to take her cues from other people's initiatives. She was quick to notice details that she could use to manipulate the other children, teasing them on sensitive points.

The two sisters stopped their play to watch me pass on my way to Um George's, and Lisa turned expectantly to see the reaction on Miriam's face. Miriam's dark skin turned a crimson red in an unmistakable blush, and she turned quickly to run away and hide behind the wall where we could not see her. I said hello to Lisa, who stood firmly holding her ground and shyly twisting the corner of her coat, but she did not answer.

Within half an hour, as if drawn by a magnet, the shadowy figure of

Miriam slipped quietly into the family room where Um George and I had settled and nestled in her customary place by my side. I dared not move for fear my notice of her would cause her to run away again. As usual, she watched me closely and began imitating my actions, slowly and unobtrusively so as not to attract her sister's notice. Her sister, however, soon saw what was happening and exchanged glances with her, Lisa's a triumphant "caught-you-in-the act" look and Miriam's a threatening "I'll-kill-you-if-you-say-anything" return look.

Still, Miriam couldn't resist. I crossed my legs, she crossed hers. I smoothed down my skirt, she smoothed down her skirt. I folded my hands, she folded hers. I shook my bracelets loose from my sleeve, and she shook imaginary bracelets loose. In a few days she would be wearing plastic bracelets she had begged her mother to buy for her at the village "boutique."

I slowly pulled out my embroidery along with the special piece I had bought for her and slipped hers into her lap. The stitches had been started that would form a butterfly in the middle of the hoop. She was startled that her game of imitation has been interrupted but picked up the embroidery. I showed her how to pull the threads through the holes to make the pattern, explaining that the picture would become a butterfly when she filled in all the markings on the cloth. I helped her take the first stitches, and she settled in to work.

There were troubles with her mother almost from the start. "Oh, Um Dawud, it's very nice of you to bring her the embroidery, but really, she is too young to learn how to do embroidery." "I will teach her, Um George, don't worry. Won't it be nice that she will be able to do it by herself?" Um George looked unconvinced. I sat patiently, with little Miriam by my side doing a reasonably acceptable job on her embroidery. Every now and then I rescued her from a minor mistake, but she had ability, as I suspected, and did well under my supervision.

That evening I visited Um George again, but the embroidery was nowhere in sight. "We need to continue the lesson, Um George," I said, and she took the missing embroidery from a high cupboard, where I also noticed some stuffed animals and the Legos that the children's father had given them. "She gets it all mixed up," Um George said impatiently, and I learned that in my absence Miriam had come to her mother a number of times for help in untangling her thread.

I spent some time correcting the problems in the embroidery, and soon Miriam was at work again, this time with Muna also sitting at our elbow offering advice. Miriam did well for a while but soon tired of the work and put it down to go to the bathroom. Immediately Muna seized it and started to work on it herself—a somewhat aggressive act yet not remarked by the sleepy Miriam when she returned. The pattern was not very large, and I began to worry that the competent Muna would complete it and spoil Miriam's sense of accomplishing the work herself. But I didn't say anything—and Miriam passively watched while Muna continued to work on the piece.

Each day it became more and more difficult to find the embroidery when we went to look for it, and Um George was obviously reaching a level of irritation with the project that did not bode well for its completion. In the end, it became such a problem to retrieve the embroidery against Um George's resistance that both Miriam and I resigned ourselves to its disappearance— I with disappointment and she without any apparent emotion.

Later, thinking back over this episode, I saw that I was again setting up a learning experience for Miriam that didn't work very well for either her or the others around her. I assumed that the younger she was, the more everyone would be impressed that she had learned such an intricate skill. Even though the task was difficult, I thought that my one-on-one attention would enable her to succeed. I wanted her to feel she could successfully complete the work alone. If she had finished it, I would have told everyone, "Look how clever she is—only five years old, but she can do embroidery all by herself." I wanted it to be her work so I could emphasize the "all by herself" part. That was why I was unhappy when Muna took it over.

I also was pleased with myself to be taking the time to teach Miriam— pleased with her company and pleased I would be able to leave something tangible after I had gone. I assumed that Miriam's mother would be happy for her to learn this nice womanly skill. After all, both Um Abdalla and Um George were proud of the sequined Madonnas they had embroidered to hang on the walls of their parlor. They must have believed this was a skill that every girl needed to know before she married.

What I didn't count on was her mother's disapproval. Um George judged a child's efforts by how much she contributed to, or at least didn't detract from, the family welfare. Children shouldn't be asked to do work or learn skills until they were old enough to do them properly. She believed that a child who was too young to manipulate thread and needle well should not be asked to do embroidery, since learning when too young took longer and consumed the energy of others in trying to ensure a successful product. She didn't feel that embroidery was important enough to consume adult time in something that, at best, might produce only indifferent results.

On her side, Miriam was not used to having something of her own, separate from the other children. She didn't feel the sense of "ownership" in the embroidery that I was expecting. Instead, she was perfectly happy to let Muna work on it and finish it. Furthermore, what for her had been an interesting activity—helping a fascinating foreigner with the adult activity of stitching a fine embroidery—lost its appeal when it became a child's activity with coarse cloth and thick thread that she was supposed to do herself. With this embroidery, I not only drew her away from the more pleasurable activity of doing things with the other children but also removed her from the work we had been doing together on my embroidery. I tried to individualize the lesson—to make it hers while keeping the other children away. They, of course, could not help gravitating to a place where an interesting activity was going on and were puzzled at their exclusion from Miriam's work. As a consequence, the embroidery drew the rapt focus of their attention—in much the same way they had watched the Damascene children next door with their commando games—waiting to see what would happen next but knowing they had not been invited to join. I should have figured out a way to make it more fun for everyone, including Miriam, by making it a joint project. It took her sigh of resignation at being handed the embroidery for me to realize what a burden I had imposed on her. She did it to please me and not because she enjoyed it.

Eventually, we reverted to the old pattern of Miriam's helping me, and soon she was happily back at my side taking a stitch or two every now and then. I drew Um George's attention to the rather sweet way she imitated me, but Um George barely responded. Children were given to impractical and frivolous behaviors, and "cuteness" was not something the practical Um George found very interesting. She ran a house, and what interested her was the contribution that each child made to its smooth functioning or, because of age and limited capacity, to the workload she faced. The embroidery increased her burden because of the time and energy required to untangle the incorrect stitches and the distraction it created for George in doing his homework. Homework was the only children's activity to which Um George adjusted her household activities.

It was easier for me to communicate with the girls at Um Abdalla's, partly because we all were females and therefore shared an unspoken though clear assumption of mutual interest. But there was another reason, too. The girls were demonstrably more voluble than their brothers, as was clear when the children began squabbling. The girls' quarrels, when they had any, usually came near the end of the homework period, at the end of a long day of sitting in class, working on household projects, and studying in the homework room. By that time, the children were badly in need of a diversion.

The girls usually fought with words. Lisa, assuming a parent-like posture, would become impatient with the fidgeting Muna and shout at her to sit still and study. She felt responsible for seeing her sister take a more serious approach to schoolwork and seemed embarrassed as much for herself as for Muna when her sister came home with poor marks. It irritated her to see Muna waste so much time in the study room when she might be memorizing her schoolwork and getting better grades.

Muna chafed under her older sister's reprimands but usually did not respond with more than a quick retort. She knew her parents would support Lisa's "bossing," which reinforced their own interest in making Muna study harder. On her side, Muna might still be smarting from the fact that Lisa had worn the socks to school that morning that she had been intending to wear. Although she rarely confronted her older sister directly in front of her parents, she would sulk for a while and then, in retaliation, disturb the careful alignment of books Lisa had piled up in anticipation of school the next day. Lisa would order her to stop and then, escalating the conflict, tell Muna that her uniform stuck out in a peculiar way in the back—knowing full well how important appearance was to her sister. Frustrated, Muna might shout at her cousin little Ilyas, further down in the age line, for breaking her ruler and complain to her mother that she would get in trouble with the teacher. Both girls felt a strong tension in regard to school, Lisa because she was obsessed with doing well and Muna because she was not doing well. Each had a major point of weakness that the other knew how to exploit—the older one, her need for order, and the younger one, her concern with appearance.

Being less verbal, the boys were more difficult to understand. They released their pent-up energies in physically aggressive behavior. Boulos, who usually finished his homework first, might grab a plastic playing card, one of a deck that Hanna had been playing with. Hanna would sit on top of him, not because he wanted the card, but because he needed a way to retaliate; later, the cards would be sitting in the middle of the floor, and Boulos would take them up again without resistance. Or Abdalla might accidentally poke his pencil into Hanna's arm, causing the latter to retaliate with a harder poke that would begin a series of pokes back and forth until their parents noticed. Abu Abdalla would finally say "Abdalla!" in warning tones, focusing on the older of the provocateurs, who should have known better. Hanna would snicker and look triumphantly at his brother, who had been singled out for reprimand.

Although household items might be involved in squabbles, rarely were they the main cause for a quarrel between siblings. Because the children considered very little in the household to be their own private property, there was little reason to fight over ownership. Household items, including the rare toy that was available, were used by everyone, individually or collectively as it seemed appropriate at the moment. The major exceptions were schoolbooks, notebooks, and writing equipment, all of which were the personal property of individual schoolchildren and a generally overlooked way that education may exert an individualizing effect on families. The reason, of course, was a system that required different books and different equipment at each grade level.

I was intrigued by what seemed to be the children's lack of possessiveness. As I noted earlier, there were few "toys" around the house, and when Abu Adil brought something back from Saudi Arabia for the children, like the Lego blocks, they played with them for a few days, and then they disappeared, in the same fashion as the embroidery, to a high shelf in the family room. On one visit to the village, I decided to see what would happen if I brought a single toy as a gift for all the children. Would there be arguments over its use? Would one child take it for his or her own private use? What would the children do with the toy, and how would they relate to one other when playing with it?

Feeling somewhat guilty at experimenting with them, I nevertheless set about making my preparations. I chose a toy with no predetermined pattern for its use, so that all the children, regardless of their ages, could play with it. The toy I choose was a stick of wood, shaped like a piece of molded bannister, with a rubber wheel fixed at the middle. It was commonly used in the States as an aid in exercise: the hands were supposed to be placed on the protruding handles, and in the motion of a push-up, the user rolled back and forth on the wheel. The toy had been a "bonus" thrown in with a bicycle bought for my children when they were younger.

I presented the wheel toy to Um George's family on the first evening of my return from Damascus while the older children were still studying. This gave the younger children a chance to experiment with it alone. At first, they tumbled around with it, swinging it over their heads and rolling it on the tiled part of the floor. The older children glanced up from their studies now and then to watch, and Um George, as usual, looked at it with irritation for the disturbance it was causing the students.

After George and Boulos finished their schoolwork, they joined the play, with some creative new uses for the toy. The younger children willingly relinquished the toy and stood watching to see what the older boys would do. First, they stacked their schoolbooks in piles to make a base for inclining some cushions off the floor. Tentatively, they rolled the wheel down the incline, but there wasn't enough pitch, and so they had to build the book base higher. They tried different angles of incline, discussing how many books they would need to make it move fast enough to continue to the other side of the room. There was cooperation in the venture: whoever was closest to the top of the incline would be handed the wheel and would start it in motion down the slide. Another child collected it at the bottom. Adil, Lisa, and Miriam were attracted back to active participation by the excitement of trying to make the wheel reach the wall. Adil would collect the wheel at the bottom of the incline and run back to give it to the other children to start it rolling down again. The older boys adjusted the incline with each roll until the incline was enough for the wheel to smack into the wall with each trial, and then they told Adil to leave it alone to see if it would roll that far. Adil did as he was told. By about the fourth successful trial, when the outcome was no longer in doubt, Miriam, sitting along its path, stuck out her foot and deflected the wheel. The big boys were losing their enthusiasm for what had become a successful roll, and when Miriam interfered, they sat back on the cushions and ignored the wheel.

The older Lisa, sensing Miriam's desire to try something new, asked if she would like a ride on the wheel. Miriam nodded agreement, and Lisa told her to balance her feet on the handles while she held her up and gave her a "ride" across the room. Adil wanted Lisa to give him a turn, too, and waited patiently until Miriam had finished her turn. Lisa alternated back and forth between the two until they were tired of the rides. Then, with George's help, Lisa lifted baby Ilyas onto the handles, but he was so limp in her hands that after a minute or two of trying to give him a ride, they gave up the effort.

George and Hanna then attempted to do the same thing, first one and then the other, without much success. First, one tried pushing while the other balanced. In this way, the toy continued to pass from hand to hand smoothly with no quarrels about who should use it next. One took it until he or she was done, and then another would either take over or join the first. Others watched until it was free. A younger child might snatch it from an older child, and for a while, the older child would help the younger child try something new until the younger one tired of the play and turned to something else. Later, the older one would disentangle the toy from the younger by saying, "Look, I want to show you something." By the end of the evening, the toy sat alone in the corner. I watched Um George returning the sitting room to a semblance of order with resignation, since she didn't want to offend me by complaining about the damage the toy had caused. One by one she replaced the cushions in their proper places and straightened the rug which had bunched up at the edges near the tiled floor that had served as the roadway for the wheel. Feeling guilty about the shambles that "my" toy had produced, I went to help her straighten up.

The next morning, while the others were at school, the four preschoolers took the toy outside. Adil sent it down the three outside steps between the upper garden and the porch at Um Abdalla's. It bounced in spectacular leaps, to the children's excited amusement, before it bumped against the house. They tried this several times before turning to something else. Next, Miriam helped Adil find a board which they laid down one side of the stairs. They dragged the wheel to the top and let it go. This time it moved in a smoother trajectory across the veranda. Adil tried to sit on the wheel before it moved down the slide, but Miriam showed him that it wouldn't work. He accepted her guidance and was content to roll the wheel down the board for a while. Meanwhile, his brother, Ilyas, barely toddling around, sat on the ground sucking his thumb and looking sleepy. Little Lisa halfheartedly helped out by collecting the wheel and returning it to Adil but then retreated to the observer's role she often adopted around the more aggressive Miriam.

After a while, Miriam realized that they could use the board that had acted as an incline as a seesaw, by putting it across the stool that sat under my window. Adil and Miriam dragged the stool to an open spot, and Miriam showed Adil how to sit on one end of the board while she sat on the other. They seesawed awkwardly up and down for a bit, giving Lisa a turn and then, with Miriam's help, a turn for little Ilyas. As they had the night before, the children moved smoothly from activity to activity, allowing all the children who wanted one a chance to participate in each intriguing new invention.

Miriam eventually wandered off and noticed a small onion with its stem still attached lying on the back porch. She picked it up and fingered it absently and then swung it around in the air a few times while she watched an argument developing between the boys. Adil accused Ilyas of sitting in his way as he tried to climb up and down the stairs. He was about to push Ilyas down the stairs when Miriam intervened to tell one to walk down one side and the other down the other side. They began to make the stair climbing a game of up one side and down the other, in faster and faster steps. Ilyas crawled partway, and Adil caught up and tumbled over him.

Miriam returned to her preoccupation with the onion. She walked up the embankment to the upper dirt area and, with a stick she happened to find there, dug a small hole in the ground and put the onion in it. Then she carefully replaced the dirt around it and stamped on it. Next she went over and picked up a can that was used for filling the *tanakas* of diesel fuel for the stoves, filled it with water from the outside tap, and took it over to water the onion. She returned several times with tins of water to pour on other, dry wintery sticks of the previous year's garden. The other children followed her in a little troop from faucet to planting. When they finished the watering, they all moved off toward home and out of my view from the back window. The wheel lay abandoned at the foot of the stairs.

Perhaps the answer to my question about possessiveness was that the children rarely took, or felt they had a right to take, exclusive control of any possession. My new toy—even though novel as toys generally were—was treated like furnishings and other household items, common to all. The children did not articulate "fairness" rules about its use. Rather, they assumed that the toy was to be shared instead of being used in "turns," during which one individual was given exclusive use in timed intervals of equal duration. The children never showed any inclination to do this kind of accounting, nor did they play with the toy alone. Indeed, they went out of their way to elicit cooperation from the other children or, if they were older, to help the younger children enjoy the play at a level that was suitable for them.

This behavior in the children seemed almost "too good to be true." But as I thought about it, the logic was apparent. The sharing came from three sources in the children's upbringing: being accustomed to approaching any activity as a group; not seeing toys or anything else as private possessions; and the older children's ingrained sense of responsibility for the younger children. These guidelines for behavior were already so strongly inculcated in these children—all less than six years of age—that they automatically conformed to them in play.

There also was probably one more important point that contrasted with the context in which my own children operated, and that was the absence of the parental factor. Parents kept out of children's play by neither remarking on it nor becoming arbiters in what the children did. The children, therefore, did not keep an ear tuned to their parents' reactions or expect their parents to intervenc in their affairs.

ELEVEN

Lessons

Culture hides much more than it reveals and strangely enough what it hides, it hides most effectively from its own participants. Years of study have convinced me that the real job is not to understand foreign culture but to understand our own.

— Edward T. Hall, *The Silent Language*

It was my last week in Wusta and I was reluctant to go. I was too enmeshed in the lives of the families to leave easily, and it seemed an especially bad time to go because of the many unresolved episodes in their lives. Um Abdalla was about to have her baby, and I had hoped it would come while I was there so I could repay her kindnesses by helping out with the children. (Instead, the baby came a week after I left.) All the schoolchildren were about to take their exams and would then know whether the long evenings in the "study room" had been worth the effort. For Lisa and Muna, at least, the results were crucial—Lisa, so she could move on to high school, and Muna, because she was so close to failing a grade. Once again, Abu Adil had taken his truck off to Saudi Arabia, and we were especially concerned because of the tension building up along the borders at that time. I didn't know it then, but in a matter of days, in June 1982, Israel would invade south Lebanon and among the many disruptions that followed was the effective cutoff of trade in fruits and vegetables coming out of Lebanon. Also, the supply of chicken feed almost entirely dried up, leaving Abu Abdalla wondering how to continue raising chickens. There were already enough signs of politically troubled times ahead to warn me that as an American and an "enemy of Syria," according to the rhetoric of the press, it was better for me to leave the village before I caused embarrassment to my hosts.

For a few hours every morning for a week, I reviewed what I had learned in Wusta and found to my surprise that I had learned more than I thought about family life in the village. To understand the fundamental differences better, I continually asked myself, "How would I, or Americans like me, react in this situation?" The purpose was not to judge the rightness or wrongness of either of our actions but to try to understand both our worldviews better. By carefully analyzing the behaviors of the Wusta parents and children, I felt I would find consistent elements leading ultimately to some of the general principles organizing their worldview. Then, by noting the different way I would approach the same issues, I might better understand my own behavior as a parent. Hall's comment about culture's hiding itself most effectively from its own participants often proved true in my immediate reactions to what the Wusta parents did. Being a parent is an intimate and personal experience that is not easily distanced or objectified.

In Wusta, people believed in a family ideal—which could not always be realized—that family members should remain close, physically and emotionally, all their lives. In theory, the composition of families changed only through natural causes like birth and death even while living members were actually moving in and out of households for compelling reasons like marriage and distant employment. Most parents hoped their sons would bring their wives to live under the family roof, even though they knew that modern couples preferred to live in separate homes of their own.

Parents acted on their hopes whenever they could. They built additions to their homes for sons and tried to contract marriages for daughters with nearby relatives or other villagers so that they, too, would stay in the vicinity. If circumstances forced grown children to establish families outside the village, the children would feel obligated to visit frequently and keep in touch by any means possible. For grown children, any inconvenience there might be in the obligation to stay close to parents was tempered by their belief that the parents' home was the place where they found the best food and the warmest welcome and were most at ease.

My American friends and myself expected something different. All else being equal, American parents and children were expected to live together under one roof only until the children were old enough—usually in their twenties—to support themselves elsewhere. Parents groaned when an adult child unexpectedly returned home for an extended stay, and although they took them in, it was always in the expectation that the stay was temporary until they "got themselves together again." Those who stayed too long with parents ran the risk of being considered pathologically dependent, in the sense that the aging postman in the popular television serial *Cheers* was an object of ridicule because he could not live without his "Ma." Also different from Wusta, the adult children of my friends frequently lived with others of their generation, not because, as in Wusta, they felt a compelling bond of blood or marriage, but because sharing living space was a temporary convenience for housekeeping, sex, companionship, or sharing expenses. It was a practice that would have been incomprehensible to the Wusta villagers.

In Wusta, there were three types of family that conformed with people's notions of what family life should be. The most ideal was exemplified by the family of the wealthy Abu Ilyas, in which several generations lived under one roof. A second was extended in the limited sense of Abu Abdalla's and Abu Adil's households. Even though they were living under separate roofs, they still cooperated in many daily activities. The final type, exemplified by Nabil's family, was one in which the married sons established self-contained households away from other family members. Although this last kind of family had the smallest number of cohabitating persons, the essential members—mother, father, and children—were present. Other household arrangements, such as a widow living with her children or someone living "alone," as was the case of Um Yusef and her grandson or an elderly couple without children, were seen as arrangements that arose by accident and not by choice. Villagers viewed such people as *miskiin*, a word meaning being both pitiable and miserable.

It would be difficult to predict what kinds of families the children of Um and Abu Abdalla would form as they grew older. Circumstances might lead them to options different from those offered to their parents. Abdalla, Hanna, and Boulos, for example, might decide to bring their wives into the family to help run the many family enterprises, thus becoming an extended family similar to that of the rich Abu Ilyas. Or alternatively, they might set up separate households near one another and run the various family businesses independently. In that case, they might merge some of their activities in the same way their parents did with Um George and Abu Adil next door. Perhaps Boulos would become the professional the family hoped for and would move to Damascus to be nearer his work. Many factors were likely to influence these decisions, such as whether Abu Abdalla remained alive and exerted the authority to keep the boys under one roof, whether everyone in the household remained compatible, and whether the main income came from businesses whose profits could be shared easily. With foresight, Abu Abdalla was building a variety of options for his boys that might encourage them to remain at home. The girls, of course, would eventually settle in those places chosen by their husbands.

With so much emphasis on family, the people of Wusta viewed members of the family circle as "insiders," a category distinctly different from that of "outsiders." In the exceptional case in which people did not fit, it was possible to reassign them to a more appropriate category in order to maintain the correctness of the theory. Accordingly, Um Abdalla's estranged mother could be treated as an outsider, and someone like Abu Munir who spent a lot of time around the house could be drawn closer by emphasizing his distant blood relationship.

The family behaved differently toward outsiders. They were suspicious of them and consciously controlled their interactions with them. Normally, relationships with outsiders were manipulated toward specific objectives, and in theory, relations that were no longer important could be terminated simply by letting the time between visits lengthen indefinitely. In most cases, people "balanced" their relations with outsiders. That is, what they gave was reciprocated equally by the other—the same number of visits, an equal value in gifts, one favor for another, and so on. When one side "unbalanced" the relationship by giving either more or less than was due, the other looked for an explanation: "What do they want?" or "What is the problem?" Consequently, outsider relationships were precarious, since one side was always in the position of "owing" something to the other.

Events that required obligatory visits, such as marriage, illness, death, and birth, gave a family the chance to find out the status of relationships among their circle of acquaintances. Weddings offered an especially concrete accounting in the value of gifts. Families kept mental notes so that when they gave return gifts, they could be sure to select something of similar or greater value. Almost as tangible were events like illness, where the number and length of visits substituted for gifts as a measure of friendship. For example, when Abu Abdalla was sick, he knew who wanted to maintain friendly relations with him by the stream of well-wishers who came to visit. Many came not so much out of concern for his health as for the power he wielded in his government job. Abu Abdalla kept mental note of who came and went, as did Um Abdalla and Um George when they discussed the list of visitors each morning at our coffee break. Each "active" acquaintance was expected to come at least once during his convalescence and would store up more "credit" if he came several times. Those who were continuously present at the sickbed, like Abu Adil and Abu Munir, were people with a special relationship whose closeness with Abu Abdalla others noted as potentially useful if at a later date they wished to conduct business with him.

An alternative to conducting "balanced," evenly reciprocal relations with outsiders was for the two sides to agree tacitly that one occupied a superior position. In such cases, the "weaker" was always obliged to visit the "stronger," since it was the weaker who hoped to gain the most by the visits. As the Arabic proverb says, "Call even a dog 'Sir' if you need something from him." The powerful Abu Abdalla rarely made visits around the village unless he needed something in particular. Instead, petitioners came to him with requests. One day, however, he visited a distantly related man and brought him a chicken as a gift because he needed the man's truck to carry chicken feed back from Damascus. The truck owner didn't return his call because lending the truck more than compensated for Abu Abdalla's gift and visit. This was one of the few times that Abu Abdalla went as a petitioner; almost always he was the one petitioned.

There usually had to be some common interest that initially brought outsiders together: distant kinship, business connections, childhood friendships, contemporaneous schooling, or other similar interests. Neighborliness was one of the best reasons for maintaining close relations. Praised in proverbs ("Choose your neighbor before you choose your house") and in the warmth associated with the term *jarti* (neighbor), neighbors were sometimes expected to be even closer than kin. For instance, when Abu Antoine was bedridden, his claim on Um Abdalla for a visit was that he had been a friendly neighbor to her family when she was growing up. Um Samir and Um Munir could justify their close friendship because they were neighbors. Neighborliness was the excuse for the deaf Um Yusef to stop by regularly and for me to take the liberty of becoming so much a fixture of the family's activities. After starting out as outsiders, we became "honorary" insiders based on our proximity as neighbors—with a formal accounting of our visits no longer necessary. It took me time to realize that her use of the term *neighbor* for me was the way that Um Abdalla included me in her close circle of friends.

Although relationships with outsiders usually started because of a broad mutual interest, actual visits took place for more focused reasons: conducting business, returning a necessary visit, looking in on an ailing member of a family, offering condolences at a death, or taking part in events like a wedding. The unstated reason for these visits was that others would reciprocate at a later date. Because there was usually a motive for visits, the hosts remained somewhat reserved if they were not sure why their guests had come. Too effusive a welcome might make it easier for the guest to request favors that would be difficult to refuse. This was the awkward situation that Abu Abdalla faced one day when a visitor wanted to borrow his tractor, and as a host he felt required to grant his guest's request. Requests were hardest to refuse when people of status—like the summer visitors—came to call. In this case, the honor of important people "humbling" themselves to visit made it hard for Abu Abdalla to refuse them.

People who considered themselves "friends," that is, visited one another more frequently, expected to have special happenings shared with them. It was incumbent on Um Abdalla, for example, to share the experience of having a resident foreigner in her house by taking me around to see her special friends. These friends invariably complained that we hadn't visited them soon enough or stayed long enough, implicitly comparing themselves with others who were visited earlier or received more of our attention. By means of these complaints, they sought reassurance from Um Abdalla that nothing was wrong with the friendship. Relations with outsiders could easily intensify or diminish, and so people were anxious to determine where they stood at a given moment.

Relationships with outsiders took effort. If Um Abdalla or Abu Abdalla ignored them for too long, the relationship would cool and eventually die, usually with hard feelings on the part of the slighted individual. To reassure each other that the relationship was still going well, the first words between host and visitor at any visit were, "We haven't seen you for a long time. Where have you been? Why haven't you come?" The explanations for the absence had to be convincing. By contrast, relationships between kin could be revived whenever necessary and didn't require the same kind of effort or accounting. It was simply assumed that they would endure.

Visits with outsiders were formal. The visitors dressed up, stayed for a reasonable length of time, and were expected to accept the prescribed hospitality. On their side, the hosts showed how they felt about the guests by the kinds of food they offered and the elaboration of its service. High-status summer visitors received the full array of "courses" on the best china—soft drinks, coffee, nuts, fruits, and sweets—whereas the neighbor Um Yusef received only a cup of tea and nuts from a common dish. The visitors also showed their feelings of intimacy with the household by the way they approached the house—which door they used and whether they knocked, called out the name of the owner, or simply entered. Other signs of intimacy were the terms that guests and hosts used to address one another, the way that the guests were seated, and the amount of attention directed toward making them feel comfortable. Hosts judged visitors by how often they came, how long they stayed, how cordial their conversations were, and whether or not the visit was undertaken out of strictest obligation.

When people had difficulties with relatives, they used outsider rules to signify their problems. This was what happened with Um Nabil, the mother of Um Abdalla. As her relationship with her daughters deteriorated, she visited them less frequently, entered through their formal front door, and took pains to divide her time equally between the houses of both daughters. In return, Um Abdalla and Um George visited their mother in her son's home only on certain "occasions," such as when their brother's child was born or he returned from a trip. Thus, their visits to her, like those with outsiders, became both formal and purposeful.

Marriage offered one of the rare opportunities to cement permanent relationships with outsiders. The neighbors Um Samir and Um Munir secured such a relationship by marrying a daughter and a son to each other. Other parents, according to Um George, who wanted a stable marriage for their children would select their spouses from families with whom they already had a strong relationship. This might mean pairing cousins whose common family interest would keep a marriage stable. Multiple marriages between families were supposed to have a similar effect, as in Um Abdalla's and Um George's case, in which two sisters married two brothers.

In general, the family was wary of outsiders. They treated them formally and, with few exceptions, initiated and maintained contact with them only when there was a good reason to do so. By the way in which they interacted with outsiders, they made it clear that they viewed them as different from family insiders in a number of important respects.

Relations with family members were the diametric opposite of relationships with outsiders. Instead of being malleable, balanced, and easily terminated, as were outsider relations, relations within the family were fixed, unbalanced, and permanent. They were "fixed" because each member of the family behaved toward each other member in terms of "fixed" behavior rules relative to their age, sex, vested authority, and permanent relationship (how spouses, parents, children, and siblings should behave toward one another). They were "unbalanced" because any two members of a family did not have the same obligations to one another. What an older sister "owed" in the way of responsibility and care to a younger sister was different from the obedience and respect the younger child owed to her older sister. The relations were "permanent" because the kinship connection endured forever and could not be discarded even when there was no active contact. These three characteristics fit together nicely because family relations were supposed to be fixed and permanent, and so the fact that they were unbalanced at a particular moment did not make them "unfair" for a single individual. By the time a person's life span was complete—assuming that all family members were present and carrying out their obligations to one another—a person should have passed through all the stages of authority and deference, and the obligations he or she owed to others would roughly balance what was received from them. Children who deferred to their elders would eventually occupy similar positions of authority as they aged, unless, of course, views about conducting relationships should change. It thus was in the interest of everyone to see that the same patterns continued.

This way of looking at others, unconscious as it was, had two important effects. First, it diffused the tensions that family members might have felt toward one another if they had expected their exchanges to be roughly equal. Um Abdalla, for example, expected a family member such as Abu Abdalla to meet the obligations inherent in their specific relationship and not to match equally what she gave to him. Second, such a system strengthened the family's general bonds, by encouraging its members to seek satisfaction not from their own efforts or from relationships with single individuals but from across the entire family group of people exchanging obligations and receiving what was due to them.

Two conditions kept this system from being the same for all family members. The first was gender. The sexes climbed different ladders in their lifetimes, which meant that they did not experience the world in exactly the same way. Each gender assumed positions of authority and control, but not in the same arenas of household activity. If the Wusta villagers had been reflective enough to argue their own case, they might have justified the difference in the gender ladders by pointing out that one was not less valued than the other, that each had its advantages and disadvantages. Both were necessary to the family's well-being and could not be measured on a single scale of value because it would be like comparing "apples and oranges." They might have said, as Abu Abdalla implied in conversations with me, that Western scales didn't apply in Wusta because Western women had "thrown out the female ladder" and were vying for a place on the "men's ladder," on which, as he saw it, Western society placed the higher value. A more relevant single standard for Wusta, because it focused on family life, might have been one typically used to evaluate feminine characteristics: success in nurturing, caring for, and raising children, which both men and women in different ways were expected to care about.

The second source of "unfairness" came when important family members were missing—through death or absence or, when present, were not playing the part expected of them. Nurse Miriam's family faced this dilemma when her father died. There were no sons to support them, and therefore the daughters had to assume roles not rightfully belonging to women. Um Abdalla's mother was an example of the other kind, a person who, though present, did not fulfill her motherly obligation to help her daughters. They genuinely missed her contribution, which, in theory over the long run, would have balanced what they gave in services to their own daughters.

One consequence of these specialized family roles was the ease with which the lowest denominator of family could be recognized. As far as the villagers were concerned, a "complete family" existed when the people living together covered the necessities of daily living with conventional income earners and household caretakers. By this measure, Um Abdalla's and Um George's families were separate entities and not one extended family living under two roofs. When Um George's first husband died and she no longer had a means of support, the families merged for a time until they worked out a way to make her family "whole" again, by arranging her marriage to the third brother, Abu Adil. In Wusta, the lowest common denominator of satisfactory living was complete families with all the essential members present.

Roughly speaking, an immediate family was also defined by the people who pooled their resources without expecting an accounting of who used how much. For example, the sons of the wealthy Abu Ilyas contributed their earnings to a common bank account, and Abu Ilyas distributed the money as he saw fit, according to need rather than the share of the earner. By contrast, the finances of Abu Abdalla's and Abu Adil's households were kept strictly separate. When Um Abdalla sent Boutros to buy bread for both families, Um George paid the small amount that was her share. When Abu Abdalla took care of Abu Adil's family while he was on the road, Abu Adil brought gifts to compensate his brother. When Um Abdalla helped Um George cook for Abu

Adil's trip, Um George gave us all a noonday meal. By this accounting, they maintained the essential separateness of the two families.

A characteristic of these families—one that cannot be emphasized too much—was the importance of the unbalanced relationships and specialized roles in holding family members together. In Wusta, by the time children became adults, they saw themselves as "merged" with other family members. I could imagine Um Abdalla's being asked the question a Western reporter once asked an Egyptian woman I knew: "Do you feel you realize your full potential as an individual in what you do?" The Egyptian woman was confused by the concept, not commonly understood in Arab countries. "I am a daughter, wife, mother, sister, aunt, grandmother. What else do you want me to tell you?" she retorted. What was true for her was also true for Um Abdalla. She thought of herself mainly in terms of her relations with others, and any independent self outside these relationships was difficult for her to imagine.

These were some of the complicated ideas about relationships that children learned growing up in Wusta and watching the adult world. The learning was made easier, coming as it did from ideas of a single piece—that is, from uniform conceptions about the nature of the world and how human beings should operate effectively within it.

In the Wusta households, there were numerous ways that children learned to put the family's interests before their own individual needs.

Children learned early that parents and, in extended form, the family provided them with the major necessities of life: marriage, work, shelter, clothing, emotional support, and moral guidance. The reverse of this was also true—if they broke the rules, as happened with the young Samir who wanted to become a truck driver against his father's wishes, families could withhold their help and banish the transgressor from family life.[1] This punishment was a serious one, for there were few opportunities to participate fully in adult life without the family's active support.

Children also learned quickly that their futures were inextricably bound up in other peoples' perceptions of their family. Wusta family members suffered their family's collective behavior, both good and bad. Children were marked by family reputation just as surely as though they were solely responsible for it. Accordingly, a single major lapse of any member could wipe out a reputation built over generations. Even a minor incident like Muna's too-tight pants could become a concern if the family became known as one that allowed its daughters to wear provocative clothing. Such indiscretions could influence the other children's marriage negotiations, from the contagion of an "immoral" sister and parents who allowed such behavior. Lisa did not go visiting with us because young men who were potential marriage partners (or their mothers) might be present. Um Abdalla didn't want to appear to be "advertising" her daughters. A noticeable change came over the children when they appeared before guests—they became deferential and excessively polite, and the girls sweet and demure in a good imitation of the heroines of the nightly Egyptian television serial. The fear of tarnishing the family's image was a strong inducement to self-control among the children.

Among my own American friends, the situation is quite different. Parents feel only limited responsibility for the actions of their adult children, expecting them to find spouses, work, and even emotional support on their own. If the children make mistakes, the parents may feel sad or angry but would not expect their own personal lives or careers to be affected. When a family member is in trouble, others may help, but only temporarily, especially if the fault lies clearly with the individual concerned. Generally speaking, people evaluate others according to their own personal efforts and skills, and not their family background and status. They are likely to forgive isolated mistakes no matter how serious they are if people later prove themselves worthy. Mistakes are just a part of growing up.

These American parents teach their children not to be "hypocritical," that is, to follow a single set of standards in all situations and not just when the behavior takes place in public. Not used to cultivating public images, the children treat outsiders in virtually the same way as they do members of their own families. To observers coming from Arab cultures, American children's lack of special respect toward guests and elders seems like unforgivably bad manners.

Behavior in Wusta was judged as good or bad depending on how it affected the family. Parents disapproved if children took more than their share within the family, such as eating greedily at dinnertime when we dipped into a common pot. When Abu Abdalla's brother decided to sell his piece of what had been their father's land, against the wishes of his brothers, he lost their support perhaps irrevocably. On the other hand, people considered it commendable if a family member commandeered a disproportionate share of resources in the outside world. Villagers admired bold, illegal initiatives outside Wusta, thereby implying that to take advantage of the authorities was a good thing if one could get away with it. Why else would the brother of the rich Abu Ilyas take the risk of smuggling goods across borders that eventually landed him in jail? Abu Ilyas was angered by the problems it caused him but was obviously proud of the daring his brother displayed and his own initiative in paying for a substitute prisoner. People were supposed to improve the position of their families, for a higher morality lay in how well they managed to do this.

Looking at this from the broader perspective of community, I was forced to conclude that there might be disadvantages in strongly knit families' competing with one another for resources and reputation. It would be difficult, for example, to develop cooperation among families for other than temporary purposes. Where could one find a leadership that looked beyond narrow parochial interests? Wusta, indeed, had little sense of community that I could discern, and what goodwill did exist in visits between families hid a more natural tendency to view outsiders with suspicion and hostility. The "selfishness" expressed in competition between individuals in American society—and held in check by a rule of laws—in Syria seemed concentrated in competition between family groups. The competition was restricted in Wusta by the families' need for one another in marriage, business, and special services, as well as by the government's authoritarian force in regulating the conduct of public affairs. Any attempt to integrate Syrian society at the community and national levels would require an appeal to the interests of "collectivities" rather than just to the interests of individuals.

Um Abdalla and Abu Abdalla expected their children to find companionship, like other needs, within the family, and they arranged their daily schedule so that the children had little time for outside friends or even for a part of the day that could be called "leisure."

The household's almost continuous work schedule made it virtually impossible for the children to become intimate with anyone but closely related family members. And the limited free time during class breaks and coming and going to school also left little opportunity to develop intimacy with schoolmates. On rare occasions, a schoolmate was permitted to visit Lisa for a compelling reason like preparing for major school exams. A consequence of this isolation from after-school contacts was that same-age peers from outside the family had little influence on the children's way of thinking and so parents were able to retain strong control over their children's behavior. It also meant that because of their experiences with relatives in the two households, the children were comfortable with people of all ages and both sexes. They were expected to show respect to elders but were not required to be socially distant from them.

As with everything else, parents kept their children from outsiders because "it was the right thing to do." It never occurred to them that children would want companionship with anyone other than family members. Because this did not occur to the parents, it did not occur to the children. Highly selective actions such as these normally reinforce cultural "purposes," and in this case it is not necessary to search far for reasons that insularity might be useful to the family. Many proverbs in Syria encourage good relations with neighbors, but just as many warn strongly against the damage neighbors can do, such as "Close your door and watch out for your neighbor" or "The passing of a neighbor by a neighbor begins and ends in infamies." These admonitions, of course, also hold true for "children's friends," who with their "different standards" and the potential for hurting a family's reputation if they "know too much," are better kept at a distance. The children were considered too young and inexperienced to be entrusted with the subtleties of distancing potentially dangerous outsiders. It was simpler if everyone in the family kept a reasonably formal relation with people outside the family.

When my children were growing up, I thought it was "right" that they be given a special time for play, free from housework and even schoolwork. I thought it was "good" for their physical and social development to play with other children of similar age and sex, and I would go to great lengths to see that children of the right kind played with my children. I drove my children to meetings with friends and arranged "play groups" of others of the same sex and age. I thought it was good to match children's capabilities and interests, in order to make their play "more fun." As a result of so much outside contact, my children found a powerful base in groups other than our family and developed sources of value independent of ours. As adults, they still stick to their same-age friends and tend to tolerate mixed-age groups mainly at holidays such as Thanksgiving and Christmas. Perhaps American society more readily accepts change in succeeding generations because of this focus on age-graded relationships. The fashions initiated by young people—from the family-oriented 1950s, to flower children hippies, to Wall Street yuppies—have been a source of both creativity and instability in our society.

The daily schedule of Wusta families didn't draw a distinct line between times for work and times for play. Children willingly spent many hours in housework or schoolwork at least partly because there was nothing they would rather have been doing. Although work took up most of the waking day, it was carried on in such a measured way, with frequent stops for tea and talk, that it was difficult to say when the work stopped and the leisure began. Work came to a complete stop only about an hour before bedtime when the children put away their books and Um Abdalla finished folding the laundry. Otherwise, Um Abdalla and Abu Abdalla kept the children busy and felt no obligation to entertain them or give them time off to do what they liked. The children's entertainment came from being together and talking or watching a special television show. There were no places to go or friends to see that competed with life at home. Household chores took priority, and parents did not hesitate to ask children to take care of what was needed. Muna was taken from her homework to serve guests; Lisa stopped her studying to make dinner. The boys were called away from a soccer game to clean the chicken sheds. They did not yearn for leisure time, since to all intents and purposes, they had never been exposed to it.

Americans distinguish work from leisure more clearly than the Wusta families do. Their days are divided into blocks of time: working hours, coffee breaks, weekends, school hours, lunch breaks, after-school events, summer holidays, all with implications for the kinds of activities that should take place. Although the contrast is partly due to differences between Wusta village and American urban ways of life, this reason alone does not account for the entire phenomenon. Damascene shopkeepers who sip tea with their customers and office workers who run personal errands during business hours mix work and personal social life with a casualness that indicates little respect for the distinction. Even when Americans find their work rewarding and enjoyable, most look forward to a leisure time that is their "own time" to do what they want. The same is true for children for whom the school day delineates work time from fun time. In their minds, leisure is associated with certain activities—movies, ball games, "hanging out"—and, by association, with certain people, preferably from outside the family, such as neighborhood kids, schoolmates, and others roughly matched in age.

Because the American parents I know work long hours, they don't want to spend more of their leisure time engaged in housework than is necessary. They certainly do not want to spend much time in the tension-fraught activity of getting children to do their share of housework. These parents maintain that their time with the children should be "quality" time, which usually translates into activities that entertain the children—going on trips, reading stories, going to the zoo or movies, or whatever. Even though the adults may

prefer to do other things after work, they feel guilty about being away from
their children so much of the time. The fact that they so consciously distinguish activities as belonging to either adults or children may make certain
aspects of adulthood seem more appealing to children. At the same time,
however, it may make the transition between childhood and adulthood more
difficult. Among the children of my friends, some run into difficulties trying
to cope with the full range of adult responsibilities before they are ready;
others try to hang onto childhood and delay adult responsibilities for too
long; and still others vacillate back and forth between the two worlds before
finally feeling comfortable as adults. There is no clear rite of passage in
American society after which it is possible to say that the transformation to
adulthood has been completed, unless it is the transition from university to
jobs.

Most of the activities of Um and Abu Abdalla's household in some way reinforced the stability and cohesiveness of family life. This is not to say that life
was always perfect but, rather, that these patterns existed to defuse conflict
and encourage mutual reliance.

The work of the household was routinely carried out by groups of adults
and children: cooking, cleaning, eating, taking care of the chickens, and
doing other chores. A child might learn how to perform one part of a major
task well and each time contribute that same part, but it would take the contributions of several people to complete the task. Children developed ownership of family work and made sure it was done even when the parents were
not present. As a matter of course, they joined in without being asked when
they found their parents working, So ingrained was the sense of working
together that even individualized tasks like schoolwork were completed
with the whole family sitting together and the parents helping with the
work. So strongly did they feel the importance of being together that anyone who sought to be alone was considered sick or depressed.

Perhaps most reflective of their family's style of living was the way eating
was arranged, around a central pot from which everyone ate at the same
time. There were no separate plates, separate portions, separate foods for
children and adults, or even separate loaves of bread, and there was no
accounting of how much each took. Politeness required that everyone show
restraint; they should dip up small portions of food with bite-size pieces of
bread; they should use their right hands so as not to offend the others with
the hand reserved for bathroom functions. They should refrain from eating

in a hurry or from greedily taking excessive amounts. They quietly absorbed themselves in eating and talked little during mealtimes.

The requirement that everyone eat together meant that meals were served only when everyone had assembled. No one delayed when the noon meal approached. Abu Abdalla rarely stayed at his office for pressing business; Um Abdalla kept her mind on the cooking so as to have the food ready on time; and the children did not linger with schoolmates on their way home from school. Despite a seeming casualness about timing, everyone appeared promptly for the meal.

Among the American families I know, my own included, a respect for privacy and difference makes family members spend considerable time alone working on their own projects. The idea that people should develop independent skills means that they need time to practice on their own. Meals may even be taken separately to accommodate the different tastes and conflicting schedules of household members. Parents may eat later than their young children because they want a relaxing, quiet mealtime or because they want to eat foods that do not appeal to children. In American families, individuals are given as much choice as possible in how they spend their time.

Um Abdalla's children were encouraged to perfect their talents for the service of the family rather than for their own personal development. The parents assigned the children tasks based on their capacity to perform them and not because they felt the children needed to learn every skill for their own self-improvement or because work should be shared equally. Because they were good students, Lisa and Boulos were relieved of housework they might otherwise have been required to do if parents had thought it necessary to be "fair." Muna was good at serving guests, so she was "relieved" of homework to do this task. Hanna did a good job of installing the stoves so it was not necessary for anyone else to learn how to do this job. Even as adults in separate households, Um Abdalla and Um George made their *kibbee* together so each could do the part she did best. Parents made no effort "to even out" the work. In the process, if some family members "actualized" certain kinds of potential more than others did, their successes would reflect on the rest. For example, if Boulos became a doctor, everyone would bask in the light of his accomplishments. When members of a family are taught to do some kinds of work and not others, they assume the long-term survival of the group as a whole.

On the other hand, I tried to distribute the burden of housework equitably among my children and to rotate chores so no one had more than his share of the onerous tasks. For the most part, my children were expected to complete these tasks on their own, to "develop a sense of responsibility." As a consequence of this emphasis on "fairness," my children developed an "accounting" mentality by which they kept tallies of their treatment compared with that of their brothers. They also competed for recognition from us that they had mastered important skills better than their brothers had. American parents are greatly impressed when their children learn a skill, like reading or sports or music, at a young age, or when they show responsibility by taking on a task like mowing the lawn or delivering newspapers and complete it efficiently by themselves. We look for evidence that our children are developing their talents and learning enough basic skills so they will not have to depend on others. This kind of approach to child rearing assumes that family members do not constitute a group that will survive for long as a physical entity.

One of the fundamental lessons that the Wusta children learned was how to carry out their obligations to others. The emphasis on obligations charged relationships with expectations different from an emphasis on rights, or what is due someone. If I owe you obedience, it is incumbent on me to make sure I obey you. On the other hand, if I have the right to be obeyed, I must concern myself with whether or not you obey me.

Um Abdalla and Abu Abdalla, of course, did not lecture their children about obligations. Rather, they believed in them and encouraged the children by their actions to follow them. Since children's obligations changed as they grew older and family members were added to or subtracted from the household, they had to learn generic "rules" governing family roles, as well as the details of occupying a single role at any given time.

For example, the children learned "rules" relating to age, experience, and commitment. Older members of the family were reliable "experts," not only because they had experienced a great deal in their lifetimes, but also because they could be trusted with the family's best interests. Younger persons should, therefore, respect and obey older persons without question, and older persons should exert authority, make decisions, and guide younger persons in responsible ways. In most respects, Wusta was an "age" rather than a "youth" culture, in that people moved "up" the age ladder to positions of greater responsibility, respect, authority, and wisdom.

Older people were considered the masters of complicated jobs that required experience. Younger people specialized in less skilled tasks. Lisa cut the salad ingredients; Um Abdalla, the expert cook, put them together. Abdalla and Hanna took the water to the chickens and ground the feed, but Abu Abdalla decided the proportions of the grains in the feed and when and what kinds of vitamins to give the chickens. The boys would seek his advice about feed, even when they were adults, just as Lisa would consult her mother about food even after she went off to a separate home with her husband. Eventually, as the children became skilled themselves, the consultations would become courtesies showing respect for their parents' superior experience.

Children expected their parents to initiate and supervise work and did not feel responsible for the final products themselves. A consequence of close parental supervision was that the results were not a clumsy child's products but the adept products of a specialized and competent household workforce.

My experience in America is that people are generally appreciated for the efficiency with which they achieve results. In many fields, young adults with the latest knowledge, technical skills, and energy are more productive than older workers and therefore are more greatly appreciated. Old age is perceived as a time of weakness and decline, and to prevent themselves from appearing elderly, people sometimes go to absurd lengths to appear young and still in possession of youthful faculties. But this view of aging erodes the authority of parents and older people and reinforces in young people the desire to seek models in their own generation. "New" is equated with "improved" in our fast-moving economy, and "old" is considered "out of date."

Besides bringing greater authority and respect, age had other implications for the way the Wusta household was managed. In activities requiring family members to take turns, an age rule was often invoked. One modest example was the family bath, when one by one, from youngest to oldest, each child bathed, sometimes in the same water as the one before. A more important example was marriage, in which, barring special circumstances, children were supposed to marry in sequence, with the oldest first and the youngest last. At the time of the wedding, the child would receive the financial assistance the family could muster, which might mean that not all the children would receive equal amounts, since the family's wealth was likely to vary over time. But such differences were not viewed as favoring one child over another, since the children knew that their parents would do the best they could when their turn came. On the contrary, this age sequencing was

an equitable way of focusing family energies on one child at a time and diffusing conflicts that might arise from unregulated marrying (or bathing) in
any order. Practices like these focused the attention on family needs rather
than on individual family members who might feel they were ready to marry
or bathe at a different time than expected.

Even in unusual circumstances, families tried to abide by age sequencing.
The woman who came to explain why her prospective husband was such a
good man held up the exemplary behavior of how he and his brother had
waited to see all their younger siblings married before they themselves
sought brides. Without this explanation, the brothers' late marriages might
have made them seem like inferior marriage candidates. Because they had no
parents, the older children were expected to be responsible for the younger
children, and if they neglected this responsibility, it would reflect badly on
the whole family.

My children and my friends' children in the United States felt differently.
They expected their family to help—to pay school bills or wedding expenses
—when personal circumstances required it and not in any particular order.
As parents, we tried to be equitable about the amount, giving the ones with
lower college bills a little extra to make a down payment on an apartment
later on. At the same time, our children felt responsible for their expenses
up to what they could manage with their limited income-earning capacity;
each worked during summer vacations to pay some of their bills. It was not
a foregone conclusion for any of us parents that our adult children would
receive the full amount they needed, even if we could afford to be generous.
Rather, they were expected to contribute and to show that they were making good use of the opportunities we offered them. Most important was the
fact that each child expected equal treatment and was likely to feel slighted
if his or her share were not the same as that of another sibling. Most of the
problems we had while the boys were growing up were caused by "fairness"
issues—of thinking they were in some sense not given equal treatment.

I see now that this approach of ours—which was designed to reduce
competition—did just the opposite. It created an environment of comparison and competition, a fact perhaps consistent with a society that values sep-
aration, self-reliance, and self-improvement. It encouraged the boys to take
the initiative and to struggle for what they wanted, also useful if individuals
are expected to succeed on their own in a competitive world. Unlike the
Syrian case—and I think now of the older brother helping his younger
brother cross the street in Damascus—the American children I knew were

so focused on their struggle to be "special" that it was difficult for them to help their competitors, whether siblings or outsiders, to "cross the street."

After age, the second major characteristic around which Wusta family obligations were organized was gender. Females had certain responsibilities, and males had others.

Barring unusual circumstances, gender defined the obligations and skills that children had to learn. A singular advantage was that people knew precisely how these responsibilities and tasks should be divided, and so no time or controversy was wasted in deciding who must do what. Girls knew that most of what they needed to know they could learn from their mothers, and boys knew that the same was true for their fathers. Even when a new activity appeared, it was immediately clear to everyone who would be responsible. Um Abdalla had earlier raised chickens informally for household consumption, but when large-scale chicken farming became the new income-earning occupation for the family, the job—by the logic of clearly defined gender roles—became an activity that Abu Abdalla would manage. People did not find it difficult to locate new responsibilities within old gender categories.

Although the Wusta parents did not explicitly lead the children to believe that the functions of one sex carried a different level of importance than the other, it was evident that the advent of a more moneyed economy was giving greater importance to outside sources of steady income. The significance of money in modifying old gender roles was, of course, more obvious when finances were a problem, as in nurse Miriam's family, in which the women were pressed into "male" support responsibilities. However, in households like those of Um Abdalla and Um George, in which the incomes were relatively assured, there was little reason for women to want to assume "male" support roles. They would have been amazed at anyone who suggested that their lives were incomplete because they didn't work for wages outside the family. Rather than envying the men the opportunity to work as they did, the women talked sympathetically about the difficulty of their husbands' jobs and usually expressed satisfaction at doing women's work which allowed them to be continuously at home. The reluctance of Abu Adil to go off on his trucking trips suggested that he, too, would rather be at home, albeit not necessarily doing women's work. At other times when comparing men's and women's work, the women complained that women's work was never done, whereas men could take time off for sickness or to rest between trucking jobs. The women's complaints, however, seemed more to be pointing out advantages and disadvantages in both kinds of work rather than a serious desire to trade their work for men's work. Neither sex felt a compelling attraction in the work of the other sex, even though they saw the advantage of their daughters learning skills that would help them earn a respectable living if male support were not available.

What my American friends might have considered to be negative aspects of segregated gender roles were not seen that way by the Syrian families, for at least two reasons. First, Syrian society was so focused on the family that what went on outside the family was usually of less interest to people than what went on inside the family. People in Wusta did not take their sense of importance from their personal accomplishments outside the family, as Americans often do, and therefore women did not feel that they had to occupy "men's jobs" in order to realize a sense of worth. Indeed, just the opposite may have been true, for women dominated what was the socially more important arena of family life.

When Lisa or Muna talked about employment after they finished school, they were not thinking about personal fulfillment for themselves. Few jobs, in truth, offered this kind of professional reward (including professional jobs, which tended to be routine and circumscribed). Rather, they wanted to ensure their economic security if a husband or father died. If they had been married, they might even have rationalized employment—as one often hears Arab women doing—in terms of their feminine roles of "being a better wife" or "being a better mother" and not as "being a better person." With an additional salary in the family, they could purchase extras for the family. They would not, however, consider their contribution a major income support of the family. Support was a male function, and if women assumed this role, it would make it look as though the men in the family were not adequate to their roles. If women spoke of their employment tactfully in terms of their female roles, it would no doubt help them gain a broader acceptance of the idea of women's income-producing work while at the same time keeping the support function securely attached to the men's domain.

The second reason that female roles may not have seemed so burdensome in Wusta was that they were adopted matter-of-factly, with few opportunities to experience any contradictory way of life. If the adult females in the two households had worked outside the family to earn money, they might have discovered, as women elsewhere have, that women end up with two jobs instead of the one held by men. The "inferiority" of women's work would become more obvious when men disdained to do household work to help a working wife for fear of diminishing themselves in front of others.

Maintaining a difference between male and female roles—whatever people may think about its fairness—has an important stabilizing effect on families that is rarely recognized. The more that males and females need each other to perform tasks they cannot do for themselves, the stronger family ties become. It is little wonder that the Arab world has at times resisted efforts to narrow the differences between men's and women's roles, especially through universal education and employment, both of which enable women to support themselves without male help. When the family is as central to a society as it is in the Arab world, attacks on its vital relationships—in this case, the connection between males and females—come to be seen as attacks on the society itself.

In the United States, my friends and I took an alternative approach to gender, by saying that it made no difference because everyone was equal. As much as possible, all our children, male and female, learned to do whatever it took to survive on their own. By implication, this meant that since individuals could stand alone, there were few compelling reasons to make permanent alliances with others, that is, to marry or establish families. In America, "self-sufficiency," "equality," and "independence" are qualities as positive for girls as they are for boys, whereas in Wusta, these same words express the meanings "selfishness," "disorder," and "indulgence."

In Wusta, the parents made decisions for their children in all the large and small matters of daily life. Children were not encouraged to think independently. Parents decided what their children would eat, when they would eat, what they would wear, what tasks they would do, and so on throughout the day. A constant stream of directions punctuated their time together. The children were supposed to obey their parents' orders and not to express their own opinions. This did not mean that they never made decisions—older children were constantly making minor decisions for younger children. These decisions, however, were not "real" in the sense that issues were weighed and decided; rather, they were attempts by the older children to anticipate what their parents would have done if they had been present.

Since comparative age carried with it the right to make important decisions, adult children might never have the chance to make some decisions as long as their parents were alive and living nearby. Even when children developed expertise beyond that of their parents, they continued the fiction that their parents knew better. They might avoid discussing certain topics, but it would have been unusual for them to go against a parent's wishes. The seriousness with which Samir's rebellion was greeted should be seen in this light. Rather than rebel outright, children were likely to negotiate a way through problems in order not to upset the relationship of respect with a parent.

Children treated in this way look to others for direction. Not being accustomed to weighing the pros and cons of an argument, they are inclined to accept authoritarian statements as true in the most absolute sense. George accepted without comment my request to install my stove in the wrong place—I was an adult and therefore I must know where it should go. As a consequence of this attitude, there was little rebellion accompanying adolescence in Wusta. Parents expected to be obeyed without question, and the children's sense of obligation meant that they would do so.

Most parents I know in the United States, by contrast, feel better when their children, from an early age, actively participate in decisions about themselves—it makes the parents feel more egalitarian and less authoritarian. One conversation I overheard between an American father and his four-year-old son illustrates this tendency: "Don't you think it's time to go home from the beach now, Johnny?" "No," was the emphatic answer. "What do you think we might be having for dinner—aren't you getting hungry?" "No" again. "Our friends will be there, and it will be nice to sit around with them." "No." "Susy's mother says she has to go home, too," said the father, winking conspiratorially at Susy's mother, "so there won't be any one here to play with." Recognizing his advantage, the child bargained, "If I go home now, can I have Susy come to our house to play tomorrow?" "Yes," said the father, happy that the child at last had endorsed the decision to go home.

When children are made participants in decision making and are given the chance to make choices on their own, they develop a sense of themselves as separate beings with thoughts that count. This practice emphasizes their individuality and their right to decide their own independent fates. It produces children who at adolescence, often before their judgment is fully mature, continue to believe that they are capable of making their own decisions, as their parents have taught them. Not to do so would be an infringement of their rights and everything they have been taught so far. This kind of treatment builds a strong persona in children that may at times lead to conflicts with adults.

The American public schools that my children attended encouraged them to become this kind of independent person. It did this by teaching them to have their own separate opinions about the instructional materials they were given, by reducing the difference in authority between teachers and students, and by assigning children independent work, including cut-and-paste projects that encouraged them to execute original designs they created themselves. No matter how critically Americans may view their education system, there is one thing the system accomplishes well: the production of independent, competitive children. This fact is particularly visible abroad in international expatriate communities in which schools of different nationalities stand side by side.

The Wusta children had little reason to compete with one another for the attention of adults. As I mentioned earlier, the children expected to receive benefits in a particular order based on the arbitrary fact of age—they waited patiently for their turn to come, and no amount of wishing themselves in a different position would change the order rule. Parents expected different types of performance from each child and therefore did not compare them all against a single standard. Children had few personal belongings to quarrel over—the few toys that existed were commonly owned, and clothing was shared—socks belonged to the one who came to the clothes closet first. Schoolbooks and uniforms temporarily belonged to particular children, but even they might be handed on to the children next in line the following year. Personal space did not exist. The children shared rooms and might find that their bedroom on the sunny side of the house was suddenly converted into a sitting room for the whole family in the winter months. The children did not even have a place that was customarily theirs in a bed shared by siblings.

Parents were also not given to rewarding children for work well done around the house. Proper behavior was expected rather than remarked on. Therefore, children were not constantly looking for adults' approval or vying with a sibling to attract adults' attention. Instead, they worked to avoid adults' displeasure by carrying out their obligations correctly. Hanna or Abdalla would be scolded for forgetting to fill the water tanker during the noonday meal and thus delaying the trip up to the chickens, but there was no notice taken when they did the task correctly. Parents rarely intervened in quarrels between children, and when they did, it was likely that they would hold the older children responsible for not resolving the problem first. Parents would say, in effect, "You are older, and therefore more is expected of you." Consequently, it was not realistic for children to compete with their siblings for equal treatment when the parents' expectations for each child differed, depending on those arbitrary facts of age, talent, and sex. Children learned that their accomplishments were important only insofar as they furthered family interests and that therefore there was no use in vying for attention that was not likely to be forthcoming.

At an early age, Wusta children fit themselves into hierarchical arrangements during play. The leaders were, by definition, the older children, and the followers, the younger children. These arrangements changed depending on which children were together at any given moment. Of the pairs of same sex-siblings at Um George's, Miriam directed little Lisa, and Adil directed Ilyas, or if Lisa and Adil were alone together, Lisa became the leader and Adil accepted her leadership. The expectation that age and authority were related forced all the children to practice roles they might not have assumed were they to act according to their natural inclinations. Miriam, by nature, was much quieter than little Lisa, yet as the oldest of the preschoolers, she readily accepted her role as leader, and Lisa deferred to her because she was older.

When Miriam stepped in to resolve an argument between her younger siblings, her parents didn't need to intervene. Rather, the parents were there to take care of creature comforts like food, drink, sleep, and cuddling. When the small children had a disagreement about the new toy I brought them, Miriam suggested a new way to use it and then stepped back and seemed to take satisfaction in seeing the idea work. Then, in the afternoon when the schoolchildren were at home, Miriam retreated into a follower role, taking directions from the older children. All the children in the household thus became both parents and children to their siblings, diffusing the parental role and making it a less sensitive one. During their lifetimes, people thus assumed most if not all of the major roles associated with their gender. Each role had clear obligations that when accomplished well could create a sense of fulfillment, comparable to the rewards that I and my friends might find from professional competence in our society.

As parents, my friends and I found ourselves frequently becoming the arbitrators of fairness between children. The children knew that outstanding accomplishments gained our appreciation. They knew that they would be noticed if they were unique, precocious, or outstanding, even if these traits were expressed in a negative way. Because arrangements for relating to one another were not fixed as clearly by age or gender, the children had to jockey for position based on personal characteristics—sports abilities, looks, artistic accomplishments, intellect, personality, sociability, and so on. In many households, younger children may even have a hard time finding an unfilled niche, other than that of "baby" of the family. To hold the parents' interest, each succeeding child may find it easier to shine in a new way rather than compete with a sibling with age and development advantages. For instance, if the oldest child is a scholar, the next may become an athlete, and the third an artist, in order to distinguish themselves in their parents' eyes. As adults, their need for attention continues—to make more money, to excel in an occupation, to contribute good works to the community. Partly for this reason, I feel, many women in my generation, myself included, started working outside the home, since unlike Wusta, there was little reward in America for fulfilling "women's roles."

In Wusta, the point at which a child became an adult was obscured by the fact that from an early age children absorbed and honored the same obligations as adults did. Technically, perhaps, the point of adulthood was reached with marriage and parenthood, when the scheme of obligations expanded to add new responsibilities to spouses, in-laws, and children. Even after marriage, however, people never stopped being children to their parents and parents to younger family members. The transition to adulthood was therefore almost seamless, generated from rules that applied similarly across childhood and adulthood, causing each person at the same time to be parent or child to specified others.

The fundamental difference between the Wusta families and the Americans I knew was that Wusta people believed their lifetime interests were best served through long-term commitment to families, and Americans believed in forming individuals who eventually could cope on their own outside the parental family. The measures of success for the two were different: the Wusta parents were satisfied when their children conscientiously carried out their obligations to family members, and the American parents were proud when their children coped well with their personal and professional lives outside the home.

The behaviors described here for Wusta—those that strengthened family ties and those that reduced competition among family members—were organized by a common rationale. Not all people at all times in Syria "accomplish family" in precisely the same way as did the Wusta families I lived with, nor do all American families conform to the practices described here for my friends and family. It would be a mistake, however, to become too caught up in the superficial details of behavior and fail to recognize the extent to which people's actions in each society are organized by powerful understandings about life. Um Abdalla is driven ultimately by rationales common to others in her society, just as I and my friends are motivated by tendencies that characterize elements of American society.[2] There appears to be much less choice involved in culture than one supposes.

In general, the Syrian village child does not measure well on a scale of individualism, nor does the American child measure well on a scale of collectivism. The question remains whether the people of a society can consciously choose to become more of one thing than another or, instead, whether the consistency organized by the culture's deep-seated rationales doesn't exert so compelling a control over conscious behavior that few choices are possible. In this book, I have tried to show the pervasiveness of culture in organizing daily life. When daily behavior is organized into central themes, the skewing of all social behavior to those themes becomes itself a powerful means of embedding the themes in growing children. Vast ranges of behavior are drawn together by these means in consistent and reinforcing fashion, leaving little contradiction to mar the complacency of each "true" design.

This book has also tried to make clear that as yet there is no revolutionary worldwide convergence toward anything like a single family type. Finding similar numbers or kinds of family members residing together in two societies is not enough to signal true convergence. On the face of it, Abu Abdalla's family in Wusta may be called nuclear, just as, on the face of it, my American family of similar composition may be called nuclear, but forces more important than composition need to be considered when determining congruence. Even when American and Syrian families maintain an outward semblance of similarity, they are organized by very different views of what is important in life and what families should be. There is a danger in viewing them as similar because when we do, we are suggesting that only the surface characteristics are significant.

At the same time, having scope to manipulate aspects of family—its composition, its economy and its authority—seems, from an evolutionary standpoint, to be a potent tool for conducting the business of life. Generally speaking, the ability to vary family forms gives options to earn, to conserve, to expand, and to regroup that otherwise might not be available to its members. The many faces of family thus act as a flexible strategy for coping with the difficulties and uncertainties in a rapidly changing world. Abu Abdalla's children are poised on the edge of decisions that in a few years time will determine whether they throw in their lots together or separately. Even knowing many of the elements in these choices does not make it possible to predict what they will be.

There is no way to organize family life that is better than all others. Each form has significant costs and benefits that need to be weighed. Can Americans, for example, continue to bear the social costs of each person pursuing his or her own individual interests? Can we alleviate the specter of loneliness that haunts the individualistic spirit of American life? Can the government continue to bear the burden of services that families provide in other societies? On the other hand, Syrian culture has not dealt well with the individual needs and creative impulses of its members, nor has it been able to lighten the sometimes tedious burden that falls on the shoulders of the capable who care for many "nonproductive" family members. Neither culture has addressed adequately the question of women's roles, nor perhaps can they if some of their fundamental perspectives remain as they are now.

Every variation of family has advantages and disadvantages, and each creates sets of consequences that enhance or detract from it as a choice. From the evidence of Wusta and my own limited experiences with child rearing, both our cultures, with their powerful rationales, seem destined to suffer the blessings and penalties of their own forms of family life for some time to come.

My work the next year kept me traveling to other countries in the Middle East and left me little time to make the frequent visits back to the village I had intended. I had fallen behind in the news of the families, and so only a few days before I was leaving Syria for our summer holidays, my husband and I returned to the village just at the time in the afternoon when the family's main meal would be finished. Rounding the corner from the main road, I immediately noticed the addition of a porch on the cool north side of the house. It was early summer and the day had the breathless quality of stifling heat. The two families sat in a line of new aluminum chairs along the wall of the house in the shade afforded by the porch. Sitting with them was an almost unrecognizably sober and much-aged Abu Munir. They looked as though posed for a formal photograph. The young children clambered over the adults, and on one side, Lisa, in a characteristic pose with her book in her lap, was pointing out something on the page to her friend, Muna, sitting next to her. Before Muna could reply to her question, the noise of our car wheels on the gravel of the drive caused them both to turn to see who was coming down the road. I realized that it must be exactly the same time as when I had left the year before—with final exams imminent and the whole family engrossed in studying. Only the additions to the house and the slightly older versions of each child indicated that so much time had passed in the meantime.

I felt unfamiliar with this spot on the north side of the house that we had ignored during the winter months, but I was even less prepared for the lack of enthusiasm in their greeting. I had steeled myself for their reproaches at the unconscionable amount of time I had let pass since last seeing them, but I hadn't expected this. They said all the right words: "We missed you, neighbor. Why did you stay away so long? Where have you been? What is the news of your family?" but there was a remarkable quiet about the way they asked the questions; even the children down to the youngest Ilyas clinging to the skirts of his mother were uncharacteristically silent.

Something was wrong, but what? Had I offended them so much by my long absence? Had I committed some other offense that I was unaware of? I felt this was a lukewarm reception for someone who had been away so long. I talked on for a while about how busy I had been with my work in the intervening period, about how I had been in bed for three months with a bad case of hepatitis, about my boys and their exploits during the year, and about my husband and our plans to return to the United States temporarily for the holidays. I knew I had talked more than I should, but it was from anxiety that my absence had offended them. I feared that when I stopped, we would lapse once again into the uneasy silence.

Finally I said, "Now I want to hear your news. I have missed you, too, and want to hear everything that has happened since I left." They were distracted for a few minutes as I was introduced to the new baby, now almost a year old. Lisa had taken her from her stroller to sit in her lap, and when I turned to her, she smiled warmly, engendering smiles from the rest of the group, who were obviously very fond of her. As if finding it unbearable to be without her, Muna stretched out her arms to the baby, who went willingly to her. I asked about her name, and they said it was Reem, "little gazelle," a flight of fancy in this family of sturdy villagers. Already, Reem possessed the square stocky shape of her mother and the dark hair of her father. Yet her skin was an alabaster white, not freckled like Lisa's, Muna's, Hanna's, and Abdalla's, all of whom had inherited their mother's red-headed genes. Bright red cheeks completed the picture of a child who had all the right attributes to grow up to be a village beauty. I was careful, though, not to exclaim too much over her, for fear of eliciting the evil eye, and automatically pronounced a *mashalla* of protection.

They began to tell me about the events in their lives. A few weeks after I left the village, Abu Abdalla had had a mild heart attack, which the doctor said was due to the stress of working too hard. He spent many months recuperating, and the boys had taken over much of the work of the chicken houses while he continued to give directions from his bed about how many chickens to raise and what they should be fed. He seemed more stooped than I remembered him and also, like Abu Munir, considerably older and more tired. Um George was pregnant with what would be her sixth child; the idea seemed to please her. All the children were doing well in school this year, including Muna, who had had to repeat a grade after failing her exams the summer before. Now that she was older, she had settled down and was working harder. She blushed when she heard the news about herself but looked pleased with her success. Lisa had gone on to the secondary level and continued to get above-average grades. Abdalla also was doing well in school. Then suddenly I noticed, "Where is Hanna?" I asked. "He is sleeping," they replied but didn't elaborate and continued with the news. Boulos, as usual, was doing well, as was George in the other house. The two little girls, Miriam and Lisa, were now going to school. I could picture them in their uniforms going off to school and no longer leading the little boys around the yard on their play mornings. I complimented Abu Abdalla on the new porch and the extensive vegetable and fruit gardens that had been planted in front of the two houses. I remembered these areas as rough, uncultivated places that they had just begun plowing when I left.

Um Abdalla, her usually jovial face set in grim lines, suddenly sprang up and left the group. Lisa and Muna went conscientiously to get us drinks. Um George immediately turned to me and blurted out, "It's Hanna. He's very sick, and Um Abdalla is upset. She has gone to him." With a rush of understanding, I knew then that this had been the problem. Hanna must be seriously ill for them all to have been so affected. When Um Abdalla returned after some time, I asked her about Hanna, and in a torrent of emotions it came out. "Oh neighbor, the doctor says he is very sick. He had headaches for a long time that we thought were due to studying so much, but when we took him to the doctor in Damascus for an X ray, the doctor said it was serious—that there was something bad growing in his head." She couldn't bring herself to say the word *cancer*. "But can't they operate?" I asked. "The doctor says there is no use in doing anything." "Are you sure there is nothing that can be done?" I asked, not wanting to give up so easily. "Well, someone we know has a relative in America who knows a doctor who specializes in these things.

He says we can send the X rays to him, and he will tell us if there is anything we can do. Look, I will show you the X rays," and she left to get them. Abu Abdalla remained silent, but Um George said sympathetically, "She is wearing herself out with this problem. If we could only do something for him, but we have tried everything, asking this and that doctor in Damascus, including the ones who come here for the summer, but no one has anything new to say." Um Abdalla returned with the X rays, pointing out to me the white patches on the image. It was obvious that the case was advanced. She looked anxiously at me for a sign of hope. "Look, I'm not a doctor, and I don't know what this means, but I can take the X rays to the doctor in America so he will receive them quickly." She focused on this as a ray of hope and agreed that when the latest set of X rays came the next day she would send them to my house in Damascus so I could take them with me to America. "Would you like me to go see Hanna?" I asked. "No, he is sleeping now." She sat quietly for a while and then turned to me. "You know how it is with me, Um Dawud," she began, using the name that connected me to my children instead of the familiar *neighbor*, "My heart cannot stand suffering, and it overflows easily."

I left and went back to America, taking the X rays with me, and found, as predicted, that nothing could be done for Hanna. My last view of Wusta was the poignant one of a mother whose "heart was overflowing," unable to do anything to protect a beloved child. It was a sad ending to such a pleasant interlude in my life. I wondered who would install the winter stoves at Um Abdalla's when winter came and knew, as they all would, that no one could do it quite as well as the responsible, capable Hanna.

NOTES

Chapter One

The epigraph is from Ellen Goodman, "Our Finding Fathers," *Baltimore Sun*, July 1, 1985, p. 9a.

1. The names of villages and individuals have been changed to protect their privacy. *Wusta* means "in the middle," and *Mafraq*, which appears later, means "crossroads." The population of Wusta at that time was estimated to be around eight hundred to one thousand.

2. *Um* means "mother," and *Abu* means "father." In most Arabic countries, parents are addressed as "mother or father of (the first son's name)." In this case, Abdalla (a pseudonym to preserve the family's identity) is the oldest son of Um and Abu Abdalla. A younger son's or even a daughter's name may be used when this is the oldest child left at home. For example, a younger boy's name may be used when an older son has left home, and the neighbors are more used to seeing the younger boy around, or a girl's name may be used when no sons are present.

3. During my stay in the village, the American dollar was worth approximately S£4.

Chapter Two

The epigraph is from Dawn Chatty, "The Anthropology of Syrian Society," Report of U.S. Agency for International Development, p. 40.

1. Charles Lindholm, *Generosity and Jealousy: The Swat Pukhtun of Northern Pakistan* (New York: Columbia University Press, 1982).

Chapter Three

The epigraph is from Clifford Geertz, *Islam Observed* (Chicago: University of Chicago Press, 1968), p. 4.

1. Syria and Egypt merged into the United Arab Republic on February 1, 1958. After a military coup d'état on September 28, 1961, Syria seceded and became the Syrian Arab Republic.
2. Frederick C. Huxley, "Wasita in a Lebanese Context: Social Exchange Among Villagers and Outsiders" (Ph.D. diss., University of Michigan, 1978), p. 67.

Chapter Four

The epigraph is from Ellen Goodman, "Our Finding Fathers," *Baltimore Sun*, July 1, 1985, p. 9a.

Chapter Five

1. This estimate was provided by an official in a local government office, but it seemed high to me. The upper limit probably includes those currently living outside the village who still consider themselves inhabitants. Army recruits would also be in this category.
2. A commercial distillery processing a large portion of the grapes grown in Wusta also failed during this period, villagers say, because of stringent government regulations concerning the production of alcoholic beverages and the heirs' general lack of interest in continuing to run the plant. Whatever the reasons, its closure made one more reason to abandon large-scale agriculture production.

Chapter Six

The epigraph is from Marvin Howe, "Year of Family Wins Friends and Some Foes," *New York Times*, November 9, 1988, p. A13.

1. Another source estimates that in the previous fifteen years, the number of commercial freight vehicles expanded sixfold, from 2.1 in 1963 to 3.2 vehicles per 1,000 persons in 1978. See L. Berger International Inc., "Comprehensive Transport

Study," U.S. Agency for International Development Report, March 1981, pp. 2–5.

2. In one year alone, between 1979 and 1980, according to the Syria Market Profile put out by the American embassy in 1982, corn imports increased from 127,000 metric tons to 141,000 metric tons, and barley from 5,000 to an astonishing 205,000 metric tons. By the end of 1982, it was estimated that Syria would need to import 300,000 tons of corn and an unknown large quantity of barley, mainly for livestock and poultry.

3. Less than 10 percent of agricultural land in Syria is irrigated.

4. Volker Perthes, "The Syrian Private Industrial and Commercial Sectors and the State," *International Journal of Middle East Studies* 24 (May 1992): 210.

5. About 80 percent of the trucks entering the northern ports of Syria by ferry during this period were transit trucks, and of these about 60 percent were destined for Iraq and the rest for Saudi Arabia and Jordan. The Saudis did not admit trucks from communist countries, which ruled out major truckers to the Middle East— the Bulgarians, who operated about five thousand trucks, and the Hungarians, who together with the Bulgarians dominated more than half the routes between Europe and the Middle East.

6. It should be stressed that these stereotypes were a reflection of Christian perceptions rather than of anything real in the differences between the groups. Most of these values could be seen as either positive or negative, depending on the person and the context in which they were articulated.

Chapter Seven

The epigraph is from Sigmund Freud, *Civilization and Its Discontents*, trans. J. Strachey (New York: Norton, 1961), p. 50.

Chapter Eight

1. True to her promise, she stayed in her apartment when the rest of the family moved to the new house.

2. Years later, when Samir was released, they were told that because his case was connected with the Iraqi regime, it could be decided only by the Syrian president.

3. In 1920, French forces seized the newly established independent Arab kingdom of Syria from the Hashemite King Faisal. France occupied the country with minor interruptions under a League of Nations mandate until Syrian nationalist groups forced it to leave in 1946.

Chapter Nine

The epigraph is from Edwin T. Prothro, *Child Rearing in the Lebanon,* Middle East Monograph 8 (Cambridge, Mass.: Harvard University Press, 1961), p. 133.

1. In Egypt during the last several decades, education more than any other fac-

tor has determined the social dividing line between the lower and middle classes.

2. An article by an American psychologist reinforces this point. He states, "A preschool child should be offered clear alternatives: would you like to wear the blue shirt or the striped shirt? By the time the child reaches adolescence, he should feel comfortable determining whether he needs more information before making a decision." Lawrence Kutner, "Parent and Child," *New York Times*, December 31, 1987, p. C8.

3. Edward T. Hall, *The Silent Language* (Greenwich, Conn.: Fawcett, 1959), pp. 69–71.

Chapter Eleven

The epigraph is from Edward T. Hall, *The Silent Language* (Greenwich, Conn.: Fawcett, 1959), p. 39.

1. Bouthaina Shaabaan, *Both Right and Left Handed: Arab Women Talk About Their Lives* (Bloomington: Indiana University Press, 1991), gives a number of examples of Syrian women cut off by their parents because they made choices, usually about whom they married, without their parents' permission.

2. Ethnic communities in America may be less likely to conduct their lives according to these mainstream values, but they inevitably come into contact with them through their children.

REFERENCES

Chatty, Dawn. "The Anthropology of Syrian Society." Report for U.S. Agency for International Development, 1978.

Freud, Sigmund. *Civilization and Its Discontents*. Trans. J. Strachey. New York: Norton, 1961.

Geertz, Clifford. *Islam Observed*. Chicago: University of Chicago Press, 1968.

Goodman, Ellen. "Our Finding Fathers." *Baltimore Sun*, July 1, 1985.

Hall, Edward T. *The Silent Language*. Greenwich, Conn.: Fawcett, 1959.

Howe, Marvine. "Year of Family Wins Friends and Some Foes." *New York Times*, November 9, 1988.

Huxley, Frederick C. "Wasita in a Lebanese Context: Social Exchange Among Villagers and Outsiders." Ph.D. diss., University of Michigan, 1978.

Kutner, Lawrence. "Parent and Child." *New York Times*, December 31, 1987.

L. Berger International Inc. "Comprehensive Transport Study." Report for U.S. Agency for International Development, March 1981.

Lindholm, Charles. *Generosity and Jealousy: The Swat Pukhtun of Northern Pakistan*. New York: Columbia University Press, 1982.

Perthes, Volker. "The Syrian Private Industrial and Commercial Sectors and the State." *International Journal of Middle East Studies* 24 (May 1992).

Prothro, Edwin T. *Child Rearing in the Lebanon*. Middle East Monograph 8. Cambridge, Mass.: Harvard University Press, 1961.